Analyzing Public Discourse

'In *Analyzing Public Discourse*, Ron Scollon puts his own brand of discourse analysis to work in the world to actively engage public policy and make change. In the act, he transforms the field of discourse analysis, infusing it with a new and exciting relevance.'

James Paul Gee, Mary Lou Fulton Presidential Professor
of Literacy Studies, Arizona State University, USA

'In this outstanding book, Ron Scollon lucidly shows how discourse analysis can be used to protect both democratic liberties and the environment. It should be key reading both for discourse analysts, and for environmental activists.'

Guy Cook, The Open University, UK

Analyzing Public Discourse demonstrates the use of discourse analysis to provide testimony in public policy consultations: from environmental impact statements to changes in laws and policies.

Discourses are in collision in our world: democratic society is based on free and open discussion of public policies but governments, democratic or not, achieve and maintain power by holding their cards close to their chests. It is, however, a requirement of the law in many democratic nations that governments, resources developers, and NGOs seek public responses to their proposed actions especially where those actions are expected to have an environmental or a social impact in the communities where the actions occur.

In *Analyzing Public Discourse*, Scollon asserts that it is in the best interest of democratic public discourse for all participants in the process to be working with a common discursive framework. He puts forward a strategy by which discourse analysts can become engaged in this framework as participants through the process of public consultations. Using documents which are publicly available online from specific consultative projects, Scollon provides the reader with concrete examples and introduces basic skills for discourse analysis.

Accessible to readers who are new to discourse analysis, *Analyzing Public Discourse* will be of interest to students of linguistics and language studies as well as to those on environmental studies courses. *Analyzing Public Discourse* can also be used as a guide for any public consultation which calls for public responses.

Ron Scollon was Professor of Linguistics (now retired) at Georgetown University. He is the co-author (with Suzie Wong Scollon) of the Routledge titles *Nexus Analysis* (2004) and *Discourses in Place* (2003).

Analyzing Public Discourse

Discourse analysis in the making of
public policy

Ron Scollon

Routledge
Taylor & Francis Group

LONDON AND NEW YORK

First published 2008
by Routledge
2 Park Square, Milton Park, Abingdon, Oxon OX14 4RN

Simultaneously published in the USA and Canada
by Routledge
270 Madison Ave, New York, NY 10016

Routledge is an imprint of the Taylor & Francis Group, an *informa* business

Typeset in Bembo by Bookcraft Ltd, Stroud, Gloucestershire
Printed and bound in Great Britain by Biddles Ltd, King's Lynn, Norfolk

British Library Cataloguing in Publication Data
A catalogue record for this book is available from the British Library

Library of Congress Cataloging-in-Publication Data
Scollon, Ron.
  Analyzing public discourse : discourse analysis in the making of public
  policy / by Ron Scollon.
  p. cm.
  1. Discourse analysis—Political aspects. I. Title.
P302.77.S36 2007
401'.41–dc22   2007014084

ISBN10: 0–415–77094–7 (hbk)
ISBN13: 978–0–415–77094–1 (hbk)

Contents

Preface   vii

Acknowledgements   xii

1   Alaskan oil, Scottish scallops, and German paints:
    public consultative discourse analysis   1

2   Action in critical discourse analysis   14

3   The representation of action: summarization, framing,
    and synchronization   42

4   When discourses collide: politics, law, science and
    government in the sale of oil and gas leases   73

5   Document types: who says so? who do they think I am?   97

6   Modes and modality: the multimodal shaping of
    reality in public discourse   128

7   Documents to mediate action (PCDA)   151

Appendix   163
Notes   166
References   174
Index   183

Preface

Discourses are in collision in our world. Democratic society is based on free and open discussion of public policies. Governments, democratic or not, achieve and maintain power by holding their cards close to their chests but democratic ones must do so within a broader discourse of full disclosure, public consultation, and consensus-based management. Political power, now so closely allied to the forces of globalizing economic production, uses the discourses of advertising, marketing, and branding to achieve its hegemony by persuading the public to acquiesce in its ideology. The discourses of law and science stand to one side under a shroud of neutrality, objectivity, and measured certainty even while they often are blended and bent to become mere tools of public coercion in the service of these other powerful discourses.

This book is based on three assumptions about public discourse in a democratic society: (1) public discourse is always and inherently political, (2) stakeholders in the political process may operate from positions of power or from minority positions, and therefore, (3) all participants in public discourse as well as all citizens must face up to the difficult dilemma of trying to win, on the one hand, but, on the other hand, insisting on preserving open, free, non-coercive negotiation of their positions to enable democratic processes for making decisions. The book argues for and presents an action strategy by which discourse analysts can become directly engaged in public discourse, though as a distinctly minority voice.

In our contemporary political environment this position may be thought to be naive, idealistic, or even quixotic. Free and open public discourse must never be let slide to become simply a rhetorical catchphrase in the sale of political ideologies. Genuinely public discourse – discourse of and among the public, not just media shows of rhetorical positioning on issues – must be practiced throughout the society for that society to be and to remain democratic. Readers who feel this position is untenable have no reason to read or argue with this book. In *The Prince* of Machiavelli or *The Art of War* of Sunzi they have ample reading more suited to their ideological position of political victory at all costs. It is a viable position, all too viable, that power and only power matters in politics, but this book takes the position that the experiments with democratic public discourse of the past two or three hundred years or so have not yet been concluded. At the same time, there is an urgent need to revamp our systems of public discourse and restrategize the ways in which minority voices can come to be heard within the political processes of democratic nations.

This book puts forward a strategy by which discourse analysts can become engaged in public discourse as participants, not just as discourse analysts, through the process of public consultations: Public Consultative Discourse Analysis. For our purposes this includes any process in which an agency – government or commercial – opens a public consultation for the purpose of receiving and reacting to public comments on a policy or action proposal. By far the most common of these are the public consultations connected to the preparation of environmental impact statements (EIS).

The focus for this book is on the action taken by a discourse analyst within the consultative process. From one point of view this opens up an arena for analysis that widely expands work that is commonly done within the field of discourse analysis so that it includes any issue of public policy on which a public consultation is opened. From another point of view the focus on action narrows the perspective of topics, research theories and methodologies to those which may be usefully applied in just this situation of preparing and engaging in a public consultation. Readers will find that this focus on action, however, gives a very wide range for the eclectic garnering of crucial and effective theory and practice in discourse analysis. While on the one hand time limits and other constraints on the public consultative process virtually guarantee that an analysis can never be as fully developed as one might wish, on the other hand, the focus on action sharpens the process of selection by which events, actions, documents, and policies are brought into the analysis.

Analyzing Public Discourse: Discourse analysis in the making of public policy arises out of the author's own concern to engage in the maelstrom of discourses in collision surrounding the US government's sale of oil and gas leases in the fragile ocean of ice off the Arctic Coast of Alaska, the Beaufort Sea. Neo-cons and world environmentalists, Alaska Native indigenous communities on the Arctic Coast and the largest of the world's energy corporations, minor government bureaucrats and powerful media and legal apparatuses here come together in direct conflict.

The many stakeholders use all means at their disposal to win in their sometimes fierce struggles with each other. Chief among the strategies and tools which are used in these struggles are spoken and written language. Neo-conservative political forces which are hegemonic in US politics at the time of writing want oil development offshore in the Arctic Ocean and just onshore from there in the Arctic National Wildlife Refuge. The Secretary of the Interior and the Director of the Minerals Management Service, the government agency for these sales, are political appointees of this administration which is frequently accused of basing its domestic and foreign policy on the profits to be made from oil. Environmentalists representing world non-governmental organizations who have never set foot in Alaska, much less on the sea ice of the Beaufort Sea, marshal their forces and don their petroleum-made fleece parkas to appear in public meetings to stop these sales at all costs. The indigenous people who have hunted bowhead whales on the sea ice as well as inland animals for centuries, not only as their economic and nutritional base, but as their central action of cultural cohesion, are faced with the construction of short-term industrial zones which threaten to destroy the animals and their cultural base forever, but at the same time they choose to live in homes which are built of materials imported by jet-fueled airplanes and heated by natural gas which oil companies have extracted from under their foundations. Government officials who began their careers under environmentally more benign governments must be responsive to mandates which are not in keeping with their personal environmental positions.

I have been caught up in this swirl of colliding discourses because of my own personal history. My first arrival in Alaska was in December of 1964 when, coming from Japan, I spent the 12 hours of a fueling and aircraft repair stop in Anchorage looking for a job. I failed in that instance and so my first job in Alaska came four years later, in January of 1969, when I was hired onto a crew of a geophysical prospecting company as a surveyor looking for oil in the Swanson River field on the Kenai Peninsula. Now it is nearly 40 years, three university degrees, and many years of anthropological linguistic research with Alaska Native people later. Beyond my academic research I have also served one three-year term as an elected official in one of these small Alaskan communities. I now have what amounts to a lifetime concern for communication between local Alaskan communities and the organizations and agencies of government and commerce. The extraction of natural resources, from the gold rushes of a hundred years ago to present-day development of oil resources, is always a central concern.

Because the purpose of this book is to outline a general form of discourse analysis, it cannot be a full analysis of any single policy consultation, nor a direct contribution to it. The book does, however, make use of documents which are publicly available online from specific public consultative projects which were current at the time of writing, in order to provide concrete examples. The point of view I take reflects my personal history, from those early experiences in Alaska to my present concern to use my professional work in trying to solve problems of social injustice. I have written the book because I am convinced that the field of discourse analysis not only can be, but should be, directly engaged in the processes of developing public policy, of democratic public discourse, and of social justice. The book outlines how a discourse analyst can locate an important arena of involvement, can become engaged in the public policy process, can produce a pertinent analysis, bring that analysis directly into the process, and continue in engagement as the policy develops. This is not discourse analysis at a distance but discourse analysis as part of the process.

It will, perhaps, surprise you that I believe from a democratic-process point of view that it is more important for the analyst, that is you, the reader, to be committed to engagement in the process of policy development than for you to be a highly specialized and credentialed discourse analyst. The kind of discourse analysis that I propose here can be done by anybody who has just the basic tools of discourse analysis at hand and who has access to a public consultative process. The book introduces these basic skills and shows how to develop your ability with them. As I will show in the practical activities given, public consultations are now abundant in many countries and easily accessed via the internet.

Although the book is not written to be used outside of a public consultation concerning a public policy – that is, it is not written to be used where an engagement in the process cannot be assumed – nevertheless it will also be useful to readers both within (whether or not in support of) and external to (whether or not in opposition to) governmental or non-governmental policy development. While my personal concern is to try to alleviate social injustice through the use of discourse analysis, this book takes the position that it is always in the best interest of democratic public discourse for all participants in the process to be working with a common discursive framework. Whether the openness originates from within organizations and agencies or is politically demanded from outside parties and interests, this book takes the position that democracy demands such openness and that an essential tool of openness in public discourse is the sort of discourse analysis process developed in this book.

As I have worked on this book I have talked to people about it. One question which I have heard frequently is: wouldn't it be much more effective for a discourse analysis to be based on work within an organization such as the Food Standards Agency (UK) or the Minerals Management Service (US)? Wouldn't an ethnographic study of day-to-day practices be more effective than just studying the texts which are made public? In some ways I agree with that position, and it is how I have done most of my previous work. But this is a position weakened by three constraints: access, confidentiality, and the conflict between professional expertise and democratic, non-specialized decision making. First is the problem of access. It is very difficult, though obviously not impossible, for an external ethnographer to gain access to organizations which are central in the development of public policy. And if the ethnographer is or becomes a regular employee of the organization, such organizations are extremely busy. Time constraints on simply doing one's job pretty much preclude ethnographic work.

This limited access is compounded by a second important and necessary requirement, the requirement of confidentiality. Good ethnography is never, in my mind, a kind of whistleblowing. In exchange for access to an organization or a community the ethnographer takes on ethical constraints to treat what one learns with great respect for the needs of the individuals one works with, the organization or the community. Such limited access means that a close and inside ethnography is not nearly as attractive a basis for public discourse analysis as it might seem to be in theory.

Those two problems lead to the third concern. A fine-grained ethnographic discourse analysis can never be predicated as the basis for democratic public participation in public discourse. Nor can institutional position. Very few people have the training, the resources, and the time to produce such a study; few citizens can be members of any particular policy-making organization. Democratic public discourse must confront a dilemma: if only those on the inside really understand the situation and to be effective must keep that understanding confidential, how can ordinary citizens be sufficiently involved that they can participate in the democratic discussions necessary for informed citizen discourse? For public consultations to be anything more than empty charades, ordinary citizens must have the confidence that they have the knowledge to be able to make their own analysis and to make their own judgments about public policies.

What this book offers is a process of discourse analysis – a Public Consultative Discourse Analysis (PCDA) – which is open to a very wide range of public participation. A PCDA is a means for the discourse analyst to engage in a particular kind of mediated action, providing testimony in a public consultative process.

A Public Consultative Discourse Analysis as I have described it in this book works only with publicly available documents within a public consultative process. From the point of view of public discourse this means that a PCDA is a process which does not require and normally does not even allow extended periods of study and credentialization, lengthy commitments to a research project, nor extended periods of seeking access to research sites.

Throughout this book I have worked within these constraints of a PCDA. The case study which I use as the core of the analysis is based entirely on documents which are posted for public consumption on the website of the Minerals Management Service of the US Department of the Interior (USDOI/MMS; citations for specific documents are found in the Appendix). In some of the exercises I have used documents from other agencies around the world as well. The analyses are entirely my own and should not be construed as representing either policies or practices of any of the agencies from which I have accessed documents.

In writing the book I have not used any inside access to the Minerals Management Service, to any of the communities in which oil and gas leases were offered for sale, to any of the energy corporations, nor to any of the environmental groups which have been involved in these sales. Jim Sykes of Oil Watch Alaska generously responded to an email request concerning statistics on US oil usage which he had cited in his public testimony. My research assistant at Georgetown University, Lou Jia, was most helpful in searching the internet for existing public consultations and in making the practice activities I suggested into ones that would work with students. Dawn Weyiouanna, a former research assistant at the University of Alaska Fairbanks kindly let me use her photographs of activities in the Iñupiaq Heritage Center, Barrow.

I have had the good fortune of finding friends who are willing to read and, better yet, offer candid and frank comments on my work. In this case the comments of Sigrid Norris, Tom Bartlett, and Najma Al Zidjaly have strengthened this book substantially. Even rarer among writers is that my family have not just tolerated yet another book when they thought I might be getting over this affliction, they have been very helpful in reading and in discussions of the contents. And finally, three anonymous readers for Routledge provided a number of incisive views of the manuscript that have helped to make it what you see here. I only wish that I had been able to rise to the occasion of writing the book these readers have all suggested that I write.

Acknowledgements

Figures 1.1, 1.2, 2.1, 3.2, 3.3, 3.4, 3.5, 3.6, 3.7, 6.1: Minerals Management Service, US Department of the Interior.
Figures 2.2, 2.3, 3.1, 6.3: *Federal Register,* accessed through GPO Access.
Figures 2.4, 2.5, 4.1, 6.4, 6.5: author.
Figure 5.1: Independent Petroleum Association of America
Figure 6.6: © Topographic map reproduced under licence from Her Majesty the Queen in Right of Canada, with permission of Natural Resources Canada.
Figure 6.7: photographs courtesy of Dawn Weyiouanna.

1 Alaskan oil, Scottish scallops, and German paints

Public consultative discourse analysis

The oil tanker the Exxon Valdez ran aground on Bligh Reef in Prince William Sound, Alaska, on 24 March 1989. Crude oil gushed into the near freezing water and spread with the tides poisoning 500 miles of sea and beaches down the Kenai and Alaska peninsulas. The spill has cost billions of dollars to mitigate and a decade and a half later as much as 80 percent of the spilled oil remains in place in the sub-soils of those beaches.

Scottish scallops contain toxins which may cause amnesic shellfish poisoning (ASP). Symptoms of ASP include nausea, vomiting, stomach cramps, diarrhoea, dizziness, weakness, and lethargy. But the toxins are unevenly distributed; very low amounts are in the main muscle, the part normally eaten by humans, but there are very high concentrations elsewhere. The Food Standards Agency (FSA) Scotland called for public commentary concerning loosening the standards for testing because standards in force in 2001 prevented the harvesting and sale of Scottish scallops which tested for such toxins in any part. The industry was hoping the public would accept more variable standards set by tests taken only in the main muscle.

In October 2003 the German Federal Environmental Agency called for a study of the dangers of paints and varnishes and of cleaning agents and detergents for both manufacturers and downstream users. Because consensus could not be reached among the scientists and members of the advisory board, public commentary and discussion were called for on their website.

Complex science, public policy, and democratic public discourse

Massive oil spills and tsunamis, shellfish poisoning and toxic paints, varnishes and cleaning agents, genetic modification of foods and other life forms, global climate change, and the corporatization of democratic politics are problems which affect each of us as citizens of our own countries and of the world. Whether as citizens or as members of concerned organizations we want to know what we can do to be engaged in the processes of decision making when our lives and the life of our earth are at stake.

Accidents like the Exxon Valdez oil spill catch our attention because of the catastrophic loss of resources, the destruction of the environment and habitats, and the enormous dangers and costs of trying to set things right when they happen. In the United States, the United Kingdom, the European Union and its constituent nations, and in many other places in the world citizens have demanded that they be informed of policies or actions of governments and other organizations which have the potential to cause damage to human life or to the global environment.

Many strategies have been adopted for coming to grips with the need for democratic participation in public policy making. While some argue for working within government agencies, non-governmental organizations (NGOs), or corporations which are responsible for public policy actions, others have chosen confrontational political activism to catch the attention of the world's media in resistance to what are perceived as non-democratic hegemonic public policies. This book presents one strategy for increasing democratic participation in the making of public policy: Discourse analysis in engagement with public consultations on public policy or Public Consultative Discourse Analysis (PCDA).

PCDA is predicated on four principles which are basic to fields as divergent as critical discourse analysis, linguistic or rhetorical analysis, or advertising, marketing and public relations:

- Language is a central means by which we construct our conceptual worlds.
- Our conceptual worlds form a template we use to engage in common day-to-day actions.
- Language can be used either to open up avenues of communication and democratic negotiation or to obfuscate, confuse, or dissemble.
- Those who are adept at using and interpreting language are at an advantage whenever language is the means of setting, consolidating, or undermining sociopolitical positions.

The use of discourse analysis in public consultations is a strategy which can be used equally by government officials or private citizens, corporate public relations officers or environmental activists, professors of discourse analysis or students who are new to the discipline. Government offices, corporations, and most activist NGOs already employ communication specialists, designers, and legal analysts precisely to make sure that their communications are effective. They strategize their own interests whether these are internal communications or communications directed toward the public. This book is designed to make the analytical strategies which are now well established within academic discourse analysis publicly available. It provides a clear and workable method for bringing discourse analysis directly into the setting of public policy through the widely established practice of public consultations.

What is discourse analysis? An opening example

The term discourse analysis covers many different approaches to the study of language as it is used in speaking or in writing. Public consultations consist mostly of documents, and so our central concern with discourse analysis in this book is with the study of documents, though, as we shall see in Chapter 2 and following, it is not just the documents themselves which interest us, but the ways in which documents can be used to direct and enable or to inhibit and block the actions of social actors.

Before going into the overall structure of the book we will first take up a specific example of just one part of a document, the letterhead, to illustrate the way in which we will analyze documents later in the book. This first document is a news release which was issued by the Minerals Management Service of the US Department of the Interior (USDOI/MMS). The MMS is the US government agency which manages the actions of the petroleum industry on the US Outer Continental Shelf. The MMS is responsible for selling leases for exploration, permits for development, environmental impact statements (EIS) and for handling billions of dollars in revenues from sales and royalties. This news release announces one of the actions of the MMS.

A news release is a document which is used to communicate organizational or corporate actions to the public. These documents are written so that the main text can be used as the basis for a journalist to write her or his own story about the action. As it happens in very many cases, the text is not used just for information but is actually published exactly, word-for-word, with the journalist's or publisher's own byline as if they had written the story themselves. From the point of view of discourse analysis news releases are interesting because it is often difficult to find an answer for the common and simple communicative question: who is telling me this? We judge the reliability and the interest of something we read or hear partly on the basis of knowing who is saying it. What comes from one source might be trusted when the same words from another source would be treated with careful doubt. So from the point of view of discourse analysis in a public consultation two points are important: 1) news releases are widely used in such consultations and 2) this genre normally obscures the central communicative question of who is responsible for the contents of the document.

If we read a news story on the *Petroleum News* website it would be fair to assume that the story would reflect the interests and goals of the world petroleum industry. But if the story in the *Petroleum News* is printed word-for-word from a news release issued by the US Department of the Interior's (USDOI) Minerals Management Service (MMS) can we assume that the interests of the petroleum industry are the same as those of the US government? If it represents the interests of the petroleum industry when it appears on industry websites, does it also represent those same interests when it is 'merely' text in an MMS news release? When the same news release is also published on the MMS website, whose interests does it represent?

Discourse analysis is helpful in untying this tangle of representations. As we shall see in Chapter 5, it is essential to be able to analyze who is responsible for the ideas expressed in a document (the principal). This is often confused with the identification of who has created the wordings or the design that we read or see (the author), and with who is merely the mechanical producer of the material object (the animator). A discourse analysis provides the tools for identifying the principals in any communication and to distinguish these from authors and animators.

With this in mind we can look at just the letterhead of a news release in Figure 1.1 from the MMS mentioned above, which was posted on 19 September 2001. The design and layout is much like the letterhead of a common business letter in having the name of the organization as well as a contact name and other contact information. The words 'News Release' in a large sanserif typeface signal clearly what sort of document this is – at least it does for those who know the genre. Even if we did not know about news releases the format would tell us that it was not a common personal or agency letter.

If we ask who is responsible for the communication, this is clearly shown to be 'MMS Alaska OCS Region', even though a reader might not know what 'MMS' represents or 'OCS Region'. Only the '.gov' in the website address, in fact, explicitly signals that the principal who is responsible for this news release is the US government. From there one might work out that the MMS was a sub-agency of the Department of the Interior and that the 'Alaska OCS Region' (Alaska Outer Continental Shelf Region) is a sub-agency of the MMS. For those who know the telephone area code (907), this indicates that the office issuing this news release is in Alaska as does the '/alaska' in the website address.

The only person who is identified is Robin Lee Cacy but there are no indications of this person's role, whether that is as principal, author, or animator. One needs to know two acronyms and an area code to pin down this responsibility. From a discourse-analysis point of view, all of this adds up to indicating that this is an insider's communication. It is designed for an audience which knows these acronymic identifications and what authority they carry. It is a document that enables action only for a specific user, but one who is not explicitly identified.

MMS Alaska OCS Region

News Release

For Immediate Release–September 19, 2001

Robin Lee Cacy
907-271-6070
1-800-764-2627
www.mms.gov/alaska

MMS Announces Multiple Sale Process for Alaska's Beaufort Sea

---

Figure 1.1 Minerals Management Service, US Department of the Interior

While the news release was published on the MMS website, it was also printed verbatim on the *Petroleum News* website (Vol. 6, No. 9, Week of 23 September 2001: www.petroleumnews.com). But when it was published by the *Petroleum News* Kay Casman was identified as the author. The news release was not picked up or published by any other media source insofar as can be determined by an internet search. We can ask again: who is it giving us this news and what responsibility are they taking in this communication? Who is engaged in what action here? With just this analysis to go on at this point all indicators are that this news release is a joint government–industry announcement. It appears almost simultaneously in a government document and in an industry document word-for-word as 'the same text'. While it may not be dramatic news that the MMS and the petroleum industry are working hand-in-hand in the multiple sale process which is being announced, this discourse analysis gives documentary substance to that claim. This claim could be important, given that one mandate in the establishment of the MMS is to regulate the petroleum (and minerals) industry, particularly in respect to environmental protection.

Multimodal discourse analysis or visual semiotics (Kress and van Leeuwen 1996, 2001; Scollon and Scollon 2003; see Notes section for further notes on sources) has become an important analytical perspective when dealing with complex documents that use both texts and images. One more news release from the MMS will show how a discourse analysis which uses these tools can tell us even more about the people who stand behind communications that are produced as documents.

Four years after the news release shown in Figure 1.1 the same MMS issued a news release on 24 February 2005. This is shown in Figure 1.2. This news release also concerned the sale of oil and gas leases in the Beaufort Sea off the Arctic Coast of Alaska. It was published on the MMS website and was taken up and published by 'RIGZONE, your gateway to the oil and gas industry' (www.petroengineers.com). Again this news release was not published by any

Figure 1.2 Minerals Management Service, US Department of the Interior

other media sources insofar as an internet search was able to establish. The content text was published word-for-word but with no author byline.

The most striking aspect of this news release is the newly designed full-color MMS letterhead. In this new design for the letterhead what had been obscure and 'insider' in the old news release is open and explicit. The USDOI is plainly identified and hierarchically listed above the MMS and that is above Robin Cacy's assignment in the Office of Public Affairs. There are two differences, however, that are worth noting. Alaska itself is much less visible in this news release and US national politics is very much more visible. Only the telephone area code (907) now indicates that this news release originated in Anchorage and not at the MMS national office in Herndon, Virginia. Alaska and the outer continental shelf, including the Beaufort Sea, have been subsumed to the nation of the United States. The lease sale is no longer displayed as a regional issue but as a national one.

Playing up the nation and playing down the region is most strongly signaled in the full-color images of the new and highly designed image collage of the letterhead. We now see images where before we saw only text. While the images and the grammar of this design will be taken up in detail in Chapter 6 on 'Modes and modality', here two points can be made: first, the design is centered on the US national flag and a slogan has been added. This slogan, 'Securing Ocean Energy and Economic Value for America', has also been added to the MMS website. The mandate of the MMS for environmental protection is invisible. US national (energy) security and US national economic policy are highlighted.

A discourse analysis of text and image in this news release shows an important shift in national–state relations which is graphically given in the center–periphery composition visual grammar of the letterhead (see Chapter 6). It is a shift from a difficult balancing of development and environmental protection mandates in the earlier news release to the assertion of the US government political position on national security and the US energy policy through the office of the US Department of Interior, the home office of the MMS (USDOI/ MMS). Perhaps it is not surprising that the significant political events which have occurred between these two news releases are the US war in Iraq and – just a month before the switch to this new letterhead in February of 2005 – the second inauguration of the political administration of George W. Bush and Dick Cheney, both strong, vocal advocates of just the political positions signaled in this news release.

Discourse analysis gives us analytical tools to examine such issues in documents like these news releases which make up the documents of a public consultation, as we shall see in the chapters to follow, especially in Chapter 5 on 'Document types'. We will examine questions such as: who says so? That is, who are the principals who are taking responsibility for this document? Who are the actual authors? In this case of the shift to the new letterhead along with the new slogan we can guess that it was mandated from the national office, but the text for publication was authored in the regional office in Anchorage. Whether we have inside access to that information or not, it is clear that there has been a strong shift toward the declaration of the US government as the principal as well as of that principal's political ideology.

We shall also see that we can develop an analysis from the point of view of the reader or viewer of these documents as well. We can uncover answers to questions such as: who do they think I am? That is, who is being addressed by this document? What am I supposed to do or what am I being prohibited from doing? Who is supposed to act on this? What am I not being told? Why?

As preparation for this analysis of the document types in Chapter 5 we will take up the question of discourses themselves in Chapter 4. We will examine questions such as: what discourses are present? Is this science or is it politics using science rhetorically? Is it politics or is it science in the service of politics? Who is authorized to use this discourse, who is discredited? What arguments 'count' in this discourse and what arguments are discredited? How do these issues enable some actions and prohibit or limit others, and for which social actors?

What is public consultative discourse analysis (PCDA)?

Discourse analysis has many forms. These include the analysis of specific conversations in spoken discourse (conversational analysis, pragmatics, speech act theory, interactional sociolinguistics, variation analysis) and the analysis of texts and documents (genre analysis, text analysis). All of these are most closely tied to the field of linguistics. At the same time the term encompasses the analysis of social discourses such as we find in political science, communication, literary criticism, cultural geography, cultural studies and semiotics. Critical discourse analysis, which is central to this book, bridges these two ends of the spectrum, though commonly with a stronger focus on text analysis than on spoken discourse. Much linguistic anthropological research also bridges the spectrum from careful analysis of face-to-face communication to the production of more fixed texts and practices. The discourse analysis which is presented in this book lies closer to the linguistic and text-analytical end of this broad spectrum because of the emphasis, in public consultations, on written documents.

This is not to suggest in any way that document approaches to discourse analysis are somehow either more scientifically reliable on the one hand or more pragmatically effective on the other. Public consultative discourse analysis (PCDA) is oriented toward bringing discourse analysis in any relevant form into the process of the making of public policy. This book focuses on the more linguistic end of the spectrum simply because the theoretical positions as well as the methodological tools which can be brought to the table are considerable, on the one hand, and, on the other, have not yet been much utilized in the processes of public discourse.

The form of discourse analysis most used in *Analyzing Public Discourse* is the discourse analysis of documents, though this is principally within the framework of mediated discourse analysis and the methodological extension of nexus analysis, as will be discussed in Chapter 2. This is because most public consultative processes are based on written policy statements, written responses to them, and then, in turn, adjustments or responses in document form to that feedback. Even where spoken testimony is taken at public hearings, as we shall see in Chapter 2, only formally transcribed written testimony which is authenticated as the on-record positions of the participants is regarded as relevant and the only responses which are given are to such written or transcribed testimony.

But it is not just the analysis of texts or documents nor the mediated discourse/nexus analysis perspective which constitutes the basic strategy of PCDA. Nor is it the focus on the analysis of issues of public discourse, as we see in the work of Fairclough on the language of 'New Labour' in the UK, Wodak in studies of policy making in the European Union, Van Dijk together with Wodak in the study of racism in six European states, Flowerdew in the analysis of the British strategies for withdrawal of sovereignty in Hong Kong, Smart on the ways in which global economic policies are crafted in the internal workings of the Bank of Canada, or Hensel in the study of public hearings concerning subsistence hunting and living in Alaska. Studies such as these are important resources for this book and for PCDA. The way in which PCDA augments these other forms of discourse analysis is the strategy of returning the analysis to the actual practices and actions of the policy-making process through the practice of public hearings or public consultations. The studies just mentioned, crucial as they are both for discourse analysis and for the development of a critique of the process of public discourse, stand at a distance from the process itself. While public officials, citizens, and interested organizations may read these academic research reports and perhaps even be influenced by them, there is no established mechanism for these discourse analyses to be inserted into the policy-making process itself.

As has happened in the European Union, the UK and numerous other political jurisdictions, since the passing of the National Environmental Protection Act (NEPA) into law in the US in 1969, the process of producing an environmental impact statement (EIS) is the main way in which public commentary on potentially dangerous environmental impacts is to be received. As the website of the USDOI (www.doi.gov) puts it,

> NEPA describes a vision for balancing environmental, cultural, and economic goals. It provides the primary basis for public comment on agency decisions through consideration of the environmental effects of federal actions.

Regulations concerning the EIS, and which are binding on all agencies and organizations who are required to file them (http://ceq.eh.doe.gov/nepa/regs/ceq/1502.htm), state that:

The primary purpose of an environmental impact statement is to serve as an action-forcing device to insure that the policies and goals defined in the Act are infused into the ongoing programs and actions of the Federal Government. It shall provide full and fair discussion of significant environmental impacts and shall inform decisionmakers and the public of the reasonable alternatives which would avoid or minimize adverse impacts or enhance the quality of the human environment ... An environmental impact statement is more than a disclosure document. It shall be used by Federal officials in conjunction with other relevant material to plan actions and make decisions.

The key phrase here is the first: the EIS is to 'serve as an action-forcing device.' An essential part of the process is that it must be done in two stages. First a draft environmental impact statement (DEIS) must be made, then a call for responses from all interested or affected parties, individual or group, is made and a reasonable time is given for them to make their responses, either in writing or at a publicly convened hearing. The final statement (FEIS) must then incorporate the texts of these responses as well as responses to points raised and these become binding on the actions enabled by the process.

The term 'public hearing' is most commonly used in the US. A very similar process has been adopted in the UK and in the European Union under the term 'public consultation' (http://www.consultations.gov.uk and http://europa.eu.int/ yourvoice/consultations/index_en.htm). All three of these cases as well as others now in action in other nations and also in the United Nations call for public commentary on issues of importance to society and to the world. While not all calls for information, responses, or public commentary throughout the world are as closely bound to response as the EIS process in the US, in all cases these consultations and hearings are a significant mechanism by which discourse analysis may be brought into direct engagement with the process of policy making.

Against this background of a well-established public consultative mechanism it is striking, then, that no examples of the use of this kind of discourse analysis were found in a rather extended search of public consultations including commentary from NGOs and other activist organizations either as a tool in support of or in resistance to the policies or actions under consideration in the consultation. To put this another way, while much communicative effort is expended in advertising, lobbying, legal analyses, and other forms of promotion by the agencies and organizations seeking to bring a policy or action into being, none of this promotion of policy positions is being examined *within the process itself* as part of that process. The goal of this book is to augment the public consultative process by introducing discourse analysis to this process.

As we shall see in Chapter 4 on discourses and Chapter 5 on document types, in the case study of the EIS prepared by the MMS for oil and gas leases in the Beaufort Sea, there was much blending and bending of discourses both in the documents presented by the MMS and in the testimony given by interested parties in the public hearings. As that analysis will make clear, even though the USDOI intent is to balance environmental, cultural, and economic goals of all stakeholders through the mechanism of the EIS, in fact, science and law become hegemonic discourses in the process. Members of the public who gave testimony based on cultural or economic arguments were sidelined as not addressing the so-called scientific findings of the EIS. The EIS had been blended into the scientific discourse and then the scientific discourse was bent to the service of political goals. What is striking is the extent to which most participants simply accepted this discursive strategy as given and then failed to make their points heard because these points were disallowed as non-scientific. A clear discourse analysis of the documents and of the testimony would make this discursive strategy visible and would then become a factor in itself that must be taken into consideration in further development of public policy.

PCDA as it is presented in this book is designed primarily so that it can be used in an individual project of activist engagement in a public consultation. Naturally, this will place limits on the size and scope of the project that can be worked on. Consultations that have been worked on by the author give about two months between the call for responses until the deadline for commentary. Public hearings are held about mid way in this two-month period. This is obviously a short time period in which to conduct a full-blown analysis of thousands of pages of documents as well as to do the background research into the issue itself under discussion. Nevertheless, much can be done in this amount of time and in the following chapters strategies for getting the most effective analyses done in a relatively brief period will be presented.

PCDA may also be used, perhaps even more effectively, in a group project. This is particularly good if the group is constituted as an interdisciplinary group where the discourse analysis provides one tool of analysis among others such as research on organizational development, public policy formation, mass communication and media analysis, environmental design and the sociopolitical environment within which the actions or policies are proposed to take place. Such a team or task-force structure would be well suited to placement within an agency or NGO as it develops its own policies and practices and seeks to strategize ways of engaging these in negotiation with the policies and practices of political opponents. Many currently existing research or study projects being done under rubrics of critical discourse analysis or (critical) mass communication research would be highly amenable to adding PCDA as a component of existing development strategies.

Finally, there is a recent move not just in governmental agencies such as those mentioned above in the US, UK, and Europe but also within the corporate world which is being called corporate social responsibility (CSR). While this movement should be approached with caution because of the tendency inherent in it to pre-empt critique by a relatively shallow display of self-criticism and analysis, this is one further area in which PCDA has the potential of making an important contribution to a democratic and public process of policy development.

The structure of *Analyzing Public Discourse*

This introductory chapter has presented a sketch of what PCDA is and a brief overview of how it can be used in practice. Throughout the book examples are drawn mostly from one basic case study having to do with the sale of oil leases in the Beaufort Sea. First, I prepared analyses of the documents in this case study. A draft of this analysis was circulated among a number of friendly readers. That discussion led to major revisions in what has become Chapters 2 and 3. Those comments also isolated three factors that might be most productive for further development: the multiple discourses which circulate through these documents, the wide array of document types or genres, and the variety of modes in different modal configurations. These then became the contents for the analyses of Chapters 4, 5, and 6. The final chapter distills this process into a form that can be used by readers for their own PCDAs.

The approach to discourse analysis on which the book is based is mediated discourse analysis as extended through nexus analysis. This is because that framework is organized around the social action as its unit of analysis rather than documents, or texts, or face-to-face social interaction as in other frameworks of discourse analysis. This, then, is the substance of Chapter 2. The chapter begins with a theory and case study section which outlines the theoretical foundation of mediated discourse analysis, and shows how it is related to other forms of discourse analysis which are used in this book. The chapter then introduces the case study, the multiple sale process for oil and gas leases in the Beaufort Sea, 2001–7, and the documents themselves as they have been used in the research underlying the book. The practice section of Chapter 2 then gives three assignments which will guide the reader in beginning a PCDA analysis. The assignments are based on the theoretical foundation, and the reader will select a real social issue or public policy on which to focus. A central problem with studying action is that action always stands in complex relationships with the language we use to talk about action. While on the surface of it we can easily tell the difference between an action such as speaking in a public hearing and an account of that action (a transcript) which is made and entered into the public record, or the summary of that account which forms part of an FEIS or the response to that summary which also occurs in the FEIS, these accounts are also actions in themselves. Action in the world and actions accomplished through discourse are just two of many types of action and so Chapter 3 begins by calling attention to the need to be aware of the relationships between documents and the actions they take or account for.

A consultation on public policy or actions inevitably engages in anticipatory and retrospective accounts of actions. Because these accounts do not occur within the same time and space of the actions themselves, they inevitably must summarize actions, frame and reframe them, and ultimately synchronize multiple actions that occur across different time spans within a single space-time-action space. The theory and case study section of Chapter 3, then, takes on this problem of reframings of actions that occur not only in public consultations but in the discourse analyses themselves. The contribution that PCDA has to offer to this inherent problem of discourse and action is to bring together explicit alternate accounts of the actions under consideration into the democratic dialectic of the public–agency dialogue.

The practice section of Chapter 3 provides four activities which examine and compare multiple accounts of 'the same' action as found within existing documents taken from recent public consultations. In this chapter activities are also directed to assist the reader in locating and comparing the full panoply of relevant documents for a specific social issue or consultation. These are designed to begin the reader's engagement with a concrete instance of PCDA of his or her own interest.

The central analytical concept used in PCDA is interdiscursivity. The democratic consultative process brings together many different stakeholders, each of whom may be grounded in a separate discourse in a public negotiation which is attempting to achieve different goals, partly through the force of law, partly through the evidence of science, partly through social and cultural conventions that are encoded in political discourses, and partly through rhetorical persuasion. Interdiscursivity is the term used in critical discourse analysis to refer to this mixing of different discourses through processes of blending, bending, or eclipsing. Chapter 4 begins with a theoretical discussion of interdiscursivity which is illustrated through examples taken from the Beaufort Sea Sale of gas and oil leases.

In the practice section examples are drawn from a variety of other public consultations to give the reader experience first in the classification of discourses through factors of participation, agency, lexicogrammar, argumentation, genres, and modes. Then these examples are used to give the reader guided experience in untangling the webs of interdiscursivity which occur in some of the actual documents which have been chosen in his or her own project.

Discourses are always material. They may take the form of acts of speaking by humans, their memories of such acts, or artifacts in the world from highways, medicines, buildings or documents. A full, mediated discourse analysis as extended through a nexus analysis seeks to examine the cycles of discourses as they move through changes and transformations from actions to language, to documents or objects, and back into language and further actions. In this way a PCDA differs from a mediated discourse analysis: the focus is on documents, as these are what constitute the majority of the material objects in which a public policy process is instantiated. The theoretical section of Chapter 5 first introduces the basic elements which need to be established about each document for a PCDA: the function, framing and document design, to begin with, as these are the means of analyzing writer/reader (producer/receiver) positions which are established in the document. Then, with these established, it is possible to analyze which discourses are circulating within the document and what kinds of blending, bending, or eclipsing are performed by the document.

Chapter 5 examines the many different document types or genres in the case study. Six of these need to be distinguished, because they take such different stances in respect to the discourses present in the lease sale process as well as to the producer–reader relationships that are established. At one extreme are the formal and off-putting but also very accurate, informative, and legally binding notices in the *Federal Register*. At the other extreme are documents from external sources which are found enclosed as part of what are called Leasing Activities Information memos. Participants in the process are merely encouraged to pay attention to these enclosed documents.

Thus the practice session presents two activities which first assist the reader in analyzing the reader/writer positions in the document types which are present in his or her own project and then, using a news release as an example, lead the student to make an analysis of the production positions that are used in such news releases.

In the chapters which precede Chapter 6 there are numerous instances in which it is useful to call attention to matters of design and layout of documents. As we have already seen in this introductory chapter the shift from the mode of a simple, print-based letterhead to a full-color mode which incorporates a highly designed letterhead may signal a major shift in the discourses present in the document or in the relative hierarchy of those discourses. Chapter 6 takes up the theoretical framework of multimodal discourse analysis and visual semiotics as an important tool in the discourse analysis of many forms of documents which appear in public consultations. Not least among these 'documents' are the websites which are widely used to organize such consultations.

As documents in the case study show, the most powerful documents are the obligatory sheets that must be filled in and filed to accomplish the transactions between bidders and the US government for the exchange of millions of dollars. Perhaps paradoxically, these are rather plain, in fact quite ugly, documents. At the other extreme, the highly designed and colorful website and news releases provide only the merest bits and pieces of non-binding general information.

Chapter 6, then, gives examples in the practice section of different document designs for readers to examine from the point of view of a grammar of visual design. Other activities ask the reader to examine documents from his or her own project with an eye toward evaluating the degree to which the amount of attention to design correlates to the importance of the document in the consultative process.

The practice sections of Chapters 2 through 6 will have given the reader examples as well as activities in which the reader can begin to construct his or her own PCDA project. In Chapter 7 the main principles are extracted by which such a discourse analysis can be constructed. This chapter includes both pointers on how to become engaged in a consultation and how to actually write a PCDA so that it will engage the policy makers and other interested participants in the process.

The main chapters are followed by an Appendix which gives the full details of the documents in the case study which is used throughout the book. Finally there are the Notes covering points in the main body of the book, and the formal citations in the References, to which they are keyed.

2 Action in critical discourse analysis

The Minerals Management Service today issued a Call for Information and Nominations and Notice of Intent to Prepare an Environmental Impact Statement. ...

AGENCY: Mineral Management Service (MMS, Interior).
ACTION: Call for Information and Nominations and Notice of Intent (Call/NOI) to Prepare an Environmental Impact Statement (EIS).

THEORY – CASE STUDY

The two pieces of text here at the start of this chapter were published on the same day by the same US government agency, the Minerals Management Service (MMS) of the US Department of the Interior (USDOI) but in two different documents. The first is part of the opening sentence of the news release we saw as Figure 1.1 at the start of the first chapter. The second is the opening section of the notice concerning the same action which was published in the *Federal Register*. The first is written as a fairly simple declarative sentence; the second is set up as two blocks of text separated into the identification of the government agency and a statement of the action being taken. The first is a statement about an action, the second is the action. The first tells us about the action of the MMS, the second performs the action of issuing the 'Call for Information and Nominations'.

But does it perform this action? This is problematical. On 19 September 2001 when the *Federal Register* was published in Washington, as it is daily at 6:00 a.m. EST, the action of issuing the 'Call' was performed in that action of publication. But here at the top of this page or in Figure 2.2 below, the MMS is not issuing this call ever again, and again each time the text is read. Now a very different action is being accomplished with this piece of the document. We could call this action 'illustrating the concept of action-with-a-document in the book *Analyzing Public Discourse*'.

This is the problem of action in critical discourse analysis: a text or document may be performing a cluster of actions in any particular moment or instance of its use and the actions may change, indeed they are almost certain to change, with each new instance of the use of the document. Mediated discourse analysis (MDA) is the theoretical position within critical discourse analysis (CDA) which is grounded in the analysis of actual attestable actions in real time and space as they are taken by specific social actors. The question for analysis is never only: what actions are possible with this text? The question is: what action is being taken by what social actor in a concrete material place in the world at a specific time and how is the document or text (or any other mediational means) used by the social actor as a tool for taking that action? This is a difficult and complex question to answer; that cannot be denied. But it is crucial to make this analysis of real-space-and-time action in order to undertake social action in the world which lies at the center of our interest in PCDA.

Action as the unit of analysis

Linguistic actions have been the subject of linguistic analysis since the beginnings of speech act theory in the 1960s. This line of linguistic analysis is now also often referred to as pragmatics. The central concept organizing speech act theory or pragmatics is the distinction between the meaning of a linguistic structure when it is abstracted from the context of its use and the meaning of an utterance by a speaking (or writing) agent who is acting in the world. This is sometimes referred to as the distinction between the *sentence's meaning* and the *speaker's meaning* in the writing of literary theorists and philosophers. It was also prefigured by much work in linguistic anthropology, where it was insisted that the most fruitful focus of language study was not the structures of language per se but the study of language as a tool people use to do things in the world.

If we return for a moment to the two segments at the beginning of this chapter, in the news release we saw the sentence,

> The Minerals Management Service today issued a Call for Information and Nominations and Notice of Intent to Prepare an Environmental Impact Statement.

The meaning of the *sentence* (not the *speaker*) is clear enough: An agency ('MMS') has taken an action ('issued a Call'). The action taken by the sentence, however, is not issuing the call even though the sentence was produced and published on that day by the MMS. The meaning of the *speaker* (not the *sentence*) is to say that an agency ('MMS') is telling you that that agency has issued a call (elsewhere, but just where is not stated).

If we compare this with the *Federal Register* notice, there we do not find a sentence at all but rather a standard, formatted entry that specifies an agent and its action. The 'sentence' is constructed through the design/formatting of the standard *Federal Register* notice. The *speaker's* meaning reads something like:

> We (the US government) announce with this publication that we (through our agency MMS) are hereby taking the action of issuing a call.

As we shall see in Chapter 5, it is essential for any PCDA to be able to read the text, layout, and design of documents to be able to determine both what the action is and *who* is taking the action. As we saw in Figure 1.1 in Chapter 1, the news release is a specific document type in which the responsibility for the content (the meaning of the utterance) is indicated by the letterhead and by labeling it as a 'news release'. Here in Figure 2.1 is the crucial portion of the document for this analysis.

The white space between the letterhead and the title with the subsequent text is the boundary between the principal (MMS)/author (Robin Lee Cacy) and what they have to say (the text of the news release). Together this produces the complex, multimodal 'sentence' in which the subject of the sentence shifts in midstream:

> We (MMS and Robin Lee Cacy) are telling you that we/they (MMS) are issuing a call today.

The *Federal Register* is the official publication of the US government in which notices, rules, proposed rules, and executive orders are published. It is published daily at 6:00 a.m. EST and carries the force of the US government. Nowhere is this explicitly stated in the document itself. The document does not say in text, 'By the power vested in me by the Congress of the United States, I hereby notify you that the MMS is issuing a call.' But this is not absent from the document. Figure 2.2 shows how the text which appeared at the top of this chapter appeared within the standard *Federal Register* printed format.

The pragmatic function of saying 'By the power vested in me by the Congress of the United States, I hereby notify you ...' in so many explicit words is carried in this case by the page header of the document, as we can see in Figure 2.3.

News Release

For Immediate Release—September 19, 2001	Robin Lee Cacy
	907-271-6070
	1-800-764-2627
	www.mms.gov/alaska

MMS Announces Multiple Sale Process for Alaska's Beaufort Sea

The Minerals Management Service today issued a Call for Information and
Nominations and Notice Of Intent to Prepare an Environmental Impact Statement for

Figure 2.1 Minerals Management Service, US Department of the Interior

DEPARTMENT OF THE INTERIOR

Minerals Management Service

Outer Continental Shelf (OCS), Alaska Region, Beaufort Sea, Oil and Gas Lease Sales 186, 195, and 202 for Years 2003, 2005, and 2007

AGENCY: Minerals Management Service (MMS), Interior.

ACTION: Call for Information and Nominations and Notice of Intent (Call/ NOI) to Prepare an Environmental Impact Statement (EIS).

Figure 2.2

This page header, which is elsewhere authorized and mandated by the US government, carries the pragmatic load of saying who is making the notice and who holds responsibility for it.

The analyses of discourses and document types in Chapters 4 and 5 will make much use of such multimodal pragmatic analyses of how documents tell us who is responsible for saying what to whom. This much of discourse analysis within PCDA relies very directly on these earlier studies in speech act theory, pragmatics, literary theory, linguistic philosophy and linguistic anthropology of the ways in which documents and texts may take action in the world. But there is still the problem that these remain potentials for meaning, not actual meanings as they occur in actions taken by social actors. Although the news release and the *Federal Register* notice were very different in their pragmatic force on 19 September 2001, today as you read these texts they are texts which enable a very different kind of action, the illustration of pragmatic force in a textbook on PCDA.

An important influence in the development of MDA has been social interactional analysis, which has focused on the moment-by-moment construction of the social world in face-to-face communication. From the perspective

48268   Federal Register / Vol. 66, No. 182 / Wednesday. September 19, 2001 / Notices

Figure 2.3

of MDA, until a document or text is brought into a real-time, ongoing social interaction any meanings it might be said to have are merely potential meanings, not actions in the world. An environmental impact statement which is stacked in a box on the floor may be used to prop up one's feet but the text the document materializes is at most black marks on a white page under one's feet, not, as the US government would have it, 'an action-forcing device'.

To put this another way, a text or a document (or any other mediational means) participates in only those actions which it mediates, not others. So for MDA to undertake an analysis of a text or a document, the primary question is: what action (by specific social actors in the real world) is this document mediating, and how is it accomplishing that mediation? More specifically, the analysis needs to determine *how* the document is mediating the action. Is it through its material existence alone, as is the case with the EIS stacked on the floor? Is it through the text, or the images or the combination of text and images which are laid out as a grammatical whole, as we have seen in the case of both the news release and the notice in the *Federal Register* above?

MDA, then, takes the mediated action as the object of analysis. Looked at in this way we can see that an MDA requires the analysis of three conceptual entities which always and inherently constitute a mediated action:

- the individual social actor (always one or more),
- the socially organized relationship for acting between that social actor (those social actors) and any others who are co-present in the moment of action (there is no action which is not socially organized), and
- the mediational means which mediate the action (there are no actions which are not mediated).

These three theoretical concepts have been developed in greater detail elsewhere (see Notes and References).

In MDA the analysis of the individual social actor has used the term the 'historical body'. This term, developed from the philosophy of Nishida, refers to the accumulated physical and psychological history of the person which forms the basis for all actions through what Nishida calls 'action-intuition'. In other words, each action of the person arises out of this history, whether consciously or unconsciously, whether in automatic response to a situation or in thoughtful, reflective resistance to one's own history. The term is much like the term 'habitus' as developed by Bourdieu from earlier social theorists such as Elias. The term 'historical body' is different from 'habitus', however, in that it is never used generally or collectively. That is, while Bourdieu writes of the habitus of a social group or social class, historical body always makes reference only to the individual social actor.

This book is oriented toward the practical application of this theoretical approach to discourse analysis. Here, while introducing the theoretical framework, it is necessary to clarify the terms 'habitus' and 'historical body' throughout the remainder of the book; and certainly when writing a PCDA for a non-specialist reader as part of the consultative process, it is normally sufficient to use more common terms such as 'participant' or even 'person'. From the perspective of MDA the main point to be remembered is that each person in each social interaction is bringing his or her full history of experience as well as the dispositions to act in particular ways to that moment of action. Often it is important to know this life experience in order to be able to understand an action.

The analysis of the socially organized relationship for acting among social actors who are co-present in the moment of action within MDA uses the concept of the 'interaction order' as developed by Goffman. Taking Goffman's argument that all social interactions are socially organized among those who are present to the interaction, it is a central theoretical issue in MDA to analyze how the social actor is grounded in what social-interactional organization as an action is undertaken. Reading a statement in opposition to the proposal to loosen standards for testing shellfish such as Scottish scallops, which was mentioned in Chapter 1, takes on very different meanings, that is, it forms very different actions, when the statement is read alone at one's desk while writing it, when it is read out loud to a circle of equally committed members of an activist opposition, or read out loud in the meeting of a government committee commissioned to receive testimony on this policy. Even that reading may take on very different meanings depending on whether the person reading it is currently established as properly having the floor to speak or, as in a demonstration, reading it as an interruption of some other speaker who has been designated by the ongoing interaction order as properly having the right to speak. While the meaning of the text may be the same in terms of its potential for interpretation, the meaning of the act of reading depends utterly on the interaction order in place at the moment of reading it.

Finally, the texts themselves, along with all of the other mediational means that are either being used in the action or being sidelined, ignored, or disattended are theoretically pulled together in MDA with the concept of the 'discourses in place'. The two questions of concern are first, what discourses are present at the time-place of a social interaction and, second, how are those discourses used by social actors to enable, inhibit, facilitate or obstruct the action itself. As we saw with the concept of the interaction order, the meaning of an action – what kind of action it is taken to be – may be very different depending on its relation to the discourses also present in that moment. In public consultative hearings, for example, like in many other forms of meetings, there is a clear distinction maintained between talk which is on record and that which is off record. Off-record talk is normally backgrounded by whispering or speaking *sotto voce*, on-record talk is foregrounded by being directed to the convener of the hearing as well as by being spoken into a microphone for recording and transcription. Exactly the same talk would be a very different kind of action if said at home among friends while something was playing on the TV.

The idea of discourses in place at the moment of action is perhaps the most complex one of the three theoretical entities. Texts such as the documents that enable, record, or comment on a public policy form complex chains of intertextuality in which each text refers backward in time to previous texts and forward in time to texts which have not yet been produced. Each text incorporates other texts within it as quotations or as indirect references or as reactions to them, much in the way the first news release of the MMS made reference to the actual action of announcing the call that was published simultaneously in the *Federal Register* or the letterhead of the later news release (Figure 1.2) incorporated the political slogan of the current US government. These chains of texts form extended discourses.

These discourses may be the enormous, complex, and intertextual (you could even say 'intersemiotic') array of texts and other semiotic representations that exist in the world as newspapers, books, films, CDs, pixels on computer and television screens, or light-sensitive metals on photographic paper as they are largely within critical discourse analysis (CDA). But texts, as representations of discourses, may also exist materially as they do within sociocultural (neo-Vygotskian) theory, in and as the bodies (as both conscious and unconscious process) of individual social actors. They may exist materially as they do in distributed cognition theories, in the bodies of other social actors as they are integrated interactionally in joint social actions. A government bureaucrat or the representative of an NGO speaking in a public hearing does not need to know each detail of a scientific study, for example, as long as her colleague carries that portion of the discourse they are constructing together. That is, discourses become available for appropriation for individual social actors through social interactions with others in whom the discourses have been internalized.

But also discourses may exist materially as they have been theorized to do in cultural geography, for example, as the material objects and artifacts of our lives and the built and 'natural' environments in which we conduct our social action. What begins as a proposal to sell leases is transformed into an EIS, which is further transformed into a bidding process which may be followed by material operations which result in drilling oil wells. It is just this circulation and transformation of discourses into actions and objects which is at stake in a public consultative process.

These relationships among theoretical entities as they form a social action or mediated action can be suggested by Figure 2.4.

It is important to note that each of these three analytical entities is to a great extent encompassed in the others. In a social action, that is in a mediated action, the historical bodies of the participants carry in them each, independently, but also differently, the histories of their own internalizations of previous social interactions, including ways of talking about them. Each participant knows to call it a meeting or a conversation or a public consultation as well as the much finer details of habitual behavior and interpretations of that behavior in others that we think of simply as behaving normally under the circumstances. That is,

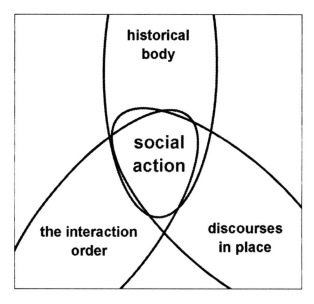

Figure 2.4

each participant has internalized both a varied array of possible actions together with others, as well as ways of talking about those actions and their meanings.

In the same way, each participant carries multiple discourses in her or his historical body, the social languages and social genres of which Bakhtin wrote. Each carries a history with tables and microphones, with particular kinds of texts and documents and of certain spoken genres, as well as various forms of architecture and building design. The discourses in place have been internalized to greater or lesser extent over the experiences of each historical body's lifetime, leading up to that moment of action.

The interaction order is materially embodied in the historical bodies of the participants (as memories and reflections on social interactions and expectations on outcomes) and concretized in the objects, artifacts, and built structures within which an action occurs. A conversation may be smoothly constructed by participants in a quiet kitchen or work against the noise and chaos of a large, public coffee shop. In each case the conversation itself will be acted within and against the jointly constructed discourses in place. The presence of other family members in the quiet kitchen or the isolation from such involvements that can be comforting in public places are both material components of the interaction order that MDA does not theoretically allow to be abstracted as simply a conversation.

As is implied in these paragraphs on the historical body and the interaction order, the discourses in place are partly concretized directly in texts, signs, objects, and buildings, partly embodied in the historical bodies of the participants, and are socially organized as action through the interaction order that is established by the participants (and the concrete spaces and objects). The discourses in place are seen within MDA as both enabling resources, such as when we speak in order to be heard, and as constraining limits, such as when we can't find the words to express ourselves.

Finally, in concluding this theoretical outline of MDA we need to note that each of the three analytical concepts (or we might have said as well each of the points of view) by which the mediated action is examined is inherently historical. The historical body of the individual social actor carries the psychological and bodily experience of this person in both conscious reflection and unconscious memory – what Bourdieu calls 'genesis amnesia'. We know how to act but have long forgotten how and when we learned those ways of acting.

Events of the interaction order, from chance meetings of friends through major ceremonial events, are inherently time-ordered sequences with beginnings, endings, rituals for joining, suspending participation, or dissolution. Discourses are, as we have noted above, extended intertextual sequences, often involving resemiotizations, recontextualizations, or revoicings which transform talk into action and again into fixed material objects, from texts to oil wells, from laboratory experiments to genetically modified foods on your dinner plate.

MDA, then, takes the mediated action (or social action) as its focal point of analysis; this is the unified entity of the social actor acting through the use of some mediational means. Three analytical concepts are used to triangulate on this moment of action:

- the historical body of the social actor(s),
- the interaction order that obtains for that moment of action among all of the social actors who are co-constructing the action, and
- the discourses in place which enable or constrain the mediated action.

Each of these theoretical entities is in itself historical, that is, each of the theoretical entities carries an inherent trajectory through time and space. Like the discourse-historical approach in CDA, MDA is inherently historical in its analyses.

The historical (and ethnographic) aspect of MDA is referred to as a nexus analysis. A nexus analysis begins, as does MDA, with the focus on a mediated action. From there a nexus analysis traces the lines of historical antecedence which have given rise to the focal action. What that means is that a nexus analysis seeks to analyze the historical experience by which the social actors have come to act in the concrete moment being examined; it further seeks to analyze the unfolding of the interaction order in that moment as well as in the history of that interaction order in the historical bodies of the participants; and, finally, it seeks to analyze the extended history (and future anticipations) of the discourses in place through which the action is enabled or constrained.

This introduction to MDA and to nexus analysis has left unanswered two questions which now need to be addressed. First, is MDA a form of critical discourse analysis, and second, is PCDA a form of either MDA or CDA or both? The answer to both questions is 'yes', but this answer needs to be qualified.

While the concept of the interaction order is derived from social interactional theories which have largely been developed as non-critical frameworks and MDA makes use of the full panoply of forms of discourse analysis, two concepts link MDA to CDA. The first is the concept of the historical body (or habitus) which directly locates MDA among practice-based theories of social action and social activity. The concern in MDA is not with humans as independent psychological entities but as socially grounded and enabled social actors who carry in their bodies the histories of their experiences in human social life and who act through the agency of mediational means from language and body idiom to documents and electronic networks.

Second, the concept of the mediated action or of the unity of the social actors and the mediational means which enable that action locates MDA as a development of what is sometimes called neo-Vygotskian or sociocultural psychology. Here the concerns are to understand how the social world and the world of individual human action are dialectically linked so that a change in one entails a change in the other. This, then, implies that MDA, like CDA, is inherently a theory focused on social change, not on plain description.

Finally, we come to the question of how PCDA as outlined in this book fits into both MDA and CDA. PCDA is a form of MDA in three ways. First, the overall concern is with the action of the discourse analyst as an action within a public consultative process. From this point of view the guiding question is: how can a particular discourse analysis be used by the analyst to mediate an action within the public consultative process? A discourse analysis of the greatest academic interest and importance might not be any more useful to an activist PCDA analyst or a government PCDA analyst than an EIS that sits in a box on the floor if it cannot be used as a tool to mediate his or her actions in a public consultation. In this way MDA provides a test of relevance for the PCDA analysis. The question is always: who can use this analysis to do what in which contexts?

The second way in which PCDA is a form of MDA is in the focus on action in the analysis of the documents. There are many perspectives which can be taken in the analysis of documents. Because MDA is focused on action the questions asked of each document follow this line: what actions are enabled, constrained, prohibited, or required by this document? What is the authorization of the principals of this document? Who is addressed as the receiving principal and what must or may they do because of this document. That is, what actions may this document mediate? In other words, the concern is not so much with what the document says as with what actions the document can mediate and for whom.

The third way in which PCDA is a form of MDA is in the use of nexus analysis to follow out the histories of the historical bodies whose actions the document mediates, analyzing what are the interaction orders within which the document is activated as a mediational means, and how are discourses in place for the actions which are enabled or proscribed by the document selected, blended together or bent to achieve these purposes.

Having said that PCDA is very much a kind of MDA, it is also necessary to point out that PCDA is limited from the point of view of MDA because it is restricted to just the publicly available documents of the public consultative process. An MDA would always prefer to know what is going on behind the scenes both in government offices and in the offices of the organizations which represent what is commonly referred to as the public interest, that is, the interests of particular polities. Such analyses have made important contributions to the development of MDA. But PCDA stops short of an ethnographic requirement in order to be able to focus on publicly available documents which are the foundation of the public consultative process. PCDA accepts this limit on theoretically possible investigation in exchange for active engagement in the process of democratic political negotiation of public policy.

Finally, we can ask whether PCDA is a form of CDA. The answer to this is that it decidedly is CDA. The analysis of language and the analysis of social life are taken to be inseparable within CDA, and it is the goal of PCDA to always go beyond 'pure' description and analysis to active engagement in the discourses being analyzed. PCDA is predicated on the idea that, as Fairclough has put it,

> language is an irreducible part of social life, dialectically interconnected with other elements of social life, so that social analysis and research always has to take account of language.
>
> (2003: 2)

From this point of view it could be argued that any analysis of language is *ipso facto* an analysis of social life and vice versa. Such analyses could, however, remain disengaged from the social worlds being analyzed. PCDA is never *just* discourse analysis but it is a form of discourse analysis which seeks to bring discourse analysis itself into the democratic and participatory negotiation of public policy.

The sale of oil and gas leases in the Beaufort Sea: a case study in PCDA

Lying off the Arctic Coast of Alaska and Canada is the Beaufort Sea, which is covered with ice much of the year. Under the floor of the Beaufort Sea are oil and gas resources. While the size of this reservoir will not be known without exploration and development, it is estimated to be significant.

In the United States, energy industry corporations buy leases from the US government which give them the legal rights to explore, develop, and extract oil and gas for commercial profit. As resources have been found, exploited, and exhausted new leases offered for sale and development have been in increasingly remote areas of the US. While the OCS (Outer Continental Shelf) Lands Act of 1953 enabled the sale of leases for offshore development, it was then and is now always a political decision of the US government whether or not to pursue further sales and further development of oil and gas.

In 1969 and through later amendments, the National Environmental Policy Act (NEPA) required natural and social sciences research to be conducted as part of the basis for decisions which would affect the environment. The Minerals Management Service (MMS) is the agency of the US Federal Government which was established both to manage the sale of leases for oil and gas development and to monitor the environmental (including social) impacts of this development. Politics, law, science, and government here meet in a confluence of discourses which sometimes produces mutually augmenting waves and surges and sometimes problematical conflicts.

In September of 2001 the US government announced that it was planning a sale of oil and gas leases off the Arctic Coast of Alaska, on the border with Canada in the Beaufort Sea. This is one of the most extreme inhabited Arctic environments in the world. This planned action was strongly opposed by most members of the three Native American (Iñupiat) communities (Barrow, Nuiqsut, and Kaktovik) who live on that coastline and who have conducted whaling on the ice and in those waters for innumerable generations as an essential foundation of their survival and of their sociocultural organization and identity.

The first step in planning the sale was for the US government to announce that they were planning the sale (as enabled by the OCS Lands Act and by the precedent of other oil developments in that region such as Prudhoe Bay and the Trans-Alaska pipeline) and to prepare an environmental impact statement (EIS) as required by the National Environmental Protection Act (NEPA). Then a draft EIS was prepared and four public hearings were held during the last week of July and the first week of August 2002, one in each of the affected communities and one in Anchorage. The hearings were open to all interested parties, encompassing not just community members but representatives of Alaska state governments, local governments, tribal governments, and many non-governmental organizations (NGOs) such as 'Oil Watch Alaska', an NGO which works in political opposition to the continued development of new oil resources in favor of energy conservation.

The documentary coverage of this process, as posted on the MMS website, runs to thousands of pages when printed as documents, including news releases, notices in the *Federal Register*, Leasing Activities Information memos, and full transcripts of public hearings which were held to receive responses to the Draft EIS (DEIS). These are the documents which constitute the case study which is examined in this book. Although there are thousands of pages, the bulk of this documentation is taken up by just four documents: the Draft EIS (DEIS), an Oil Spill Risk Analysis (OSRA), a four-volume Final EIS (FEIS), and an environmental assessment (EA) of over 300 pages which was made in preparation for the second sale. A full listing of these documents is in the Appendix.

Here in this chapter the focus is on testimony given at Kaktovik on July 26, 2002. The full transcript of the hearing is 34 pages. In this case the mediated action on which the analysis is focused begins with the testimony of Isaac Akootchook. Insofar as this action is accomplished primarily through spoken discourse our analysis does not depart strikingly from analyses which are typical of the several fields of discourse analysis. Where it departs to some extent from these other forms of analysis, however, is in considering not just the action of speaking at the hearing but, as inherent in that action, the several mediational means – the DEIS is central in this case; the interaction order that organizes the participation among the social actors – in this case the social conduct of a public hearing; and the historical bodies of the participants – in this case highly divergent personal and social histories ranging from traditional elders who have hunted bowhead whales on the sea ice for many decades, for whom the organizing motivation is to somehow stop the sale of oil leases, to US government bureaucrats and scientists for whom the primary motivation is to get public responses to the science of the DEIS. In this perspective we see several major discourses converging on this moment of utterance, the government – bureaucratic discourse of the MMS, the scientific discourse of the DEIS, the US national, Alaska state and local government political discourses, and the discourse(s) of traditional knowledge and of cultural subsistence life.

The brief transcript below records a moment in this nexus of discourses, practices, participants, and their social organization. Here the goal is to sketch out how an MDA approaches such a complex set of interacting trajectories as a way to analyze how discourses come together in a specific moment of social life. (Line numbers and format are those of the original transcript from the MMS website, pages VII–340, 341.)

> 18 MR. STANG: Thank you. Isaac.
> 19 MR. AKOOTCHOOK: My name is Isaac
> 20 Akootchook, raised here in Kaktovik. I've been here 80
> 21 years and I've look at the – having many times this
> 22 hearing, a hearing in our land and we talk about oil
> 23 development in the Beaufort Sea. Many times we opposing.
> 24 I'm always saying we oppose it. The oil development in our
> 25 area, oceans is our living. We're fishing and seal and all

00063

> 1 already we testimony about all those things already. But
> 2 this is still happening. Same old things that coming back
> 3 to us and play more – something else to give you more
> 4 testimony, but – I have a lot of big books as to how many
> 5 boxes is coming in to us. I've not really read it because
> 6 I don't know how to read much about it. But big things
> 7 arrive and I just set them up in my floor and that's it.
> 8 But one of the things is we're always saying that, is still
> 9 there, we oppose oil development in the ocean because our

10 life, living, we pass it on to our generations and
11 generations.
12 And one of the things I'd questions, always
13 is make it answer. It happened to the pipeline oil spill
14 drill, whatever, did Kaktoviks people have a benefit from
15 that? Happen to use the money for all his life? I don't
16 know. I don't think you will have answer that. I don't
17 think we will get any benefit. Happen to our yards, in the
18 oceans spill. That's how – I'm always listening to that
19 because we are government, we pay the taxes, you know.
20 Anything – there's always a government doing it, we pay.
21 Everything – the income, you know, all of that income
22 through taxes. Same thing with the North Slope government.
23 We'd like to know sometime if you come back
24 maybe you get answer for that because it's not going to
25 stop. We're going to oppose [sic] the oceans and the

00064

1 inland and we always favor to ANWR and make plans, we
2 always favor about it, but not in the ocean.
3 That's all I have to say. Thank you very
4 much.
5 MR. STANG: Thank you, Isaac.

Action as a nexus of practice: a nexus analysis

Isaac Akootchook's testimony may be summarized as follows:

1   I speak as an elder with 80 years of history in this community.
2   This hearing is one in what is now a very long series of hearings.
3   We always oppose oil development in the Beaufort Sea; I always oppose it.
4   You keep preparing EIS's; I have a large stack of them on my floor.
5   I can't read them but whatever they say, I still oppose oil development in our ocean.
6   We depend for all of our lives on the ocean; can oil development give us the living to replace that?
7   If you can answer that, come back and let us know.
8   I do not oppose onshore oil development; just development in the ocean.

The language in which Isaac Akootchook has spoken is a variety of English commonly used as a regional variety on the North Slope of Alaska. Space does not allow us to enter into a lexicogrammatical analysis, though it would bear fruit for a CDA analysis of this transcript, particularly in contrast to the language used by the representatives of the MMS which we comment on below. What we can see, however, is the careful and succinct argument structure of his testimony. He first gives an accounting of his authorization and credentialization to speak in his own historical body (1). He moves then to his conceptualization of the currently ratified interaction order (2). Within that he addresses the discourses in place, the community's opposition and his opposition (3) and the EIS (4). He brings these together into a statement of the mediated action he is taking: having the EIS (and many others), he rejects them as irrelevant to his action which remains opposition (5). He accounts for his action (6) and proposes a possible anticipated action for his hearer (7). He closes with a careful qualification of the scope of his action (8).

Isaac Akootchook's testimony occurs within the broader discursive frame of norms for Native American social interaction (and, of course, that of many other groups as well). It is commonly the role of the elders present at a meeting or discussion to stay on the periphery and to listen for an extended period of time. When the moment is appropriate they then speak both for themselves and also as legitimate spokespersons for the community, providing a summary statement of the consensus of the discussion, the views of the community, and their own stance toward proper outcomes. Isaac Akootchook's testimony at the end of this session should thus be taken as marshalling the solidarity of an entire community in the position he takes.

The action taken by Isaac Akootchook directly contravenes the limiting framework placed upon the public hearing at the outset by the representative of the US government (MMS). In opening the hearing Paul Stang says,

> 3 MR. STANG: Maybe this is a good time to
> 4 start. First I'd like to thank you all for coming. We
> 5 don't need to translate I trust, and if you do need
> 6 translation, Suzie's here to help when, and if you do. The
> 7 purpose here is to have a meeting to discuss and to hear
> 8 your testimony on a lease/sale EIS, Environmental Impact
> 9 Statement, Draft Environmental Impact Statement for three
> 10 lease/sales ... (VII–310)

> 8 goes on here in Alaska. Nathan Hile is our court reporter
> 9 and he's going to be transcribing everything that you say
> 10 – everything that is said here tonight. As I said, the
> 11 purpose is to get your comments on this Draft Environmental
> 12 Impact Statement. Now what you have in your hands is (VII–311)

Paul Stang says and reiterates that the purpose of the meeting is to discuss the EIS, no more, no less. Only talk which conforms to this purpose will be recorded as the permanent record of 'what was said'. While not made so clear in just these statements, testimony in other hearings shows frequent instances of Paul Stang going off-record for certain topics or discussions, on the one hand, and, on the other hand, asking for reiteration for the purpose of recording.

Put in terms of an MDA, the only legitimate actions will be those which use the EIS as a mediational means. It is a draft document and the purpose is to jointly edit and produce the final EIS which will satisfy NEPA requirements and which will enable the sale process. It is at that point that the document will become, in the words of NEPA quoted in Chapter 1, 'an action-forcing device'. Within this concise scope, it is clear because of the nature of an EIS as an 'action-forcing device' based on natural and social scientific research, and from the abundant comments from Paul Stang and others from the MMS, that this is most appropriately a scientific discourse to be engaged in at the service of government/bureaucratic discourse.

We see clear reflections of the discourse of science in Paul Stang's own comments, as below:

22 MR. STANG: Correct. One of the activities
23 in the Gulf of Mexico that has produced mortality is when,
24 at the end of the life of a platform, they were using
25 explosive charges to blow the legs of the platform clear

00015

1 and they were killing a lot of animals due to the pressure
2 wave in the immediate vicinity. So they made an assessment
3 of that. So there was mortality from that. The main
4 issues that we've had here in Alaskan waters with respect
5 to noise has related to seismic exploration. We have had
6 whole series of ongoing studies. What's interesting, of
7 course, is the Inupiat whalers were saying, we can tell you
8 what happens when the sound comes. We can see what happens
9 to the whales and that there's a deflection that the whales
10 in the migratory path seismic noise goes off, they deflect
11 out away and, of course, that's been a big concern.
12 Our initial science indicated that the
13 deflection wasn't particularly – the whales didn't deflect
14 that far. The whalers were saying yes it does. In fact,
15 what's happened as more and more data – we've gathered
16 more and more data and we've listened a little more
17 carefully, is I think we're closer to agreement about the
18 nature of that deflection. With respect to drilling noise (VII 316, 317)

Phrases such as 'produced mortality', and 'there was mortality from that', are strikingly scientific in contrast to the non-scientific 'killing a lot of animals' from a more informal, non-scientific vernacular form of speech. These two blendings from two very different discourses are used, interdiscursively, within the same few sentences.

More to the point, public testimony is seen as part of a larger scientific process in the contrast between science as a way of knowing and traditional knowledge, a term used frequently in MMS documents relating to this sale process. Whalers had said that noise would affect the whales; science is now coming to the same conclusion. It is important to note the phrasing here: 'Our initial science indicated' is opposed to 'whalers were saying'. Science is a speaking agent and whalers are speaking agents. He did not say, 'Our marine biologists' were saying but now 'traditional knowledge authorizes' that same conclusion.

Still other phrases show the ascendancy of scientific/technological discourse in the language of the MMS representatives: 'our science program', 'we do have a fairly decent science effort', 'our science group', 'the scientists for the North Slope Borough and our scientists are in daily', 'we have in our science studies program a fair amount of data', 'they have statistical models that are very rigorous models', 'lot of computer horsepower', 'models are fairly sophisticated', and, putting German technology at the pinnacle, 'pretty sophisticated device. It's a German device.'

Scientific discourse concerning the EIS is further ratified throughout the testimony with comments such as, 'That's a very legitimate area to testify on. It certainly is', 'good question', or 'your questions were very appropriate', when the testimony came within this range of topic and style. In contrast, then, just following Isaac Akootchook's testimony and that of several others who reiterate his statement, we see, in closing the session, the following delegitimation of non-scientific discourse in the closing statement:

> 13 MR. STANG: Okay. I would like to thank
> 14 you all for coming. I really appreciate your coming. It
> 15 certainly is a gorgeous evening to be inside and, as
> 16 Merylin said, you better enjoy it while you can because the
> 17 weather can change very quickly. But I want to thank you
> 18 for spending your time and for coming and giving us your
> 19 thoughts and your inner feelings. I really appreciate
> 20 that.
> 21 We've made a record. We've taken notes to
> 22 talk about it as soon as we get back to the office what
> 23 you've said and we have a transcript that Nathan will have
> 24 word for word. So, thank you very much.

There are legitimate areas, good questions, and appropriate questions on the one hand, and on the other there are thoughts and inner feelings. What is at stake in Isaac Akootchook's testimony is not simply the action of giving testimony but a political rejection of the frame of the public hearing itself as well as a political rejection of the process of gas and oil leasing in the Beaufort Sea. The mediated action proposed and prescribed by the MMS, the action of speaking toward the refinement of the EIS is directly rejected by Isaac Akootchook. It is rejected by his statement that he has always opposed such sales and continues to oppose them. It is further rejected by his characterization of the EIS as, not something to read and respond to, but something he stacks up on his floor. It is rejected when he credentializes himself to speak as an 80-year member of the community.

His self-credentialization here is far from a minor point. While Isaac Akootchook places himself as a community elder in his testimony here, he might equally have characterized himself in an official capacity. The Kaktovik guide (1.12.3, b) for people who would work in their region mentions that Isaac Akootchook is, in fact, their member of the North Slope Borough Planning Commission. In another place he is presented as the President of the Kaktovik Native Village. These are not insignificant bureaucratic/governmental positions and he might have chosen to ground his testimony in them and in doing so claim both North Slope Borough political credentials and also Kaktovik Native Village credentials, but he did not.

We should explore the question of the historical body a bit further because it is crucial to the way participants place themselves or are placed within a discursive moment. In the portion of transcript below, Ms Traynor undermines her own authority to raise a question about air pollution by noting that she is not a scientist. In contrast Mr Valiulis (of MMS) validates his right to speak partly by credentialization ('not an air quality specialist' implies by contrast that he is, however, a specialist in other matters) and by reference to the central mediational means of this currently legitimated bit of discourse, the EIS.

3 that it's some of the – some very high pollution just from
4 drilling oil over there. But – and I'm not a scientist so
5 I don't ....
6 MR. VALIULIS: The studies that we have
7 done, and it's one of the requirements we have and EPA has
8 to approve the permits for that. We know that the action
9 we propose would be from these leases, based on what we
10 know so far and the scenarios that we've adopted would not
11 be significantly detrimental.
12 MS. TRAYNOR: What is the actual pollution
13 from the oil if, say, a well were to be developed? What's
14 the pollution factors there?
15 MR. VALIULIS: I'm not an air quality
16 specialist and I do know that we cover this in the
17 Environmental Impact Statement but I can tell you that it's
18 a very limited affect [sic].

This brief sketch is, of course, only illustrative of how we can approach a moment of action and begin to develop a nexus analysis of that moment. The goal here in this chapter is to show that the three elements which constitute a social action – the historical bodies of the participants, the interaction order which organizes their interaction, and the discourses in place by means of which they act – reward further analysis as each sheds light on how an action is historically constituted in its discourses, participants, and their social relations. Social action may be constituted or resisted through any or all of these elements.

Historical body

In this public hearing Paul Stang quite rightly and clearly claims authorization to speak on the basis of his employment and position in the MMS, the government authority for these hearings and for the sale process.

> 11 We are from the Minerals
> 12 Management Service in Anchorage and in Herndon, Virginia,
> 13 which is our Minerals Management Service headquarters. My
> 14 name is Paul Stang, S-T-A-N-G. I'm the regional supervisor
> 15 for leasing and environment here in Alaska.

As we have seen above, Ms Traynor marginalizes her own authority to speak within the currently authorized discourse of testimony on the EIS. Isaac Akootchook squarely resists authorization to speak within scientific and government discourse by authorizing himself within a discourse of traditional knowledge and community membership as an 80-year resident of the affected community. He might have as easily introduced himself as the Kaktovik member of the North Slope Borough Planning Commission, but he did not. These speaking positions are not only taken up explicitly by the participants in this hearing, as we have seen in the cases of both Isaac Akootchook and Paul Stang, they embody much longer personal histories and identities which are evidenced in their ways of speaking both in lexicogrammar (an Alaskan regional variety of English in the first case and a bureaucratic/scientific variety in the other) but also in their use and exploitation of norms of larger forms of discourse. Isaac Akootchook speaks as an Alaska Native elder in a consensus-building, summarizing way at the end of testimony; Paul Stang speaks as an MMS official by carefully staying on topic but also signaling (in other cases) the necessity to go off-record on irrelevant topics. Their life experiences with discourse at the lexicogrammatical level and speech-event level as well as their experiences with norms for social interaction clearly place these two in discursive opposition in this encounter.

Interaction order

Different participants come to any social interaction with historical experiences (or not) of that particular kind of social interaction. They may call upon the historical bodies (including this knowledge, of course) as resources to come to agreement with each other or to strike a position of resistance. Paul Stang is relatively new to Kaktovik but the careful and professional conduct of the hearing argues that he has extended experience with the conduct of public hearings. He acts in a highly professional manner. In 1997 he was newly assigned from the Washington, DC office to the Alaska Regional office. Isaac Akootchook may have little experience with public hearings outside the scope of Kaktovik and the North Slope Borough, but from his testimony we can infer that he is something of a specialist at using the public hearing format to construct his position of opposition to offshore oil developments.

Because we have only the written transcripts to inform us in this case one cannot say very much about just how the interaction order of a hearing was constructed. This can be seen, however, across the transcripts of the four hearings concerning this proposed sale in references to 'up here' (at the front) and 'back there' (in the back) as well as requests for speakers to come to the microphone. Perhaps it is safe to infer that these hearings were structured like many we have observed face to face. Commonly there is a table at the front at which the officials who are conducting the hearing sit. This includes their transcribers and their recording equipment as well as any necessary translators. The audience is arrayed in banks or rows of seats facing these conveners in face-to-face opposition. There is commonly a chair or small table or just a microphone at which testimony is given in the space between these two territories.

In many parts of the world, but not by any means in all, norms governing such an interaction order are that one speaks to all and on-record. Side sequences are uttered *sotto voce* and off-record. Speaking turns alternate between the person giving testimony and the person or persons who are receiving the testimony. The speaking 'floor' is managed by this person who is receiving testimony. Further assumptions of topical relevance and the like are also made. These, of course, could be productively researched ethnographically for each of the social or cultural groups represented in the hearing.

In this case Isaac Akootchook provides his resistance by rejecting many elements of the structure of the action but he does not reject the interaction order. His testimony is given on-record after having been selected to speak by Paul Stang, who then thanks him and selects the next speaker. Even this aspect of the interaction order can be strategically used to resist, as in a hearing the author observed concerning a proposed copper mine in another region of Alaska. Hazel Nelson, a soft-spoken elderly woman, signaled that she wished to speak, was selected and then moved to the chair designated for those giving testimony. She moved slowly because of her age and when she came to the chair she turned the chair around so rather than having her back to other members of the community and facing the conveners, it was they who were at her back. The convener asked her to turn to face the microphone and him, 'so that we can hear you'. Her answer, which was given over her shoulder, was, 'I came here to talk to my friends here in the community, not to you.' She then went on to ask of the audience what 'we' can do about 'them', 'Is there a 911 number we can call when these people threaten us?'

As further evidence that discursive opposition may be expressed through the interaction order, we can look at a portion of public testimony from a very similar public hearing concerning Sale 170 in 1997. The hearing took place in

Barrow, Alaska. Mr Paul Stang does not play an active role in this earlier hearing although he was present. He was introduced as having just come to Alaska a few days before.

> PUBLIC TESTIMONY OF MR. VAN D. EDWARDSEN
> My name's Van Edwardsen. I am the Barrow – Vice President of the Barrow Whaling Captain's Association. And we've prepared a statement this afternoon, and I'll read the statement:
> To the Minerals Management Service, Lease Sale 170 DEIS Hearing, July 10, 1997, North Slope Borough Assembly Room, Barrow, Alaska 99723.
> The North Slope Community, including the Barrow Whaling Captain's Association and others, has had enough. The US Government, through the Minerals Management Service, has continued to ignore the comments and the personal experience of many Whaling Captains and Whalers. The Whalers have attended many, many meetings within the past twenty years, commented many, many times about disruption to the bowhead whale migrations, to no avail … It is no longer the best interest to the North Slope Communities to attend the Minerals Management Service hokey meetings. The Barrow Whaling Captain's Association strongly oppose Lease Sale 170.
> And for the record, my name is Van. It is spelled V-a-n, Edwardsen, E-d-w-a-r-d-s-e-n.
> HEARING OFFICER BROCK
> Anybody ….
> (Pause – Demonstrators can be heard in the background)

In this earlier hearing Van Edwardsen, the demonstrators who can be heard in the background, and the few other speakers all use language to state that they are refusing to participate in the hearing and deny the ratification of the interaction being sought by the representatives of the MMS.

These examples make it clear, through Hazel Nelson's and Van Edwardsen's resistance to the norms of the interaction order of the hearing, that the other speakers we have looked at here have accepted, and therefore ratified, the norm that the dialogue is between them (either as individuals or as representatives of organizations or communities) and the government (or other convening agency). Hazel Nelson has dismissed the interaction order of the hearing and transformed it into a community town meeting as surely as Isaac Akootchook used the interaction order of the hearing to dismiss the mediational means of the EIS and to transform it into boxes on the floor in his house.

Discourses in place

MDA regards any of the discourses present in a moment and place of action to be relevant to that action. An important part of acting in the world is selecting among the discourses which are available at any nexus of discourses and social actors and their practices. We have already noted that from the MMS point of view only discourse relevant to the draft EIS was considered relevant discourse. All other discourses were disattended or, more specifically, actively positioned as non-relevant, such as when comments were spoken *sotto voce* or placed off-record.

We have also noted the contention among a broad set of discourses which were circulating through the public hearing, not just the governmental/ bureaucratic discourse of getting on with the sale of leases but the more funda-mental political discourse of what might be the best course of action for the nation of the US as a whole. We have seen the struggle between scientific discourse and the traditional knowledge discourse in which Isaac Akootchook located himself.

The transcripts do not give many clues concerning other discourses present at the time of this action, particularly ones to do with the place in which the action took place. We can imagine, however, rather different material settings for these four hearings when we note that the Nuiqsut and Kaktovik hearings took place in community centers in these small and remote villages, the hearing in the larger town of Barrow took place in the Iñupiat Heritage Center, and the Anchorage hearing took place in the MMS, Third Floor Conference Room. Our own experiences tell us clearly that all speakers, no matter what discourses they position themselves within, would not fail to register the presence of US national government and political discourses in the Anchorage hearing in ways that would be largely disattended but hardly absent and without influence.

Like the Iñupiat Heritage Center in Barrow, which will be discussed in Chapter 6, the Qargi Community Center in Kaktovik where this hearing occurred is a place where a very large variety of social activities happen, according to the village website (www.kaktovik.com). This 'gathering place' is the location of annual community Halloween, Thanksgiving and Christmas parties as well as other events such as a 'Kids' Recreational Cake Walk' and a 'Gospel Sing-along'. Photos of this center on the community website show an overlay of decorations which are perennial and not attached to any specific event, those which are more occasional but either left from prior events or in anticipation of ones to come, and those which are occasioned by the event being depicted.

When Hazel Nelson turned her back on the conveners of the mining hearing noted before, above her were large representations of the high school sports symbol ('Glacier Bears') as well as other posters celebrating particularly successful past seasons of basketball. She spoke to her community against this background of sports symbols and actual games as well as the also clear memories of school dances, gradu-ation ceremonies, and even funerals. Isaac Akootchook spoke to the MMS within a context of these annual Halloween, Thanksgiving, and Christmas parties and gospel sing-alongs. For a nexus analysis of this mediated action it is important to recognize that these discourses are real and vibrant in this place for Isaac Akootchook and for his community but they are almost certainly absent for Paul

Stang and the MMS staff who are convening the public hearing we are analyzing. The material place, its structure, its objects, and its history signal and substantiate community identity and membership as clearly for him and the others from Kaktovik who speak or who do not speak as the EIS signals and substantiates the identity of the MMS conveners of the hearing.

MDA, nexus analysis, and PCDA

The focus in MDA on the social actor acting with mediational means can be critiqued by arguing from one point of view that such a concrete and narrow focus, while it may be interesting and perhaps useful at the micro-analytical level, is unable to reveal the circulation, interdiscursivity, and contestation among the powerful social discourses of our contemporary life. From that point of view MDA would fall short of meeting the goals of PCDA because such a close-grained analysis of single actions would have a slight impact on the broad policy decisions to which a PCDA is addressed.

The position taken by MDA, however, is that these broader social discourses circulate through all moments of human action and may be seen more clearly when the action is unpacked as a convergence of the historical bodies of the participants (which carry in them the histories of these discourses as well as dispositions to act in particular ways), of the interaction order which is organizing these participants in the moment of action, and of the discourses in place at that moment, whether or not those discourses are in place as actively ratified present discourses, disattended as not currently relevant, or as embedded in the objects, design, and layout of the places themselves.

A nexus analysis is the methodological strategy by which the circulation of these discourses, interaction orders, places, objects, and participants can be tracked beyond the narrow limits of time and place of a moment of social action. They can be first identified in the moment of action and then studied historically and ethnographically on their trajectories into the moment of action as anticipations and stances toward action, as we shall discuss in Chapter 6, and then as they emanate from action as its consequences. This still remains problematical for a PCDA in that PCDA accepts the constraint of working with a limited set of publicly available documents.

A critique that might be made of a nexus analysis (or of any ethnographic account of social action) is that it is too broad a mandate for PCDA or any activist discourse analysis to try to follow 'everything all at once'. There is just too much going on. The documents which form the groundwork of this case study analysis run to several thousands of pages. Even a competent CDA of such a bibliomass, without any attempt to bring the analysis into engagement as part of a public consultation, might take many years (or the work of many analysts) but remain of questionable use in addressing the question of what the analysis tells us to do.

In response to this critique PCDA takes it that, in fact, it is the unit of analysis, the social actor acting with mediational means, which theoretically limits this infinite expansion from the moment into all historical pasts and possible futures. We have not analyzed the text of the EIS in abstraction from action, not what it might mean to Paul Stang, to the scientists and editors who produced it, to the petroleum industry or even to Isaac Akootchook as potentials for action. We have analyzed how Isaac Akootchook used this document within a specific action – providing public testimony at a hearing. This document, which Paul Stang has noted at the outset cost the US government one million dollars to produce, was used by Isaac Akootchook to resist the government decision to produce oil in the Beaufort Sea. Rather than an extended analysis of the document itself, we have seen in the actions of these two participants that the document for one is his authority for speaking, for convening the moment of action, and the primary tool in claiming that the participants are engaged in scientific discourse. For the other the document is a large object in a box on his floor and he uses this claim to make his broader discursive point that he opposes the development of oil in the Beaufort Sea.

In summary, a PCDA uses the theoretical framework of MDA, which is a kind of CDA in which the unit of analysis is not the document itself but rather the social action of a social actor. The organizing question is always: how is this document appropriated as a tool for a social actor in taking some action? With that as the focus, documents are analyzed as potential tools for actions, not solely as residues or artifacts of ideological positions. Certainly ideological positions are necessarily present in any document, and, further, these positions may serve to enable or inhibit certain actions with those documents, but this is not the focus. The crucial issue for PCDA is to analyze how the document relates to human action through enabling some actions and inhibiting others, through authorizing some social actors and sidelining others. The discourses which are woven into each document give this particular texture to the document as a tool for action, as we shall see in the chapters which follow. The practice activities to which we turn now focus on the first steps, locating an issue and a public consultation, analyzing what actions are invited or available for a PCDA to be done, and finding the documents which constitute the body of the analysis.

PRACTICE

Public consultations are widely available in the UK through http://www.consultations.gov.uk, and in the European Union through http://europa.eu.int/ yourvoice/consultations/index_en.htm. In the US many public hearings conducted by the Federal Government are announced in the *Federal Register* (http://www.gpoaccess.gov/fr). At the time of writing there were 137 public consultations open in the UK ranging across issues such as 'Draft guidance on European Union hygiene regulations relating to supply of wild game for human consumption' to 'Compulsory seat belt/child restraint wearing in car and goods vehicles'. Many more consultations which are now closed are also listed. New consultations open up regularly.

Likewise, at the European Union site there are open consultations, just six at the time of writing, but 34 separate areas are listed, and an extended listing of completed consultations and their results. Using the search function on the *Federal Register* and the words 'public hearing' along with the topic in which you are interested will call up currently active consultations. Generally speaking, in the UK and the European Union 'public consultation' is used and in the US and in some cases in Canada 'public hearing' is used.

In the activities below you should focus your attention on issues in which you have a strong personal interest. You should also focus within a jurisdiction where you are most likely to be able to participate. There is no reason you should not take an interest in other consultations, of course, but in many cases consultations and hearings limit participation to specific groups of people who are normally citizens or residents of the geopolitical jurisdiction.

Overall, your goal in these activities is to locate a current public consultation on an issue in which you have an interest so that you can develop this over the activities of the next several chapters. The end result is to produce your own PCDA which can be submitted as part of the consultative process.

Activity 1:
Locating and becoming engaged in a public consultation

The first task is to find your way into an active public consultation. Figure 2.5 below shows the upper half of the opening page of 'Your Voice', the public consultation of the European Union. The URL is given just above. In the column of bulleted points on the left is a list of consultations by policy activity.

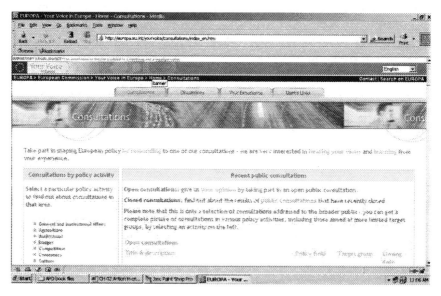

Figure 2.5

Each of these is linked to a web page with a list of current or completed consultations in that policy area. In the larger box on the lower right is a list of currently open consultations with links directly to those pages.

ASSIGNMENT

Using one of the URLs given above or another which you locate yourself, find a public consultation that is easily available on the internet. Prepare an annotated list of all of the documents which are included within the consultative process.

Observations

Your annotation should include the following (at least):

- The URL and title of the consultation
- the approximate size of each text (pages or words)
- the format (html, PDF, downloadable text file)
- the document type in each case (announcement, transcript of public hearing, letter submitted from public, map, chart)
- the availability of documents (directly readable, downloadable, or must be requested from agency)
- the timespan covered by the entire process as well as the window within which you can participate

If you are planning to use this consultation for subsequent activities, it's good to download all of the files and store them either on your hard drive or make a CD. Many websites are changed and updated or can go offline from time to time. Having the files stored offline will allow you to work without having to return to the actual website.

Activity 2:
Who are the participants, the interaction order, and the discourses involved?

Once you have located a consultation that is on a topic you are concerned about, the next task is to do a quick examination of the overall structure of the consultation. You want to know not only what documents are involved but who participants are expected to be, what qualifications they must have, and specific topics that may be or must be discussed in responses. These come down to analyzing the participants (historical bodies), the interaction order (meeting, online interaction, etc.), and the discourses in place (what forms of discourse are required or allowed to be used?).

ASSIGNMENT

Examine a consultation you are interested in by asking the following questions:

- Who (person or agency or both) is conducting the consultation?
- Who is expected to participate?
- Are there qualifying conditions, authorizations, or credentials required?
- Are there topical restrictions?
- What forms of responses will be accepted? Can these be submitted in writing, via online questionnaire, in person at a public hearing?
- Are specific forms of response prohibited?
- Are there requirements or suggestions for responding, such as the length of the document or the length of time in a public hearing?

Computer archiving

Be sure to bookmark URLs that seem promising, as you may need to return many times to complete your activities. You may also need to cross-reference between the consultation you are analyzing and others for comparative purposes. Alternatively, download the documents for your consultation to your computer or make a CD.

Observations

For an analysis to be treated seriously by the agency conducting the consultation it will need to be quite explicit and carefully documented. You cannot just say, 'there's a terrible mix of science and politics in this'; you will have to give specific examples and make an argument for why they should accept your analysis and, further, why the analysis makes a difference that they should pay attention to. This means that *from the very beginning* you should keep careful records and notes of what you are finding and where you can locate it to show others to back up your argument.

Activity 3:
What is a 'good' response?

Anticipating how your PCDA will be used by the agency holding the consultation or by other interested parties is an important aspect of developing your analysis. If the agency expects a strictly scientific response, anything else might be regarded as 'inner feelings' and so disregarded in summarizing commentary. You will need either to couch your analysis within the terms set out by the mandate of the consultation or to make a strong argument why your analysis should be considered, even though you have departed from the mandate.

ASSIGNMENT

Briefly skim at least ten completed public consultations which you find on the internet. Locate the point at which they provide their responses to the consultation. Examine these responses and write a brief (2-page at most) analysis of what factors produce the most successful comments, and thus, which elicit the fullest responses from the agency.

Observations

It is unlikely at this stage that you will find any discourse analyses as such in any public consultations you come across on the internet. Therefore, in this assignment you are only looking to see what is considered to be a relevant and effective voicing of views, what is acceptable and considered worthy of a response by the agency. Later on, in Chapter 7, we will deal specifically with how to make a PCDA so that it will be effective within this process.

3   The representation of action

Summarization, framing, and synchronization

PAUL STANG, MMS: Barrow, Alaska, 1 August 2002 ...
What we're here to talk about is this document here which is the environmental impact statement for multiple sales, three sales. The sales will occur, or
are planned to occur in 2003, 2005, and 2007 ... About 9.9 million acres are
covered, and the particular sale numbers are sale 186, which is for 2003, 195
is 2005, and 202 is 2007 ... These three sales were selected by Interior Secretary Norton, and published in final in late June of this year.

WRITTEN TESTIMONY BY MAYOR AHMAOGAK:
Even at this early point in our review of the DEIS, we have noticed many of
the same problems we have seen in previous MMS documents. Analysis seems
biased in favor of leasing.

THEORY – CASE STUDY

Our language about action can be deceiving. 'I wrote a book' is said with the
same syntactic economy as 'I ate a peanut', yet the two actions are as different as
night and day. One is a process of many sub-actions which requires many
months or years to complete and which involves other social actors; the other is
a brief process of shelling, chewing, and swallowing which is done in a minute
or two by a single social actor.

Words such as the verb 'write' or the verb 'eat' carry within them an inherent
summary of what we know about what it means to write or to eat. Equally,
nouns such as 'book' and 'peanut' summarize our experience with books and
peanuts. And so verbs and nouns and the rest of the lexicogrammatical repertory
of lexicon and syntax inherently and by their nature carry with them encapsula-
tions of our knowledge and of our experiences. We have no choice but to use
these summarizations, but their use can also lead to unwarranted assumptions
when people have different experiences.

The US government is selling oil and gas leases covering 9.9 million acres of
ocean in the Beaufort Sea to the oil industry. This is an action which is planned
to take place over seven years, to cost millions of dollars – the EIS alone cost

1 million dollars according to Paul Stang of the MMS – and to involve many stakeholders including government officials, petroleum industry corporations, citizens of the Arctic communities, representatives of environmental groups, and yet many others. When Paul Stang of the MMS summarizes the intent of the public hearing in Barrow he first summarizes the entire seven-year process as 'three sales', then further summarizes these as 'the sales'. He notes that the sales were selected by the Secretary of the Interior and published in June.

With this and no further information to go by one could be forgiven for thinking that the sales were a foregone conclusion of Paul Stang and of the Secretary of the Interior. And so from this point of view, from the language which was used in this summary, it is not surprising to see that Mayor Ahmaogak sees a 'bias in favor of leasing'. From these bits of language it seems that there is no question that the lease sales will be held and, presumably, bids will be accepted, leases granted, and then the enablement of exploration and development will follow.

Here it is important to say that within the draft EIS which is up for discussion in this public hearing are three alternatives, among which the Secretary may choose based on testimony and other evidence. One of them, Alternate II, is to cancel the plan, to have no sale of oil and gas leases. Even if we set aside the practical reasons for thinking Mayor Ahmaogak is right that the MMS is biased in favor of leasing, after all, the congressional mandate which established the MMS tasked them with conducting such sales and so they could hardly exist without sales, the language we use to talk about this action makes it difficult to keep the option of cancellation open each time there needed to be a reference to the full timescale process. We would find it very awkward if Paul Stang always referred to this as 'Sale/No-Sale 186' or even a bit more elegantly 'tentatively proposed Sale 186'.

Here in this chapter, then, we will take up the problems of summarization, framing, and synchronization. These are three important linguistic processes by which we speak of actions and which research has shown can be the source of confusion or misunderstanding among different stakeholders in a common process or task. These will be examined in the language we use to talk about action through the analysis of example documents from this Beaufort Sea oil and gas lease sale. As it has already been said that these linguistic processes are inevitable and, therefore, unavoidable, this theoretical case-study section will conclude with some suggestions of ways in which negative outcomes of these processes can be mitigated through careful attention to them. These suggestions will be essential in making a PCDA useful for stakeholders who are involved in any public consultation.

Documents as action; documents as information about action

Policy decisions are formal governmental processes by which social actors who are authorized by those policies are enjoined to take (or prohibited from taking) certain actions in the material world. As we have seen in Chapter 2, PCDA is grounded in the view that the most fruitful research and analysis is that which is located in the study of the actions of social actors in the world. As noted in Chapter 1, PCDA is predicated on the assumption, widely established in linguistics and discourse analysis, that language is a central shaping force of human action. The language we use as social actors (whether as citizens of a general public, representatives of corporations and NGOs, decision makers in government agencies, researchers, or media reporters on these processes) is transformed into the language used in the formulation of our research, our cross-group communication, and our policies and practices, and this inherently transforms those policies and practices. While this is abundantly clear in law and is pragmatically the very heart of public relations and marketing, it is less often a focus in research on the discourses of public policy.

The central distinction made in linguistic pragmatics is between language (spoken or written) which takes an action and language which is about an action. The classical example given is the difference between the sentence, 'I now pronounce you man and wife,' in which the saying of the sentence performs that marriage and 'The official at the marriage register pronounced them to be married,' which informs us about the action which was taken.

In order to make it more concrete how language is commonly tied to human action as a shaping force in public policy actions, we will examine a number of the documents connected to the Beaufort Sea Sales. This will enable us to examine the concepts of summarization, framing, and synchronization as these have been discussed in the discourse analysis research literature.

The seven-year action of this sale and its multiple constituent actions are represented in a series of publicly available documents which run to thousands of pages aggregated on the MMS website, as noted above and listed in the Appendix to this book. The actions which are performed or enabled, or about which information is given, that are documented in these pages range from the initial press releases and announcements in the *Federal Register*, the draft and final environmental impact statements (EIS), and transcripts of public consultative hearings, environmental assessments (EA), to information announcements, required bidding documents, and procedures for the closing of the sales.

Action is present in these documents in at least three different ways:

1   The document itself takes the action.

> The announcement of the oil and gas lease sale is accomplished by the publication of this announcement in the *Federal Register*. Similarly, a bid formally submitted on the appropriate documents in itself constitutes the bid.

2   The document references an action that is taken or accomplished elsewhere.

> While the announcement in the *Federal Register* is the action of announcing, it also makes reference to the sale, which is an action

accomplished across an extended range of actions and documents culminating in the payment of the bonus payment into the government account by the successful bidder. Other references include mentions of actions taken at other places and through other means, such as the reference to an ITM (Information Transfer Meeting) in a statement at a public hearing.

3   The document indirectly references or implies an action.

The officials of the MMS conduct a hearing by virtue of their official employment. This implies a long history of actions from job interviews through to issuing of regular pay checks. A meeting in Kaktovik implies an extended sequence of sometimes difficult travel actions.

Any discourse analysis, perhaps any analysis of language as it is used, always entails at least some of these relations among human actions and, more importantly, among linguistic descriptions of human actions. Actions are summarized, hierarchized, decomposed into components or constituents, sequenced, and batched. These processes entail that actions may be carried out in speaking or writing, or be referenced directly, indirectly, or only presupposed.

In these linguistic processes some of the constituent information is lost, rearranged, or re-hierarchized. One might say, 'The Secretary has approved the Beaufort Sea Sale,' and in the process drop all mention or knowledge of, for example, 1) the timing, location, and duration of the process, 2) the constituent actions required for this summarized statement, 3) the relative roles and actions of the named actor and the very large number of other participants, 4) the crucial roles of unnamed participants who are simultaneously engaged in other actions such as maintaining offices in Washington, Anchorage, Barrow, Kaktovik, or Nuiqsut; subsistence hunting or government bureaucratic work; doing scientific research or operating flight services; and running hotels and restaurants where these people work, live, and gather for meetings, 5) any other activities these participants are also engaged in at that time, such as meeting with a son or daughter's teacher at school, cooking a duck for dinner, managing resources in the Gulf of Mexico, or repairing a boat engine.

Viewed in a different perspective, a USDOI official in Washington might say at the outset or in planning these actions, 'I'd like you to hold the public hearings in May which would give us more time to digest the public responses before going forward with the final EIS.' On the surface this hypothetical anticipation of action implies an intent to be responsive to community needs and interests, but it violates the incommensurability between whaling and attendance at a public hearing. What might appear to be a statement of concern for the community in planning could also be seen in this light as a statement of ignorance about community processes and annual cycles.

In the following section we will examine three ways in which actions are in some sense distorted by the ways they are represented in language.

Three concepts of layering and sequencing in social scientific analysis

Summarization (recontextualization, resemiotization)

Any action or even a description of a prior action calls up a reinterpretation of the original action. When Isaac Akootchook testifies at a hearing in Kaktovik part of the meaning of what he says is derived from the fact that he has, by his own account, often given this same testimony. When we analyzed his testimony in Chapter 2 we transformed it from being an action he took at that time and in that place to being an example for analysis in this book.

Discourse analysis by definition is analysis which repositions or recontextualizes existing linguistic actions in the world because it is a description of those actions, as we shall see below under the topic of framing. This is done principally through processes of summarization that many researchers now refer to as recontextualization. Studies of recontextualization have spanned subject matter from unemployment policy making in European Union committees, decision making in official party and other meetings in China, the development and design of museums, hospital planning and design, the introduction of technological innovations, disability testing and tracking in education, personal identity construction, and linguistic anthropological fieldwork.

In its simplest form summarization is linguistic reduction. In the public hearing in Nuiqsut on 24 July 2002 by way of introducing the event Paul Stang, the representative of MMS who was conducting the hearing, says:

> We have three sales that the Secretary of Interior scheduled in this document that was approved in June, and we are preparing one Environmental Impact Statement to cover those three sales. The first sale is in 2003. The second sale is in 2005. The third sale is in 2007. These are proposed sales. [Translation intervenes.]
>
> Thank you. After we complete the final version of this draft environmental impact statement, then we will hold the sale in September or so of 2003, and the decision will be made to hold the sale or to cancel the sale and to pick one alternative or the other … But, after that, before we hold the next sale …
>
> (1.3: VII–288)

There is considerable, but necessary reduction in the repeated statements, 'We have three sales', 'sale is in', 'we will hold the sale', which is barely mitigated by the conditionals, 'These are proposed sales', 'the decision will be made to hold the sale or to cancel the sale', if we compare it to the statement of the Alaska Regional Director, who is paraphrased in a news release as saying:

The multi-sale process in the Beaufort Sea will incorporate planning and analysis for Sales 186, 195, and 202 tentatively scheduled for 2003, 2005, and 2007 respectively.

(1.1)

Here the sales are not asserted as existing but are considered to be part of a process. The news release continues, quoting the Director as saying:

Although we are proposing to prepare a single EIS for all three Beaufort sales in the upcoming 5-Year Program, we will not compromise environmental standards or our commitment to producing a complete scientific record on which to base leasing decisions ... After the first EIS is completed for Sale 186, we will prepare either an environmental assessment or a supplemental EIS and a consistency determination for each subsequent sale. The public will have opportunity to comment on each sale proposal.

(1.1)

In the Director's more extended and grammatically complex statement the sales are 'tentatively scheduled', not 'scheduled', the single EIS is proposed, not asserted. Other types of action are also included such as the option of either an EA or a supplemental EIS as well as a consistency determination. Further, none of this will occur without public commentary.

Again, in a summarizing statement at the public hearing in Kaktovik, 26 July 2002, the MMS representative, Paul Stang, says,

The sale will occur a little more than a year from now.

(1.1: VII–313)

His own subsequent statements make it clear that there are three options which the Secretary may exercise, the second of which is to cancel the sale. A less summarizing statement, then, would have been to say, 'If the Secretary decides to proceed with the sale, it would occur a little more than a year from now.'

Perhaps more important is the simple nominalization 'sale'. The news release has the actionally more complex phrase 'The multi-sale process in the Beaufort Sea'. This captures an importantly wider range of actions and options which take place over time and involve multiple social actors. When the MMS representative chooses the summarizing nominalization, sale, he presents a hierarchical constituent relationship among multiple actions and actors. Options for action as well as the sequential complexity of the process are obscured.

This also is a selection of some actions to the exclusion of other actions which are linked to those actions in several of the ways that have been outlined above. Though they are present by implication, this summary excludes mention of public hearings, of transportation arrangements for those hearings, of subsistence whaling, of other actions of the MMS or of the other participants, from community members to government officials.

Using 'sale' further simply presupposes and backgrounds the batched actions of scientific research and analysis that result in the EIS. Of course, that also means that it excludes crucial participants in those excluded actions, such as environmental scientists and energy industry officials. This 'simple' summarization presents us with a significantly narrowed range of actions which are given relevance and a significantly narrowed range of human participants. Perhaps equally important, referring to 'the sale' summarizes away other crucial life events and activities which enable the actions of the process of producing oil and gas leases in the Beaufort Sea. We see nothing of salary paychecks for the MMS officials who attend the public hearings, the state, federal, and corporate research grants that support the scientific projects or, conversely, the non-remunerated costs of public participation in providing public responses. This latter point was emphasized in the hearing in Barrow, 1 August 2002 (1.3: VII–412), where a request was made for 'impact assistance', that is, money to pay for the costs within the communities of public and community participation in 'the process'. While it is an accurate summarizing statement that the sale will occur in a little more than a year, it is a statement which erases a lower tier, if you like, which is not only relevant but crucial to the process.

Such reduction is both necessary and inevitable. A summarizing statement is not greatly improved in the situation of a few, orally given opening remarks by hedging and filling in the lower-level details. There is simply no summary statement which could encompass all of the actions and few a priori principles by which we can decide which social actors, which actions and events, and which materials must be explicitly included and which may be simply left implicit. A summarization is always and inherently a selection and a selection always promotes a hierarchy of perspective and focus.

Summarization cannot be avoided. One would not much enjoy discourse in which all details of action and all participants were constantly and repetitively reiterated. As Wittgenstein pointed out many years ago,

> The facts of human natural history that throw light on our problem, are difficult for us to find out, for our talk passes them by, it is occupied with other things. (In the same way we tell someone: 'Go into the shop and buy ...' – not 'Put your left foot in front of your right foot etc. etc. then put coins down on the counter, etc. etc.').
>
> (Wittgenstein 1980: 83)

The policy-making process is predicated on the concept of summarization and recontextualization. This opens up one of the essential contributions a PCDA can make to such a process by analyzing, perhaps not in each case, but certainly in crucial cases, just what the summary includes and what it excludes. This will most often consist of excluded actions, excluded participants, and excluded materials and places that are not germane in the hierarchy of the named summarized action but which are absolutely germane to the normal functioning of human action in the common flow of daily life.

But there is a more important aspect of recontextualization – what Iedema aptly calls resemiotization – which is in play in almost all forms of summative analysis. Latour was among the first to lay out how this works. An example often cited from Latour's work begins with a situation in which someone wishes to keep a door closed. At first she might just get up and close the door each time it is left open or ajar. And so in this case it is an action which accomplishes the goal of closing the door. But she might also ask people who go through the door if they would close it behind them. In this case the physical action has been transferred from one person to another by means of a linguistic request. Even further down the chain she might decide just to put a note on the door, 'Please keep this door closed.' Now this written note stands in for what was first a physical, bodily action, then a linguistic request plus an action, as a written note plus an action. In each case the situation is 'resemiotized' – that is, semiotically redistributed into different systems, codes, and modes of meaning including action, speech, and written text. As an even further extension the person might install a small piece of technology – a door closer – which now resemiotizes these prior actions, talk, and written note into an object, a technologized 'solution' to the original problem. The original action of getting up to close the door has been resemiotized, first through speech and then writing (plus action) to a more or less permanent technological object. An action has become an object.

In a parallel case Mehan detailed a sequence which begins with a child in social interaction with others in a school setting. This diffused social scene with many forms of talk and action becomes recontextualized or resemiotized – we might also say, more broadly, just summarized – as a 'problem child'. This summary of many kinds of talk, action, and social interactions leads to more professionalized analysis. Teachers, child, and parents are interviewed and a summary is made which characterizes this child as one who potentially has a 'learning disability'.

It is important to remember, before going on, that this situation might equally be summarized as a social group which has a 'socialization disability'. That is, as a group they are not competent to adapt to the needs of this child. The next stage, then, is that, armed with this recontextualization keyed by the phrase 'learning disability', a battery of professional interviews and tests is done and the child is given a formal 'score'. At this stage of resemiotization the term 'learning disability' and the test resulting in the score become a firm 'diagnosis' and an identity for the child which henceforward are regarded as a fundamental and inherent characteristic of the child, not a characteristic of the sequence of summaries and resemiotizations which have aggregated in this final diagnosis.

Such cases of resemiotization (recontextualization, summarization) highlight a crucial concern for any PCDA. While in formal description a public consultation always should retain a clear link to the original source research and documents, in practice it is rather too natural to consider a subsequent statement or summarization to be a resemiotization of all earlier tiers, players, statements, or projects. There is a kind of arrow of irreversibility in this process such that it becomes progressively more and more difficult to unpack the antecedent complexity that led to subsequent resemiotizations.

Interestingly, it is most often the case that the later, resemiotized summary is taken as the base 'condition' or situation. Problems with that condition or situation are seen to arise directly out of that stage; they are rarely traced back to earlier stages. Once a door closer is installed, the problem becomes one of keeping the door open from time to time, for which doorstops are employed rather than more basically removing the door closer. Once a child is 'diagnosed' as a child with a learning disability subsequent treatment revolves around how to deal with this disability rather than how to unpack the sequence of summarizations that led to this conclusion and then, perhaps, coming in with a different summarization that the social group has a 'socialization disability'.

There is a natural tendency toward irreversibility of all forms of summarizations, particularly when those summarizations become resemiotizations. An open-ended discussion, for example, becomes a plan; the plan then guides the construction of a new wing for a hospital; subsequent problems and solutions have to do with the new hospital wing – it is too late to dismantle the building.

This is a concern that arises because public policy develops over an extended time period which involves many different kinds of documents and many different decision makers. The continued existence of prior research, prior decisions, and prior policies in no way guarantees that later decisions, practices, and policies will have the capacity or the will to reverse this arrow of summarization to unpack hidden or obscured actions and participants. Often quite the opposite is the case. Subsequent analysis is directed toward solving the 'problem' as defined by the current resemiotization, and rarely directed toward reversing this directionality. Obviously, this process produces the strongest irreversibility when the resemiotization results in material changes such as in resource extraction, changes in the built environment, or the fabrication and manufacture of objects.

One salient resemiotization in the Beaufort Sea sale process concerns the shift from political and economic discourses to scientific discourse for which the EIS is a major fulcrum but not, of course, the only instance, as we shall see in Chapter 4. The decision to seek energy development in the Beaufort Sea is a political/economic one which was first enabled with the 1953 Outer Continental Shelf (OCS) Lands Act. Rarely do any of the documents presented by the MMS concerning this sale discuss these discourses which have given rise to the Secretary of the Interior's decision to undertake the sale. This political discourse does show up indirectly, for example, in the hearing in Kaktovik where the MSS representative says:

> Okay. The Secretary of Interior in developing a five-year program is looking at that program from the perspective of the nation as a whole. So

what the Secretary is doing is looking at what are the needs of the nation as a whole and where are the prospects for oil and gas around the nation.

(1.3: VII–328)

While this makes reference to the broader political discourse of national energy security, it is important to note that the comment is, in the first place, a direct response to a question about the political process from the audience. It is not a comment which is originated by the MMS. Further, the comment is prefaced with the discourse marker 'Okay'. Research in sociolinguistics has made clear that such discourse markers occur specifically when the speaker is making a marked departure from the line of argument or topic which has been on the floor. In other words, the MMS representative considered these comments of his to be off topic even while giving this response to the audience question. Except for such rather marked cases, references to the national political discourse are largely implicit or indirect although they can also be seen, as noted in Chapter 1, in the letterhead slogan for the MMS shown in Figure 1.2, repeated as Figure 3.4 below: 'Securing Ocean Energy and Economic Value for America.'

Other comments within the public hearings suggest that, once the political/ economic decision is made by the Secretary, all subsequent discussion is or properly should be scientific and address impacts on the natural environment. Put another way, from the outset of this process, prior political/economic discussions are eclipsed and resemiotized into a decision to proceed with the sale process. Only a window of scientific/environmental action is left open on the political process. As we observed in Chapter 2, in the Kaktovik hearing (26 July 2002) we find the following comment from the representative of the MMS:

We have had a whole series of ongoing studies. What's interesting, of course, is the Inupiat whalers were saying, we can tell you what happens when the sound comes … Our initial science indicated that the deflection wasn't particularly – the whales didn't deflect that far. The whalers were saying yes it does. In fact, what's happened as more and more data – we've gathered more and more data and we've listened a little more carefully, is I think we're closer to agreement about the nature of that deflection.

(3.1: VII–317)

It could be argued that what the whalers are primarily discussing is the threat to their cultural/subsistence way of life. What the MMS representative is saying is that only scientific studies and 'more and more data' will determine the facts of the case, even where these 'more and more data' come to assert what the whalers have said in the first place. It is only scientifically produced knowledge and statements which are given validity.

Some speakers are intimidated by this scientific discourse. For example, the citizen cited in Chapter 2 says,

I understand that it's some of the — some very high pollution just from drilling oil over there. But I'm not a scientist so I don't know.

(1.3: VII–339)

In response an MMS representative parallels this comment grammatically but with a switch of authority. He says,

I'm not an air quality specialist and I do know that we cover this in the Environmental Impact Statement but I can tell you that it's a very limited affect [sic].

(1.3: VII–339)

Linguistically, there are three things to note here. First is the adversative positioning of this almost parallel statement. The speaker simultaneously disclaims his authority as an air quality specialist but not as a scientist. Second, he then asserts that the answer is to be found in the EIS. Third, the EIS assures the reader that there is a very minimal problem from air pollution. To put this another way, the speaker from the MMS notes that it is not his credentials, or by implication the speaker's lack of scientific credentials, but this document which settles questions.

This is more poignantly clarified in two comments made by the MMS representative later in the same hearing in Kaktovik. A member of the public prefaces his comments with a question about his commentary, the MMS representative responds by saying,

That's a very legitimate area to testify on. It certainly is.

(1.3: VII–320)

Another questioner's comments are also legitimated when the MMS representative says,

Thank you, Robert. Your questions were very appropriate.

(USDOI/MMS, 30 July 2002: VII–335)

Obviously, however, not everything is considered relevant to the scientific discourse within which the hearings are expected to be performed. In closing this hearing in Kaktovik, during which there was expressed much political opposition to the sale, mostly in terms of concern for subsistence whaling, the MMS representative says,

I would like to thank you all for coming. I really appreciate your coming ... I want to thank you for spending your time and for coming and giving us your thoughts and your inner feelings. I really appreciate that.

(USDOI/MMS, 30 July 2002: VII–342)

As we noted in Chapter 2 and shall examine in further detail in Chapter 4, on the ways different discourses are blended or bent to other discourses and purposes, a contrast is set up between 'very legitimate areas' and 'inner feelings'. Legitimate areas have to do with the science of environmental impact; inner feelings are responses to the social, cultural, and political implications of the proposed sales.

The EIS, then, amasses the scientific discourse and the public responses to it into a substantial document. In public hearings the DEIS (draft environmental impact statement) is referred to as 'this thick document' (Nuiqsut, 1.3: VII–288) or even 'this baby' (Kaktovik, 1.3: VII–330) by the representative of the MMS. Its physical mass is the object which is literally pointed at to resolve points of political discussion.

> And we have it both in hard copy, which is a document here. George has a copy right here. Three volumes.
>
> (1.3: VII–311)

The public hearings make it abundantly clear that all but one or two of those who testify in the four public hearings for Sale 186 oppose the political decision. But it is also abundantly clear that only scientific arguments and objections are accepted as relevant.

Before turning to the question of framing it is important to say again that summarization is inevitable in any form of human discourse, but at the same time summarization in the form of resemiotization is a very powerful strategy for producing a kind of irreversibility in discourse. In these documents concerning the Beaufort Sea Sales the most elaborated and explicit (non-summarizing) examples are found in formal announcements and scientific papers. The least elaborated are the linguistically somewhat simplified comments made in public hearings. This introduces a dilemma for those who conduct or participate in such hearings. If you speak casually or informally you can produce rapport more easily among the participants in the meeting. But speaking in this way produces hierarchical constituent summaries of actions which are, in reality, not so closed or hierarchical. Conversely, speaking in a formal, careful manner which brings out the complexity of the actional processes introduces a stiffness and distance which lies open to accusations of non-involvement and bureaucratic lack of concern.

Framing (contextualization)

Framing is a term now used quite widely in public and media discourse. The concept of framing has been active, however, in the social-scientific literature on communication at least since Bateson's article in the 1950s on what he called 'frame' or 'metacommunication'. The crucial concept of framing, as Bateson used it and as it was taken up by others in social interactional research, is a concern with the relationship between two levels of communication. Bateson called the basic, fundamental level the message or the communication. He called the second level the 'metamessage' or 'metacommunication'. This second level, in Bateson's writing as well as that of those who followed him, was a communication *about* the primary communication, not just a second or parallel line. Most importantly, the metacommunication is for these frame analysts a message that tells us how to interpret the basic message. Bateson argued that all communications entail both a message and a metamessage. Without the second tier, if you like, there is no intelligibility of the first tier.

Examples that Bateson liked to give had to do with communication either among non-human mammals or between humans and mammals. This, he argued, was because of the need to acknowledge that this principle is inherent in all communication of all mammals and could not be factored out or ignored. In his article 'The message "This is play"' (Bateson 1972), he noted that our pet dog can signal a bite with flashing teeth and a gentle bite, but signal 'This is play' by a wagging tail and raised ears and a 'smiling' face. A very similar bite is signaled as a serious bite by lowered tail, raised hackles, and ears laid back.

These important insights of Bateson's were paralleled in literary studies by Kenneth Burke's *Grammar of Motives* (1969 [1945]) and *Rhetoric of Motives* (1950), where he called attention to the complex rhetorical grammar by which our language not only makes statements but makes reflective statements about what we are saying as we say it. Such notions, of course, are continuous within the field of rhetoric since the time of Aristotle. What is important for us here is that there is a solid line of research which takes all statements or utterances, whether spoken or written, as inherently bi-leveled. To make meaning with language is to make statements simultaneously with further cues (metamessages) about how we are to interpret those meanings. Such contextualization cues or metamessages in spoken discourse are fairly subtle matters of tone of voice, accompanying gestures, or, for our purposes, the selection of a specific style in which to couch the utterance.

While the main strand of this research literature focuses its attention on face-to-face spoken and embodied communication, and while Burke's attention was directed to matters of style in writing, a third line of analysis has been opened up by multimodal discourse or visual semiotic analysis which examines the ways in which multiple modes including typefaces, colors, and graphics perform many of these same metacommunicative functions in a range of media from print to film and video. In the public documents we can access on the MMS website we cannot directly determine, of course, very much about face-to-face metacommunicative messages. We do have, however, many examples of both stylistic and multimodal metamessages.

For example, in different public hearings the same person, Paul Stang, is transcribed as speaking in two quite distinct styles. While we do not have a record of his rhythm, pacing, or intonation, we can see significant stylistic differences in the following:

Nuiqsut, 24 July 2002: The purpose of the Environmental Impact Statement is to provide information to people and ultimately to the decision-
maker, so that person can make a proper decision.

(3.1: VII–296)

Kaktovik, 26 July 2002: Let me tell you in a nutshell the way that system
works. This document is the five-year plan for 2002 to 2007. It was
approved at the very end of June by the Secretary herself. She had sent out
three preliminary versions of this over the last 18 months or so for
comment … So she looks at those and makes her judgment. Obviously,
any Secretary who is worth her or his salt would consider what people have
said in the past.

(3.1: VII–322)

The style is quite different in these two cases, cueing somewhat different
stances or interpersonal relationships between the speaker and the audience.
The first uses a more formal style than the second: 'The purpose' is opposed to
'Let me tell you in a nutshell'. In the first instance the speaker sets himself
outside of the utterance as the simple animator of an objective statement. In the
second instance he includes himself in a face-to-face relationship with the questioner. Correspondingly, the Secretary of the Interior is presented only indirectly as 'the decision-maker' in the first case but as a known person who
commands the pronoun 'she' in the second case. Shortly after this utterance she
is, in fact, referenced by name, 'Gail Norton', suggesting, if not a personal relationship, at least an insider's knowledge between Paul Stang and the Secretary
of the Interior. Of course, such stylistic differences are clearly preserved in the
written transcript.

Comparably, two different documents covering the same action use different
linguistic forms which are further framed by the contextualization cues of
different typographic layouts and design. The notice of the Beaufort Sea Sale
186 which appears in the *Federal Register* gives the following summary as its
opening text (also in Figure 3.1):

The MMS will open and publicly announce bids received for blocks
offered in Oil and Gas Lease Sale 186 on 24 September 2003, in accordance
with provisions of the OCS Lands Act (43 U.S.C. 1331–1356, as amended)
and the implementing regulations (30 CFR part 256).

(USDOI/MMS, 21 August 2003)

This may be compared to the 'same' notice given as part of the MMS's
'Leasing Activities Information' package, which opens with the text (Figure 3.2
below):

Enclosed is the Final Notice of Sale for Sale 186, Beaufort Sea, to be held
on 24 September 2003, in Anchorage Alaska.

In addition to the Notice, this package consists of:

Lease Stipulations for Oil and Gas Lease Sale 186
Information to Lessees for Oil and Gas Lease Sale 186
Royalty Suspension Provisions, Sale 186
- etc.

(USDOI/MMS, 21 August 2003)

Federal Register / Vol. 68, No. 162 / Thursday, August 21, 2003 / Notices   **50549**

Dated: August 11, 2003.
Aurene M. Martin,
Assistant Secretary—Indian Affairs.
[FR Doc. 03–21464 Filed 8–20–03; 8:45 am]
BILLING CODE 4310-4N-P

DEPARTMENT OF THE INTERIOR

Minerals Management Service

Outer Continental Shelf (OCS) Beaufort Sea Alaska, Oil and Gas Lease Sale 186

AGENCY: Minerals Management Service, Interior.

ACTION: Final Notice of Sale (NOS) 186, Beaufort Sea.

SUMMARY: The MMS will open and publicly announce bids received for blocks offered in Oil and Gas Lease Sale 186 on September 24, 2003, in accordance with provisions of the OCS Lands Act (43 U.S.C. 1331...

Bidders may not modify or withdraw their bids unless the Regional Director, Alaska OCS Region receives a written modification or written withdrawal request prior to 10 a.m., Tuesday, September 23, 2003. Should an unexpected event such as an earthquake or travel restrictions be significantly disruptive to bid submission, the Alaska OCS Region may extend the Bid Submission Deadline. Bidders may call (907) 271–6010 for information about the possible extension of the Bid Submission Deadline due to such an event.

Note: Four blocks in the easternmost Beaufort Sea area are subject to jurisdictional claims by both the United States and Canada. This Notice refers to this area as the Disputed Portion of the Beaufort Sea. The section on Method of Bidding identifies the four blocks and describes the procedures for submitting bids for them.

Area Offered for Leasing: MMS is

available to assist in locating the blocks relative to the adjacent areas. The Locator Map is for use in identifying locations of blocks but is not part of the official description of blocks available for lease. Some of the blocks may be partially encumbered by an existing lease, or transected by administrative lines such as the Federal/State jurisdictional line. Partial block descriptions are derived from Supplemental Official OCS Block Diagrams and OCS Composite Block Diagrams, which are available upon request at the address, phone number, or internet site given above.

Lease Terms and Conditions: On February 20, 2003, MMS published a Notice of Availability (68 FR 8306) of the proposed Notice of Sale for Sale 186, which included proposed lease terms and conditions providing for a minimum bid amount of $62 per hectare and a rental rate of $13 per hectare,

Figure 3.1

Leasing Activities Information

 MMS   U.S. Department of the Interior
Minerals Management Service
Alaska OCS Region

Notice of Sale
Beaufort Sea Oil and Gas Lease Sale 186

Enclosed is the Final Notice of Sale for Sale 186, Beaufort Sea, to be held on September 24, 2003, in Anchorage, Alaska.

In addition to the Notice, this package consists of:
- Lease Stipulations for Oil and Gas Lease Sale 186
- Information to Lessees for Oil and Gas Lease Sale 186
- Royalty Suspension Provisions, Sale 186
- Blocks Available for Leasing in Oil and Gas Lease Sale 186
- Debarment Certification Form
- Bid Form and Envelope
- Telephone Numbers/Addresses of Bidders Form

Figure 3.2 Minerals Management Service, US Department of the Interior

While there are many linguistic and typographic contextualization cues that might be noted, such as the condensed paragraphing in the *Federal Register* by comparison with bullet-pointed listing in the information package, what is important here is to see that these differences convey different metamessages about the status of these texts. The *Federal Register* announcement is a formal and legal announcement, the information activities package conveys very similar information, but does so as information. In the first case the document itself takes the action, it commits the MMS to opening and announcing the bids which have been received. This is buttressed clearly by the legal basis upon which this action is grounded. In the second case the document does not take the action but makes reference to the action. The action the second document takes is to enclose information.

Perhaps the linguistic contextualization cues would be sufficient to convey the two different metamessages, 'This is an official action,' compared to 'This is information about an action,' but these two different messages are further buttressed typographically in the layout of the two documents as text on a printed page. In Figure 3.1, the *Federal Register* Notice of Sale (NOS), for example, the official status of the announcement is further conveyed by its placement within a section of the *Federal Register* dedicated to notices. The layout in three columns and within a standard format of a header, a subject line and then the sub-headers 'AGENCY' and 'ACTION' make it clear that this notice has comparable legal status with all other notices conveyed by this medium. To one who knows the medium, a glance at the page is sufficient to isolate distinct notices and to assign legal validity to each notice.

Figure 3.2, the Leasing Activities Information Notice of Sale (NOS), is presented in a format the MMS uses for documents with an information function. Again, the layout under the header emphasizes the information function and de-emphasizes the agency (MMS).

While these two examples illustrate that the contextualizing or framing cues may be conveyed by linguistic form but also by layout and page design, one further contrast will show that such framing practices may also change over time, perhaps cueing shifts in both the primary messages and the contextualizing messages. Figure 3.3 looks again at the news release dated 19 September 2001

MMS Alaska OCS Region

News Release

For Immediate Release—September 19, 2001   Robin Lee Cacy
907-271-6070
1-800-764-2627
www.mms.gov/alaska

MMS Announces Multiple Sale Process for Alaska's Beaufort Sea

---

Figure 3.3 Minerals Management Service, US Department of the Interior

Figure 3.4 Minerals Management Service, US Department of the Interior

which announces the initial multiple-sale process for the Beaufort Sea Sales. The formatting is limited to page layout and typeface differences.

Figure 3.4 shows the news release dated 24 February 2005 which we looked at in Chapter 1. As noted there, the MMS has shifted to a highly designed full-color graphic letterhead which goes far beyond both the information conveyed in the older version (agency, contact person and numbers, function, date of release, and subject) and, in fact, the framing message. From the point of view of header information, we now see both the acronym (MMS) and the full agency name 'Minerals Management Service', for example. There is also a slogan 'Securing Ocean Energy and Economic Value for America'. Both the slogan and the US national flag segment directly signal a discourse of American patriotism. These matters were left almost entirely implicit in the older news release in which the only indication that the MMS is an agency of the US government is the 'gov' in the website address.

This richly designed header not only frames or contextualizes the information within the news release as coming from a US government agency, it simultaneously sets it within the much broader frame of post-9/11 political discourses of heightened US patriotism and heightened concerns for US national security. Thus the metamessage not only contextualizes the information of the Beaufort Sea Sale 195, the message itself is appropriated as a means to mutually promote these contextualizing discourses.

A focus on the question of message and metamessage might pay attention to the ways in which linguistic style, typography, or graphic design show the announcement of a sale to be officially binding or simply informational. It is equally important to pay attention to the ways in which framing might structure or restructure relationships between the speaker and the hearer (writer and reader or designer and user), a concern developed further in Chapter 5.

The graphically designed header of the news release serves the function not only of cueing that the information is official or authorized by the US government, but also signals that both the producers of the news release and those with a potential interest in Sale 195 are equally encompassed within the political discourses of energy and national security. The relationships among the participants (MMS and potential bidders, that is, energy corporations) are placed on an explicit political footing which in the earlier news release was left implicit. A business or commercial interaction within a governmental environment is recontextualized as being at least in equal measure one that has to do with the politics of national energy security.

Beyond the issues that have been discussed above, the research on framing raises two further problems for PCDA as well as for public policy more generally:

1   contextualization cues (and participant structures) vary widely across social groups – much more widely than more primary lexicogrammatical structures or graphic design – and may therefore be easily misinterpreted; and
2   the 'style' of technical dialogue varies considerably across document types (EISs, EAs, newsletters, written transcripts of spoken public hearing testimony) and, consequently, the import of contextualization cues also varies.

That is, there is variation across both social groups and across genres and styles within social groups. As there are many stakeholder groups involved in any public consultative process and any setting of public policy, such boundary crossing is inevitable. We will examine each of these separately.

First, social groups vary considerably in their uses of contextualization cues. A smile does not universally mean happiness, but is used with other messages to produce a more complex message. Notably, for example, it has been observed frequently that Chinese may smile in hearing or speaking things that cause considerable difficulty or embarrassment. This smile does not indicate that the speaker (or hearer) is pleased with the substance of the message, but North Americans do often make exactly this mistaken interpretation. Likewise, urgency in speaking might be interpreted in diametrically opposed ways so that a person from New York who speaks with what Tannen calls 'machine gun questions' and rapid turnover of turns might be felt as showing interest and involvement within a social group of New Yorkers but interpreted as aggressive and pushy in other social groups. Conversely, many Alaska Native people, and also traditional Finnish people, who seek to show respect to others by speaking seldom, carefully, and slowly are sometimes interpreted by those outside of their social group as cold, withdrawn, uninterested, or even hostile.

Second, as we shall see in Chapters 4 and 5, genres and styles (or professional and other registers) also vary considerably in linguistic and other semiotic forms of contextualization cues. When we overhear two people talking we can tell almost immediately whether it is a casual conversation or an intense business negotiation because of the style and manner of speaking of the participants. Little more than a glance at the *Federal Register* text in Figure 3.1 conveys the message, 'This is NOT play'. The sharp contrasts between advertising text (and images) and the Surgeon General's warnings on products such as tobacco are not just design or display contrasts, they signal contrasting, oppositional meanings.

We also now see hybrid forms of styles and texts, often on corporate websites, which adopt a chatty, friendly, and interpersonal style to discuss, for example, such matters as whether or not the company does or does not produce or sell genetically modified foods. This 'synthetic personalization', to use Fairclough's term, mixes personal and formal styles or registers to provide quasi-legal information in a way that is simultaneously non-informative but gives the impression of abundant information and concern. The website of the MMS on which the documents we are discussing here are posted (Figure 3.5; see the Appendix as well) contains a complex mixture of formal legal documents and more informally informational, educational, or even entertaining documents, all of which are presented within a uniform and consistent website format which gives only minimal immediate clues about which sort of document one might be accessing.

As indicated in Figure 3.6, only the blocking of items in the site key in the left column (in blue color blocks in the original) indicates a topic or functionality difference. There is some hierarchy, with more general topics at the top, site management or forms at the bottom.

Here it is particularly important to comment on the role of multiple media and modes in contemporary communications. Metamessages about how to take primary messages are now conveyed as often through the modes of color, type-faces, graphics and other aspects of design as they are through linguistic features of text, as we have seen in comparing Figures 3.3 and 3.4 above. This leads to a second issue that must be considered, particularly in the documents relevant to a

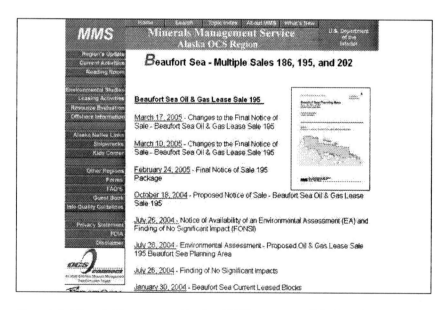

Figure 3.5 Minerals Management Service, US Department of the Interior

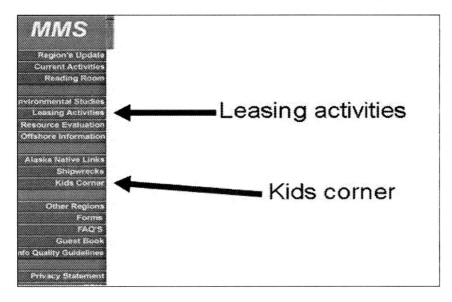

Figure 3.6 Minerals Management Service, US Department of the Interior

PCDA. Design and graphic presentation can be very expensive. If high design encodes meta-communications about care, sincerity, or truthfulness, then only those with access to those resources are able to convey these framing or contextualization cues. To raise this point more concretely as a question: would a hand-written note on some common and easily available paper from a local citizen carry the same communicative weight as a highly designed and expensively produced government information newsletter?

As a suggestive answer which is possibly counter-intuitive, it is interesting to note that the most carefully and highly designed documents within this set of documents are the news release in Figure 3.4 and the MMS website in Figure 3.6, which in themselves have a limited and purely informational function. By contrast, among the least elaborately designed documents are the formal and required bidding documents, one of which is shown in Figure 3.7.

This bid form is a simple word-processed document onto which the relevant data (the specific sale and its date) have been superimposed in bold type. The bidder fills in this document (among others) and the resulting bid is legally binding for what is often millions of dollars. In a way that inverts our contemporary 'intuitions' about graphic design: the framing cue of high graphic design signals a very low level of legally binding actional commitment; a low level of design conveys actions that value millions of dollars, engage the parties for a minimum period of a decade, and commit national wildlife and energy resources to specific lines of development and exploitation.

The research on metacommunicative differences and the consequences of misinterpretation forms a large literature. Here it is enough to note that *all*

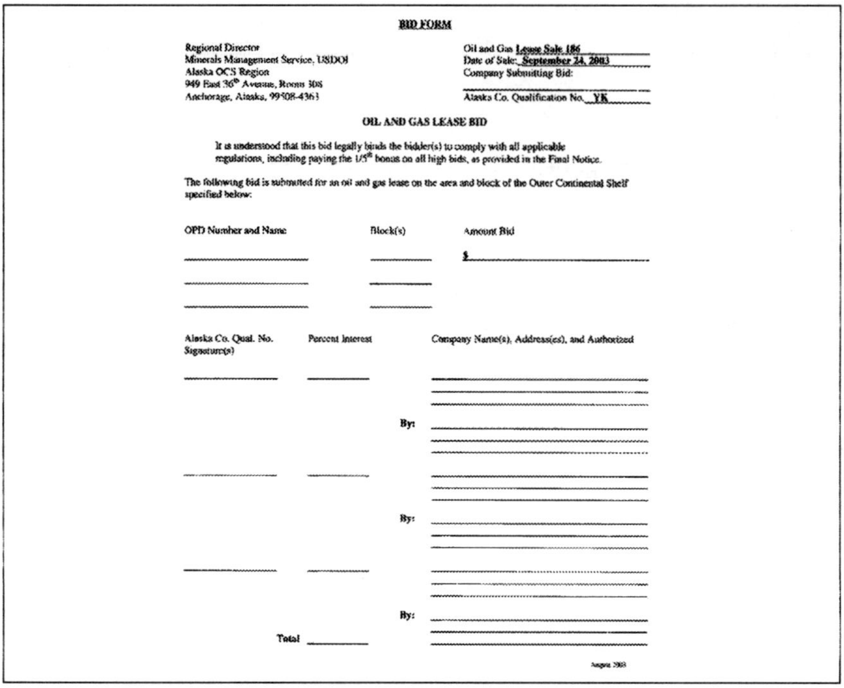

BID FORM

Regional Director
Minerals Management Service, USDOI
Alaska OCS Region
949 East 36th Avenue, Room 308
Anchorage, Alaska, 99508-4363

Oil and Gas Lease Sale 186
Date of Sale: September 24, 2003
Company Submitting Bid:
Alaska Co. Qualification No. YK

OIL AND GAS LEASE BID

It is understood that this bid legally binds the bidder(s) to comply with all applicable regulations, including paying the 1/5th bonus on all high bids, as provided in the Final Notice.

The following bid is submitted for an oil and gas lease on the area and block of the Outer Continental Shelf specified below:

OPD Number and Name | Block(s) | Amount Bid $

Alaska Co. Qual. No. | Percent Interest | Company Name(s), Address(es), and Authorized Signature(s)

By:

By:

By:

Total

August 2003

Figure 3.7 Minerals Management Service, US Department of the Interior

messages are conveyed with metacommunicative messages concerning their interpretation, but at the same time none of the metacommunicative signals (contextualization cues) cue the same universal frames. Thus, communication which crosses the boundaries of social groups from professional to layman, from government decision maker to public, or from environmental biologist to lawyer, as well as from local resident of a coastal Alaskan village to a visitor from 'the Lower 48', from the most casual conversation to legally binding documents, is prey to misinterpretations of intent, whether it is spoken or written discourse. A central goal of a PCDA is to analyze and to make explicit any cases of such misinterpretations which may be obstructing the dialogue of democratic discussion on the issue of public policy under consultation.

This literature on the framing and contextualization of messages highlights our attention to the need in any public policy analysis to pay careful attention not just to *what* is said or written but to *how* it is said or written. Because public policy analysis inherently crosses boundaries of social and stakeholder groups and communicative registers, these cross-over communications are highly susceptible to the problems of miscommunication that arise from misinterpreted contextualization, as we shall see in Chapter 4, when discourses are 'blended' or even 'bent' into other discourses. Furthermore, PCDA by definition is a form of discourse analysis that crosses levels of focus, types of data, and, consequently, presentational styles. PCDA needs to be particularly sensitive to problems of contextualization.

Finally, a central concept not to lose sight of in framing or contextualization is that an event and its context are not independent. On the contrary, event and context mutually constitute each other. As we have seen in the discussion of the letterhead of the highly designed news release in Figure 3.4, the images and slogans frame the news of the news release, but at the same time we should not lose sight of the fact that the news release gives substance to the discourses of politics and national energy security signaled by the letterhead.

Similarly, PCDA enters into the process of public consultation by recipro-cally giving meaning to the process as a matter of framing even as it is itself framed by this process. There is a systematic relationship between earlier steps in the process and subsequent developments of the policy within that frame, such as when an EIS makes use of existing scientific research, analyzes that research in relation to some proposed action, brings that analysis to a public consultative process, including a PCDA, and then takes action on the basis of this sequence of analyses.

The research on contextualization suggests that, by simply coming into exis-tence as part of the process, a PCDA signals an interpretive change in the meaning of the proposed actions of the lower or preceding tier, much in the same way that the design graphics of the 2005 news release call attention to and therefore recontextualize the low-key typography of the 2001 news release. Conversely, it is the earlier, broader, proposed-action tier that gives meaning (context) to the new tier of the analysis, in the same way that the new graphics stand out by contrast to the older typography.

Synchronization

A PCDA analyzes documents and actions which occur across several different timescales. A public consultation itself is layered in multiple tiers. This occurs when a set of previous research projects are collated, integrated, and used as the broad, programmatic under-tier for another level in which a full, broader, but necessarily less detailed study such as an EIS is prepared. This, in turn, provides the basis for subsequent, narrower, studies which are closely focused on actions which have followed the preparation of the EIS. In either case the tier which follows is more sharply focused on a specific action which has been left in the earlier tier as a proposed or potential action. This difference in timescale is not only such that the lower, earlier tier encompasses a longer duration than the specific actions and activities of which it is constituted, there is a difference of logical typing between these tiers. The lower tier is an abstract level in that it deals with potential or proposed actions, not with imminent actions. The upper tier is focused on imminent actions – ones currently impacting on people, mate-rials, and places. In the case of the Beaufort Sea Sale the three sales were grouped within a single EIS, leaving open the necessity of subsequent supplemental EISs or EAs.

Underlying all such analyses, whether tiered or not tiered, is a very much broader stratum of the world before scientific analysis is done. Research such as that involved in an EIS arises only when a significant change in existing patterns and practices of life (human and otherwise) is proposed for some reason. In practice it is not only the scientific/analytical apparatus which defines the contrast between this basal tier and the subsequent scientific research, but that is a crucial cultural difference. The scientific research analysis which is found in an EIS is parceled tightly together with the world system of sociopolitical institutions of governments and resource extraction corporations.

'Layered simultaneity' is a term which Blommaert uses to address the layering of multiple timescales in any social action or event. Events within the process of the Beaufort Sea Sales operate on multiple timescales. A public hearing operates with a timescale of a few hours to a few days, if we consider transportation time as well as the time span of the meeting itself. The meeting at Barrow, 1 August 2002, for example, began at 5:00 p.m. and the transcript went off-record at 8:34 p.m. From 6:57 p.m. to 7:25 p.m. there was a break, taken because of confusion over the starting time, which is stated in the testimony to have been 5:00 p.m. (3.1: VII–411) but had been announced for 7:00 p.m. The published transcript erroneously gives the time of the meeting as 7:00 p.m. These four hearings, as a group, comprise a larger cycle of just over a week, the first at Nuiqsut on 24 July 2002 and the last at Barrow on 1 August 2002. That cycle is set within the longer, nine-month cycle within which the draft EIS (released June 2002) and the final EIS (released February 2003) are prepared. The hearings are necessarily entrained within that cycle to intervene between the draft and the final version because the final version of the EIS incorporates a record of the public responses. Those cycles work within the seven-year time period of the three Beaufort Sea Sales.

More broadly, the cycles of this set of sales work within the several-decades cycle opened by the 1953 Outer Continental Shelf (OCS) Lands Act and, as of this writing, are projected to extend into the future indefinitely. Further, the EA which was prepared after Sale 186 and before Sale 195 assessed the published results of several global climate-change reports as a means of establishing to what extent these cycles are linked to or would be affected by climate change.

Running simultaneously, in tandem with these cycles which are directly relevant to the Beaufort Sea Sale, are yet other significant cycles. The annual bowhead whale hunt is frequently discussed in both the EIS and public hearings alike. This, in turn, is discussed within the life cycles of the whales as well as the longer cycle of the species as an endangered species. These cycles are also linked at various points with cycles of community subsistence development as well as the much longer time period of Alaska statehood within the historical life of the US.

Any of the actions have relevance within all of these separate timescales simultaneously, from the announcement in the *Federal Register*, through comments in public hearings, to the opening, assessment, and awards of leases to the best bids. This is the meaning captured with the concept of layered simultaneity. The publication of a map of the blocks available for leasing is not only an action in itself but it is a moment of ratification within the longer cycles of the sale, of offshore resource development, and of US national energy policy since the 1950s. It is also a moment within the cycles of subsistence whale hunting, Alaska statehood and US national political discourse. While at any particular moment just one or a narrow band of these timescales is the focus of attention, the term 'layered simultaneity' highlights for our attention that we are never acting in ways that are irrelevant to the other timescales also present in and circulating through that moment of action.

This conceptualization of layered simultaneity resonates with the human geographical work of Hägerstrand many decades ago and is a theoretical means of pulling ourselves analytically away from the trap of summarization which Wittgenstein noted in the quotation given above. Blommaert argues against the fallacy of what he terms 'synchronization'. This is the analytical flaw of flattening out this complex topography of multiple layers so that a single one of them is taken to encompass the full meaning of an event under analysis. To synchronize would be to say that a public hearing was just a public hearing in response to the draft EIS, not also a moment in the political discourse of the nation, the subsistence hunting of the community, and the history of tension between Alaska statehood and national priorities. Synchronization is the fallacy of flattened temporal analysis.

A PCDA needs to be alert to the problem of synchronization. It is a common problem, particularly in less formal statements such as those found in news releases. This is clear, for example, in the news release of 19 September 2001 concerning the multiple sale process. MMS Alaska Regional Director John Goll is quoted as saying:

> The multi-sale EIS will eliminate the need to prepare a new EIS for each proposed sale on issues which rarely change … If they do change, then the approach will make it easier for the public and us to key on those new issues and their effects.
>
> (1.1)

It is said that a later tier will not change or modify decisions of an earlier tier, nor change either the scope or conclusions. As Goll puts it in the news release just cited,

> After the first EIS is completed for Sale 186, we will prepare either an environmental assessment or a supplemental EIS and a consistency determination for each subsequent sale. The public will have opportunity to comment on each sale proposal.
>
> (1.1)

But, as we have seen with the concept of framing, later decisions and studies do, in fact, influence our interpretation of earlier ones. Perhaps the texts themselves of the earlier documents do not change but, as we have seen, any later analysis, comment, or statement inherently reframes, redefines, and recontextualizes an earlier one, just as that later document or statement receives its meaning, to a considerable extent, from earlier ones. To put it in terms of layered simultaneity, actions occur simultaneously in multiple layers and have their effects across all of those layers. Each layer is altered to some extent by each action, though, to be sure, because of the dampening effect across many higher and slower layers, 'small' or quick actions tend to be perceived most strongly as affecting only the layers more in rhythm with the pace of those actions.

Neither the public policy under consideration in a public consultation nor the PCDA which is entered into in that consultation should be synchronized as being in some way the final word. As Blommaert has argued, there is a teleological tendency in synchronization to read the meaning of layers of many timescales as culminating in the currently focal action as their end, purpose, and goal. We tend to see all of the history of humanity leading to this moment in which we live. It is this teleological coloring and shaping of all tiers of analysis toward the present one on which our attention is focused against which the concept of synchronization warns us. Oil lease sales are not conducted for the purpose of enjoying a public hearing, the award of a lease cannot occur without the sequence of actions leading into that moment. Likewise, public consultations are never conducted for the purpose of producing a PCDA, nor is a PCDA the conclusion of a public policy. The actions of policy makers and other stakeholders exist in a dialectic with the discourse analyst.

PCDA in the representation of action

This discussion of summarization, framing, and synchronization has shown a number of ways in which the existing sociolinguistic and social-scientific literature may be integrated into a PCDA to productively sharpen our attention to various pitfalls that can be avoided in the public consultation process. The discussion suggests a number of ways in which a public consultative process might be subjected to a discourse analysis under each of these headings.

Summarization

Key points for attention are:

- excluded actions (lower-level, enabling, alternating, or batched);
- excluded participants (participants in excluded actions);
- transformed actions (unordered to ordered, or vice versa, alternating to sequenced or co-occurring, reversing of enablements);
- irreversible transformations (talk to written policy, to material actions and objects or built environment).

Framing

Key points for attention are:

- communications across or between the documents and actions of the process itself; each action or document is a contextualization of the others;
- communication across or between the stakeholders in the analysis, including:
  - initiators of the actions requiring analysis (resource development corporations, government agencies);
  - affected populations (community groups, tribes, environmental agencies);
  - research and reporting participants (researchers, media, public relations);
- shifts in mode from speaking to writing (e.g. in transcripts of hearings or interviews), from writing to speaking (e.g. officials in Q&A sessions), or the use of more complex graphic media (images, videos, graphics);
- shifts in language or dialect used;
- shifts in style (legal; conversational; public relations; scientific).

Synchronization

Key points for attention are:

- invisibility of non-focal documents, actions, levels, timescales;
- fallacy of non-alteration of non-focal documents or actions;
- focus on different documents and actions (timescales of meaning) by different participants or stakeholder groups;
- negotiation across documents and actions rather than synchronization to the action preferred by most powerful stakeholder.

Raising attention to these aspects of the public consultative process will achieve a more robust entrainment of actions among stakeholders and processes of decision making which, in turn, will achieve a more robust practice of democratic debate on matters of public policy.

Going beyond summarization, framing, and synchronization there are three areas that are implied thus far and are in need of further analysis:

- an analysis of the multiple discourses which circulate in the documents of this leasing process, especially of the ways in which they relate to each other interdiscursively;
- an analysis of the multiple document types or genres, with a focus on how these documents take up or require different writer/reader positions; and
- the significance of the differing modes and modal configurations in which the documents and the website are presented.

These, then, are the topics which are taken up in the following three chapters.

PRACTICE

Now that you have collected documents for your PCDA project in Chapter 2 and examined the overall process of the consultation that interests you, the next task is to look for ways in which your documents take an action or provide information and to identify which ones are purely informational. That is, it is important to begin by sorting (to the extent this is possible) into pragmatic action and information categories.

Activity 1:
Action and information in documents

Some of the documents involved in a public consultation are action documents. Many other documents are purely informational. Almost always there will be a central document such as an EIS (as we saw in the case study of the MMS) or a government policy statement, a proposed rule or rule change, or a change in the law. Even if we extract just some of these primary actions, such as the action of holding the multiple lease sale (a decision of the US Secretary of the Interior), announcing the sale (in the *Federal Register*), informing the media of the announcement (news release), preparing the EIS, and conducting a hearing on the EIS, we can see that there are complex relations among these actions. Frequently a single document mixes informational sections and action segments.

As a supplementary activity to Activity 1 you could do a more extended analysis of the multiple actions performed by the documents in your project. A news release may inform the media. It also advertises or brands the agency by keeping it in the public eye. Of course, a news release also performs the action of working for a salary within the job of the public relations staff.

ASSIGNMENT

First sort all of the documents you have collected into two broad (and rough) categories, those which carry out an action and those which provide information about some action. In doing this you will find that you will probably need a third, middle category of documents in which some sections simply provide information and other sections take (or enable) specific actions.

Make a table where on one side you list the specific documents you have collected. Across the top write the three categories: action, mixed, and information. Check one of these categories for each document.

Write a brief action/information footnote for each of these documents that will support your categorization.

Observations

This matrix will give you your opening analysis, which you can then use later in Chapter 4 to start your analysis of the discourses present in each document and in Chapter 5 to start your analysis of the genres and functions of each document.

Activity 2:
In other words

Nouns and noun phrases perform a kind of summarization by encapsulating very complex processes under a single heading. Is it 'global warming' or 'climate change'? Is it the 'oil', the 'petroleum' or the 'energy' industry? If we see 'public hearing' do we think 'US', but, when we hear 'public consultation', think 'UK' or 'Europe'? What is the agency which looks after food safety – the FSA or the FDA? In the US it is the FDA (Food and Drug Administration) – the FSA is the Farm Service Agency; but in the UK it is the FSA (Food Standards Agency; but watch that you don't also get the UK's Financial Services Authority, which also uses FSA). The IRS in the US is the Internal Revenue Service, but in the UK it is the Inland Revenue Service. What is called an EIS (Environmental Impact Statement) in the US is called an EIA (Environmental Impact Assessment) in the European Union. What do these terms summarize and how do they do it differently within different agencies or political jurisdictions?

ASSIGNMENT

Find a keyword repeatedly mentioned in the documents you have browsed through, like 'sales', 'EIS', or 'EA' in the MMS case. What actions does this word represent, refer to, or imply? Unpack the actions contained in the keyword and elaborate its meaning in three different ways. Return to the original keyword, think about what actions and social actors it includes and excludes. Write a short (no more than two pages) analysis that includes these observations.

Observations

Different stakeholders may use a keyword differently or use a different term for that meaning. Compare the different terms and observe what the difference conveys about the stance of the stakeholder, e.g. 'global warming' vs 'climate change'.

Activity 3:
Ways of framing

You might submit testimony or views in a public consultation in several ways. You could submit a formally written letter on printed letterhead stationery or write it out by hand on lined, school notebook paper. You could place a tightly produced video documentary on a website or enter a few hundred words into a fixed-format online 'interactive' form. Each of these would frame your commentary very differently, as an established private citizen, a student, an activist organization with the resources to produce expensive documentaries, or a more casual drop-in respondent to a public opinion poll.

This activity will help you start to analyze both how the documents produced by others are framed and how your own PCDA might best be framed. Be sure to pay attention not just to the language of the documents but to modes (spoken or print, text only or images, black and white or color, etc.).

ASSIGNMENT

Find a document in your study, the message of which you consider important in the overall consultation process. Find documents from other sources containing similar messages. Compare these documents and notice how they are framed in terms of language, style, and mode. Through these framing devices, what metamessage does each document convey? Now imagine you are the recipient or a potential reader of the documents. What kinds of metamessage would you perceive through the framing cues? Pay attention to any potential misinterpretation. Then imagine you are the producer of the documents. What can you do to reframe the document so as to mitigate misunderstanding of the metamessage?

Use your word processor and/or photo-editing software to make a mock document that reframes the message.

Internet work

You may need to take screenshots of the web pages containing the documents to facilitate the examination of framing, particularly through graphic design. On a PC, press the Print Screen (Prt Scr) key to copy the entire screen. Open the word processor or image editing software and paste the screenshot into the document. On a Mac, press Shift+z+4. Drag the cross over the desired screen area. A PDF file of the screenshot will be automatically saved to your desktop.

Observations

This exercise enables you to see how a similar message can convey varied metamessages through different means of framing and also depending on who the recipients are. Save the screenshots you have taken. The multimodal aspect of a PCDA document will be examined more closely in Chapter 6.

As a supplement to Activity 3 you could format several mock-ups of reframed documents and then conduct a focus group to see what meanings are interpreted, based on the different framings. Write a short analysis of the focus group's comments.

Activity 4:
Resemiotization

One argument that was made for why the sale of oil and gas leases in the Beaufort Sea needed to be done soon was that the infrastructure of pipelines and the rest already existed and could be used by these new developments rather than having to be built from scratch. In this way an old political decision to develop energy resources on the Arctic Coast of Alaska had become materialized in buildings, pipe structures, and the rest of the industrial apparatus of a fully developed oil-extraction industrial site. The purpose of any public policy is to bring about a transformation from pure discussion and anticipation to solid structures, both the structures of law and government or corporate policy and the built structures of the material world.

The purpose of this activity is to think through what resemiotizations have already occurred in the process you are studying, as well as what transformations are being planned. Will buildings, roads, commercial objects, agricultural products and the like be physical outcomes of the policy? How will those physical outcomes give solidity to what is, at an earlier stage, 'just talk'? How has this 'talk' already resemiotized or transformed earlier actions?

ASSIGNMENT

Find at least two major actions that the project requires in the documents you are studying, being sure to concentrate on actions. Or, alternatively, find two actions that it is suggested should be prohibited. How will these actions result in material changes in the world which will solidify those actions (or result in the cessation of actions)? Write a two-page analysis of these actions and how they are discussed in the documents.

Alternatively, make a small website which analyzes comparable actions in other cases which are similar. A few images can often be more descriptive than pages of words.

Internet work

You can document past transformations from action through to the material by searching the internet for photographs. If you are interested in global warming, for instance, search on 'Shishmaref' for photos of a village in Alaska which is falling into the sea because of melting permafrost and rising seas.

4 When discourses collide

Politics, law, science and government in the sale of oil and gas leases

The Whalers have attended many, many meetings within the past twenty years, commented many, many times about disruption to the bowhead whale migrations, to no avail ... It is no longer the best interest to the North Slope Communities to attend the Minerals Management Service hokey meetings.

THEORY – CASE STUDY

Van Edwardsen says he is fed up with the MMS's 'hokey meetings' at the Barrow public hearing on Lease Sale 170 in 1997. In his view as Vice-President of the Barrow Whaling Captain's Association [sic] they are full of 'hokey studies conducted by Government scientists' which are done contrary to 'ethical practices used by legitimate scientists'. Are they hokey? Is the science really hokey and unethical?

In Kaktovik, just east of Barrow on the Arctic Coast, in July 2002 Paul Stang gave the following impromptu account of the MMS science program in response to a question about how research on oil spills from warmer water might be applied to the much colder water and ice of the Beaufort Sea:

> We do have a fairly decent science effort. Our whole purpose of that is to identify problems which we get here. We take information and questions like that and questions that we have ourselves back to our science group and we say, look, what are the most important key issues we need to work on. Let's devote the immediate funds to that and then we have a priority system.
>
> (3.1: VII–318)

Just a bit later in the same hearing he further develops this theme:

> The scientists for the North Slope Borough and our scientists are in daily, or not daily, but frequent communication. The fisheries people talk to the fisheries people. The oceanographers talk to the oceanographers. The acoustic people talk to the acoustic people at the staff level. We also, when

we have our studies planned as to what should be studied. That's the question. What should we be studying? We request that information from the North Slope Borough, in particular, as well as a variety of other sources. We send out these requests. What's the most important thing to be studying?

(3.1: VII–320)

Later in the same hearing he comments that MMS has a science budget in his Anchorage office of about 3 to 5 million dollars a year for scientific studies and that they work constantly together with other scientists in the main MMS office in Virginia as well as, he emphasizes, North Slope Borough scientists, and many other scientists who are independent of the MMS, the government, and the oil industry.

First an important caveat: Paul Stang's comments on MMS science are given five full years after Van Edwardsen's boycotting objection. Much may have changed at the MMS in that time. It should also be remembered that at the time of the 1997 hearing Paul Stang had just arrived in Alaska, three days before that volatile meeting. His comments five years later might well be positioned to take the wind from the sails of possible objections to the quality of MMS science. In any event, the hearings convened in 2002 were not boycotted and the objection of bad science was not raised.

Still, much of the discussion in these public hearings on the EIS concerns matters of science – both *what* science is done and *whether* science can give the most useful answers in order to arrive at the preferred decision. The MMS conducts its activities under a policy of maintaining clear and effective communication among all relevant stakeholders and with the general public to the greatest extent possible. This openness to public examination is evidenced in these thousands of pages of documents in themselves and also in their easy access in several forms in the offices of the MMS, in public libraries and other public venues in both Alaska and Canada, and, most notably, on the MMS website, which this analysis examines. Despite this commitment to public consultation and information there is still ambiguity and mutual misunderstanding in the dialogue among the major stakeholders in the process of undertaking these sales. It is this misunderstanding that is addressed in the discourse analysis presented in this chapter.

Discourse and the distortion of purpose

Macnaghten and Urry (1998) have argued that miscommunication among the public, policy makers in the government, and scientists, whether these scientists are in the employment of government management and regulatory agencies – the MMS would be an example – energy resource corporations, or environmental protection NGOs, arises from two fundamental sources. The first is the conceptualization of 'nature' which is held by members of these different groups or discourses, and the second is the degree or depth of their mutual assessment of trust, ambivalence, and uncertainty.

In one view of nature, the one which is most often held by science, it is taken as the physical world which is objectively given and which lies outside of, prior to, and independent of human conceptualizations. In this view nature is thought of as the domain of science, its theories, methods, and procedures and, by corollary, it is not the domain of the public with its unformed, often unarticulated lay understandings, nor of political or government discourses. They use the term 'environmental realism' for this view of nature. A second view, for which Macnaghten and Urry use the term 'environmental idealism', is a form of romanticism. Much as in the environmental realist position, nature is construed as lying outside of and independent of human actions but, unlike the realist position, nature is taken to be the ideal source of human values. In the third position, 'environmental instrumentalism' the focus shifts to the usefulness of nature for humans. Nature is understood to be a resource, whether for exploitation and use of its material resources, as in the energy resource extraction and development discourse, or as a cure for the ills of modernism, as in some forms of the environmental protection discourse.

Macnaghten and Urry argue that none of these positions is very useful in addressing problems of public policy, of resource extraction and development, or of environmental protection because they do not take into account the great extent to which our world, and particularly our actions in the world, are shaped by the language we use about the world and about our actions. They cite Wynne (1996), who notes that,

> What counts as authoritative scientific knowledge is, to a considerable degree, a product of active processes of interaction and negotiation between scientists and policy makers ... Yearley (1991) also examines the negotiations between supposedly universal discourses of science and the formation of policy in the fields of ozone depletion, global warming, biodiversity and sustainable development ... He suggests that in different ways standardising discourses of science can actually conceal unwarranted political assumptions, ignore local and cultural difference, and at times mask self-interest.
>
> (Cited in Macnaghten and Urry 1998: 18)

Further citing Wynne (1992), Macnagten and Urry write that assessments of trust, ambivalence, and uncertainty

> often radically conflict with the views of the lay public and that therefore the so-called experts misunderstand how people actually relate to their risk-laden environments. Public assessments of risk essentially involve judgments about the behavior and trustworthiness of expert institutions, especially of those that are meant to be controlling the risky processes involved. Thus risks are what he terms 'social relational', and involve judgments of

the quality of institutions and of one's relationship to such institutions. Such a view also emphasizes that the lay public do not simply respond to risks and assessments of risks which are simply 'out there'. The responses of the public are partly generated by the very threats to their identity which arise from the inadequate conception of the human which is deployed within and by the objectivist or expert science which is supposedly there protecting the public against such risks.

(Wynne 1996; cited in Macnaghten and Urry 1998: 18)

In the documents that enable and develop the multiple sale process for oil and gas leases in the Beaufort Sea there is a recurring problem of mutual mistrust among policy makers, government bureaucratic managers, scientists, environmentalists, resource development corporations, and the public. These problems are especially visible in the transcripts of the public hearings. Each of these groups works to a considerable extent within its own discourse system – or, for the sake of simplicity, its own discourse. Scientists speak to other scientists, government bureaucrats to other bureaucrats, and environmentalists to each other with considerable ease and comfort. This is not just because they are speaking about the same subjects but they are using the same strategies for communication, the same types of genres, and rely on the same underlying value systems of authorization, legitimization, and reward. It often happens, however, that they must speak across these lines of discourse and find that it is just there that mutual mistrust and doubts arise. When they speak or when they write to each other within the same group, they share common credentials or authorization to participate in the discourse. Further, they have agreed ideas about who should be able to have a voice in the discourse, they use very similar language, from technical terms to buzzwords, they follow similar lines of argument, they know how to prepare and read the same kinds of documents, and they are comfortable with using common modes of communication from scientific research reports for scientists, or office memos for bureaucrats, to online activist petitions for environmentalists.

In this chapter and in Chapter 5 we examine the problem of communication, especially when it occurs across the boundaries formed by these central discourses of politics, law, science, and government. While these different discourses will be defined (in this chapter), what is more important than simple identification is the processes by which these discourses are blended into each other, are bent to serve new or different purposes, or in which one or another of them eclipses another discourse altogether (Chapter 5).

This book takes the position that public discourse is always and inherently political, whatever other discourses it may borrow from or bend to its purposes. Public discourse is a process in which quite different polities try to gain the public ear and eye in an attempt to persuade citizens to agree with their own position and to support it. The public consultative process is a democratic process which is designed to bring the public, and especially the non-specialist public, into the discussion of public policy to ensure the broadest possible examination of the pros and cons of governmental or corporate action. From this point of view it is not surprising to see, as we shall in Chapter 5, the extent to which these processes of public consultation are focused on political discourse. It is the converse situation which surprises; that is, it is surprising to see the extent to which what is inherently a political process is captured and, to some extent, distorted by scientific discourse.

The analysis in this chapter, then, focuses on the central discourses which circulate in the documents concerning the multiple sales by the MMS of oil and gas leases in the Beaufort Sea (with a comparative background of the documents of the very similar process in Cook Inlet). With this analysis as background, Chapter 5 will then analyze some of the key document types which are the written field upon which these discourses play. Together these analyses highlight several ways in which the documents themselves constitute a complex and highly interdiscursive array of communications.

The discourses

Numerous discourses circulate through the documents of the MMS Beaufort Sea Sales 186 and 195. The four main discourses of politics, law, science, and government carry with them several other discourses, such as resource extraction and development, and traditional (subsistence) knowledge. The political discourse found in this sale process and embodied in these documents can be analyzed further into four main strands: US national politics, Alaska state politics, Alaska Native indigenous politics, and the politics of the world system and world economics.

While it is relatively easy to say that there are multiple discourses circulating in these documents, and this fits our common-sense notions when we read them, for a PCDA it is necessary to go beyond this simply intuitive statement to establish a set of defining characteristics. Researchers in critical discourse analysis have identified many characteristics or features of a discourse in the broad sense in which we are using the term here – the discourse of politics or the discourse of law. The characteristics used here are a synthesis of this research but the focus on aspects of discourse which are internal to specific documents, texts, or speech situations, such as the grammar of transitivity or the representation of social actors, is reduced. These aspects of discourse analysis will be taken up more directly in Chapter 5.

Our concern in this chapter is with analyzing how discourses are used and participated in by social actors. That is, we want to see how a social actor uses a discourse as a mediational means or how a social actor uses his or her authorization or credentialization within a discourse to take particular kinds of action. For this purpose we focus on features which are more pertinent to the identification of a discourse and its legitimated participants. Six features (participation, agency, lexicogrammar, argumentation, genres, and modes) provide a useful heuristic derived from the research literature for isolating discourses and participants.

- *Participation:* The system of credentialization of participants, along with their rules for participation. Only a licensed lawyer may provide a legal opinion, for example.
- *Agency:* The degree and kind of agency attributed to the 'authors' of statements. 'The passive voice is used in science,' but not 'Scientists use the passive voice.'
- *Lexicogrammar:* The lexicogrammatical shape of the language used. Science and law use highly complex and carefully stated, hedged, forms of statement while politics is governed by persuasive rhetoric.
- *Argumentation:* The type or argument structure used. Scientists use a hypothetical-deductive line of argument (theory, hypothesis, empirical evidence, cautious and constrained conclusions), but bureaucrats argue by authority of laws, rules, precedents, and policies.
- *Genres:* The characteristic genres and events. Laws, deeds, contracts, statutes, depositions and many other such genres are the stuff of legal discourse, whereas research reports published in peer-reviewed journals, lab and fieldwork reports, and scientific paper presentations at conferences are typical of scientific discourse. Government discourse deals in a wide range of documents which provide 'paper trails' of the histories of actions taken and decision-making processes from memos to minutes of meetings.
- *Modes:* The characteristic modes of communication. Scientific discourse is dominated by print in the form of the published research article. This written mode governs position in the field as well as rank and advancement in scientific and academic institutions. At the same time, scientific discourse also makes use of a wide range of other formal, coded systems, from computer modeling and mathematics to visual imaging and documentation. All of these tend to use an analytical frame that emphasizes logical relations among the objects displayed. Legal discourse tends to be codified in written modes (laws, rules, policies, statutes) but legal decisions are commonly based on the use of persuasive rhetoric in adversarial court disputes. These are ultimately resolved, nevertheless, through a written judgment. Resource and development discourse, in contrast to these, is strongly oriented toward both economic and material modes, the transfer of money and the production and manipulation of material objects – oil drilling rigs and pipelines, for example.

As we shall see, these six features allow us to tease apart the multiple discursive threads out of which these documents of the multiple sale process are woven. The analysis here and in Chapter 5 covers six types of documents:

- notices in the *Federal Register (FR)*
- MMS-originated news releases
- Leasing Activities Information memos
- the EIS and EA

- transcript of public testimony in response to the DEIS
- MMS website.

While there are still other document types in this series, the choice of these six document types was made because they are distinct in function as well as being distinct design types throughout the documents both of the Beaufort Sea multiple sale process and the Cook Inlet multiple sales being concurrently conducted by the MMS. The first two types of documents, *FR* notices and news releases, highlight some of the more interesting problems found throughout the other documents and so will be treated in considerably closer detail in Chapter 5 than will the other four types.

The blending of discourses: interdiscursivity

The general term covering the ways in which discourses are blended in actual use which has been used in critical discourse analysis is 'interdiscursivity'. This somewhat awkward term refers to situations in which one discourse is brought into an embedding or embedded relationship with another discourse, that is, two or more discourses are merged, or blended, or, as the title of this chapter has suggested, they have come into a collision.

Interdiscursivity was derived by extension from the earlier concept of 'intertextuality.' That term entered into the field of discourse analysis from the work of Bakhtin (1981) [1934–5]. 'Intertextuality' addresses the range of phenomena such as reference, allusion, quotation, citation, and paraphrase that occur when a text or a portion of a text is incorporated into another text. Bakhtin's argument was that such cross-textual phenomena are far from being the exception, they are the norm. All texts consist of such intertextual weavings of prior texts and, consequently, a wide range of histories, tensions, dialectics, and conflicts arise in the interpretation of textual meaning.

Fairclough (1992) introduced 'interdiscursivity' to extend the idea of inter-textuality so as to encompass the observation that it is not just specific words or specific portions of texts which may be brought into a text, but whole discourses may also cross-reference each other, be traded upon, or be incorporated into each other. A hospital staff meeting considering a patient's care might talk of the 'most effective treatment' for this patient. This same situation might bring up a rather different slant, however, if the question was concerned with the 'most cost-effective treatment' for this patient. The first utterance would fall solidly within medical discourse; the second has been blended with the financial discourses of hospital administration. The single word 'cost' introduces discourses of fiscal prudence or efficiency which are solidly located in financial or economic discourse, and ideally have no role in strictly medical discourse.

While in specific cases it may be a problematical matter for an analyst to decide whether one is dealing with a case of intertextuality or a case of interdiscursivity – is it just the word that is borrowed or a larger linguistic phenomenon? – in practice the use of the term interdiscursivity alerts analysts to consider more than just the words used, and to look into such phenomena as the features given above: participation, agency, lexicogrammar, argumentation, genres, and modes.

As has been noted in Chapter 1, an EIS was prepared to cover all three of the multiple lease sales in the Beaufort Sea prior to the time of the first sale. Before each subsequent sale an EA was to be prepared in which the prior EIS would be incorporated by reference, as would be other forms of information, research, and social or environmental changes which could be expected to materially alter the decisions determined on the basis of the first EIS. The EIS was prepared in two main stages. A draft EIS (DEIS) was prepared and commentary and responses were taken from the public and other interested parties. The final EIS (FEIS) then took that public testimony and other responses into consideration as part of the document itself. Thus the EA and the EIS are inherently interdiscursive as this has been defined in the discourse analytic research. Further, the general process of incorporating prior research and findings as an essential element of the current research and analysis is inherent in perhaps all scientific research. It could be argued that it is the essence of all academic scholarship. In this way government bureaucratic discourse is itself interdiscursive with academic–scholarly–scientific research discourse by incorporating one of the most fundamental and defining aspects of scientific–scholarly research.

Oil spill risk analysis

We can use one statement from the oil spill risk analysis (section IV.A.1) of the Environmental Assessment (2.5:6, also 2.5:45; citation 2.5.90) to illustrate the concept of interdiscursivity or discourse blending:

1   A recent laboratory study on the biodegradation of weathered Alaska North Slope crude indicates that low-dose oil locations are bioremediated more effectively than high-dose locations (Lepo et al., 2003).

This statement (1) from the EA is not itself an instance of scientific discourse, but it trades on the scientific research literature in three ways: it uses scientific referencing (i.e. 'Lepo et al., 2003' in the text, which is paralleled by a full citation in the bibliography at the end of the EA), it uses complex lexicogrammatical phraseology ('low-dose oil locations' vs. 'small oil spills'; 'bioremediation'), and it demotes the agency of the authors of the statement; the names of the scientists are used to index the citation but not as authors of the statement. That is, this does not say, 'Lepo and his colleagues found that', but 'a recent study indicates'.

This is neither a direct quotation nor a simple paraphrase of any comparable statement in the original article. The title of the article by Lepo et al. is: 'The Effect of Amount of Crude Oil on Extent of its Biodegradation in Open Water- and Sandy Beach-Laboratory Simulations'. The statement in the EA is a summarization of the article of twelve pages. As we have seen in Chapter 3, such a summarization runs the risk of altering the scope of the original concepts or, perhaps, of even altering the framing. A comparison with the original article suggests that these reductions have occurred in the process of incorporating that piece of scientific discourse into the EA.

The EA summary statement tells us that the study was based on 'weathered Alaska North Slope crude' [oil]; the oil used in the article is 'artificially weathered Alaska North Slope crude'. The EA summary refers to 'low-dose oil locations' and 'high-dose locations'; the scientific article uses 'low-dose experiments', 'oil doses', or 'oil dosing regimes'. The title of the original scientific article uses the terms 'open water-' and 'sandy beach-laboratory simulations' and the article follows this phrasing by referring to these simulations as the 'open-water microcosm' and the 'beach microcosm'. The summary statement contrasts 'locations' on the basis of their 'dosing'; the article contrasts 'open water' simulations with 'sandy beach' simulations.

In these summarizations we see that an experimental regime in the laboratory is linguistically suggested to be out of doors at locations where weathering might occur. We can set aside the purely scientific question of whether or not laboratory simulations in Florida with Florida sea water at a constant 20°C are a fair test of oil biodegradation in the Beaufort Sea, where the mean high air temperatures for the warmest months (June and July) are 8.3°C and 6.7°C. The linguistic question is whether or not the summary that appears in the EA is a statement within scientific discourse. The evidence so far suggests that while the statement remains approximately accurate – the article supports the claim that low doses of oil are bioremediated better than high doses of oil – further considerations support the claim that scientific discourse has been blended into the environmental/bureaucratic discourse of the EA.

The scientific article does not say that low doses of oil are bioremediated more effectively than high doses, though it does allow that summarization. The point of the article is that bioremediation is entirely ineffective and potentially dangerous for high doses (i.e. large oil spills) and for the lowest doses they were 'unable to statistically distinguish the controls from the bioremedial treatments'. Only low-intermediate doses were bioremediated by the experimental treatment. That is to say, at the lowest levels their treatments were no different from natural bioremediation, which derives from microorganisms already present in sea water. The article might have been summarized with an accuracy closer to the intent of the article by sentence (2):

2   A recent laboratory study on the biodegradation of weathered Alaska North Slope crude indicates bioremediation has no effect in large oil spills and is nearly insignificant in small oil spills.

The report itself is presented in a standard scientific format (title, abstract, introduction, materials and methods, results, discussion, conclusion, acknowledgments, and references). The lexicogrammatical features along with the scientific citation system, when located within the formal structure of a research paper, signal very strongly to any reader the message 'This is scientific discourse'.

The sentence occurs in the Oil-Spill-Risk Analysis section of the EA. This covers new information relevant to the decision which had been made on the basis of the original EIS to proceed with the oil lease Sale 186. The purpose of the EA was to determine whether any new information had become available that would require a reconsideration of that decision. In this context the bureaucratic meaning was determined to be that there was no new information that might alter that earlier decision. In the examples that follow the asterisk (★) indicates a sentence which is purely hypothetical.

3   ★*The EA prepared by the Minerals Management Service notes that biological clean-up is more effective on small oil spills than on large ones.*

Statement (3) is how we might reasonably expect the EA statement (1) to be incorporated for publication in a news release by the MMS or in an independent media report on the EA. The language is simpler in lexicogrammar and agency for the statement is attributed to the EA, not to the journalist. That is, the journalist (or public relations author) does not write, 'I read in the EA that'.

On the other hand, if the EA had produced the summary as suggested in (2), a news release might rather have said (4):

4   ★*The EA prepared by the Mineral Management Service notes that biological clean-up would not be an effective means of dealing with an oil spill.*

Finally, statement (5) is how this same statement might be processed for use within political discourse, that is, within discourse where the primary purpose is to persuade the reader or audience to accept the political position of the person speaking or writing:

5   ★*Petroleum resources vital to the Nation can be explored and developed while protecting the environment through the use of biological methods of oil spill management.*

Perhaps it might be more aggressively politicized by saying, 'We know that petroleum resources vital to the Nation can be explored and developed while protecting the environment through the use of biological methods of oil spill management.' The statement is read as political both because of the strong assertion of knowledge and fact by contrast to the scientific statements; it is, after all, only a laboratory study, not an actual oil spill, and the truth of the phrase 'vital to the Nation' is not amenable to scientific analysis but is, in fact, subject to democratic public political debate.

More importantly, had the original EA summarization gone in the other direction, as suggested in sentences (2) and (4), the statement as borrowed into political discourse would be more likely to be what we see in sentence (6):

6   *Petroleum resources vital to the Nation cannot be explored and developed while protecting the environment through the use of biological methods of oil spill management. Other means would have to be called upon.*

These examples show how different discourses may capture an idea, a thought, or a fact about the world and use it strategically within another discourse to accomplish the goals of that discourse, which are often different from those of other competing or conflicting discourses. These examples illustrate how such interdiscursivity occurs quite commonly and invisibly. For the purposes of a PCDA, we can define four main ways a discourse can stand in relation to other discourses: instantiation, blending, bending, and eclipsing. The second of these, blending (which is closest to Fairclough's concept of interdiscursivity), has three main sub-categories. These four main discursive/ interdiscursive relationships provide a terminological basis for our discussion of the Beaufort Sea Sale documents below and in Chapter 5.

- *Instantiation (independence)*: The statement is taken as being made within or as an instantiation of the discourse. It is an utterance entirely within the discourse. An example is the title of the Lepo et al. article above. The discourses of law and science provide the best examples of such independence in discourse, in contrast to political discourses where blending, bending, and even eclipsing are much more characteristic. The scientific research report is a paradigmatic example.
- *Blending*: The statement is understood to come from another discourse and it is being brought into the present discourse by appropriation or borrowing, as in (1). These blending relationships may be of three kinds:

    Subordination (binding referential incorporation): The statement is set within another, higher-level discourse. 'In accordance with the requirements of 30 CFR 218.155' (1.13) sets the statement within the discourse of US law. The statement identifies itself as part of or an extension of that larger, prior legal discourse.

    Incorporation (supporting incorporation): The statement incorporates another discourse as support for its own statements. The determination of 'Finding of No Significant Impacts' (2.4) is a government bureaucratic statement (which carries out US political discourses of energy security) through incorporation of scientific discourses, as well as several others, as supporting argumentation.

    Indexing (non-binding reference): The statement makes reference to another discourse but makes no further claim to either subordination or incorporation of that other discourse. The comment, 'a practice that has resulted in "review burnout" in Federal, State, tribal, and local governments, and the public,' in the EA (2.5) makes reference to both political and government discourses but neither gets its authority from them (subordination) nor does it incorporate them. It simply makes reference to them.

- *Bending:* The statement is presented as being within one discourse but functionally is performing within another. Examples are difficult to give because such interpretations are always disputable. The transcripts of public hearings (1.3) give many examples in which a fairly straightforward but equally deniable interpretation is that the speaker is bending scientific discourse concerning the EIS by using it for the political purpose of stopping the lease sale process. It could equally be argued that the EIS and EA are cases of using a blended scientific/government analysis for the advancement of the political discourse of national energy security. Bending is the form of interdiscursivity most given to either misinterpretation or reinterpretation and is central in the analysis and the problems of communication and dispute which arise in this process.
- *Eclipsing:* The statement takes over another discourse as its own; it obliterates the independence of the other discourse. The *Federal Register* notice of 19 September 2001 (0.1) carefully details the wide range of processes, participants, and discourses which will be involved in the multiple sale process. The corresponding news release of the same date (1.1) focuses strictly on the 'scientific record' on which the Secretary of the Interior will 'base leasing decisions'. It could be argued that in this news release the scientific/government blend fully eclipses the wider range of discourses. Like bending, eclipsing is a powerful discourse strategy, but one that carries the potential of serious interpretative and actional conflicts.

The discourses in the multiple sale documents

As mentioned above, several discourses are present in these documents: politics (US, Alaska, Alaska Native, and world system), law, science, government, energy resource extraction and development, environmental protection, and traditional knowledge. Although these discourses can be relatively clearly distinguished, all discourses (Bakhtin's 'social languages') may also be sub-categorized into component sub-discourses or may form sub-categories of higher-level discourses. In this analysis the most useful level was determined by participants' common sense and situated 'folk' categorizations where that could be determined, though in some cases, such as scientific discourse and political discourse, there also exists a sizeable literature on the forms, genres, and definitions of these discourses. In science and law, for example, gaining one's credentials rests to a considerable extent on showing that one knows, can perform, and chooses to perform within the constraints of the discourse.

As several examples of the problem of categorization, global climate change might be considered a separate discourse in some cases or a topic within the discourse of environmental protection in another. Subsistence life and activities might be thought an independent discourse in some cases but in others a subtopic of traditional knowledge or of cultural and social identity. Likewise, cultural and social (ethnic) identity is a world-wide discourse, but it is often carried out as an element of the traditional knowledge discourse (or vice versa). Similarly, Alaska Native indigenous political discourse is in some cases allied with an environmental protection discourse when subsistence issues are on the table, but in other cases it is set in conflict when safeguards on endangered species threaten subsistence ways of life. Cartography, a discipline with credentialization and a clearly defined set of skills, genres, and modes is more pragmatically subsumed within the discourse of science in these documents. Cartography is much used in the EIS, for example. Likewise cartography is an essential tool of government as well as in the discourse of environment protection, being much used in public presentations of policy.

There is also variability in the degree of isolability of a discourse. Some discourses are more formally constrained than others. Scientific discourse and legal discourse tend to be tightly constrained by professional or conventional rules of use and interpretation, but political discourses may be a rhetorical pastiche of many discourses (styles, modes, contents, etc.) which are blended in as these are required for situational effectiveness.

While these caveats on categorization could suggest that a discourse analysis of these documents is not sufficiently robust or transparent to be useful, this analysis has taken a common-sense level of characterization as the basis for the analysis. From this point of view, what is of ultimate interest is not how the analyst conceives of the discourses or characterizes them, and particularly the divergences among them, or the occasions of blending, bending, and eclipsing of discourses. What is of interest is how different participants in these events and documents construe documents, events, or particular utterances to be occasions of instantiation, blending, bending, or eclipsing. That is, what is significant from the point of view of this analysis are places or occasions where multiple and conflicting construals lead to disputes or conflicts concerning public policy.

Law and science discourses

Thus, the discourses have been identified on the basis of key characteristics largely through their contrasts and oppositions. Law, for example, is distinct from science even though the two discourses have much in common. They share some aspects of a line of argumentation, for example. Both have a concern for rules of evidence, and conclusions are constrained and evaluated by theory and method. Both pay careful attention to following the line of argument and subordinate the participant in the discourse to the discourse itself. That is, it is the law which is speaking or science which is speaking, not the individual lawyer or the scientist. They are more the vehicles of those discourses than independent agents of their own communications.

It is particularly important that participation in these discourses is authorized and credentialized by specific social institutions and academic degrees. One must enroll in and successfully complete the required post-graduate university degree in a science or in law in order to be an accepted participant in the discourse. In the transcript of public hearings on the DEIS some speakers are careful to place themselves within or outside of this system of authorization. For example, as we saw in Chapter 2, a citizen says,

> I understand that it's some of the – some very high pollution just from drilling oil over there. But I'm not a scientist so I don't know.
>
> (1.3: VII–339)

In response an MMS representative parallels this comment grammatically, but with a switch of authority. He says,

> I'm not an air quality specialist and I do know that we cover this in the Environmental Impact Statement but I can tell you that it's a very limited affect [sic].
>
> (1.3: VII–339)

But law and science are differentiated on the issue of credentialization as well. Participation in legal discourse is further authorized beyond the university degree by the law itself, through a system of examination, licensing, and debarment. It is against the law to attempt to make a legal statement if one is not so authorized. Within scientific discourse, statements are loosely checked against academic and professional credentials for authenticity but, unlike law, in science anyone who follows the rules of the discourse largely governed by hypothetical-deductive logic (hypothesis, empirical testing, constrained conclusions – another difference from law) can provide acceptable statements, though, in fact, credentials and employment tend to work as stand-ins for carefully following the principles of argumentation. That is, it is somewhat more likely that a credentialed (and employed) scientist would make a non-scientific statement of his or her opinion and get away with it than that a non-credentialed (or -employed) lay person would present a scientific finding and have it accepted without further ratification by established participants in the scientific discourse.

Note that, in the example quoted above, we do not know whether the MMS representative is qualifying himself for this statement on the basis of his employment by the MMS or of his credentials as a scientist, because he is only identified (in the transcripts) as an MMS representative. His statement is authorized not by his credentials so much as by the EIS itself. Conversely, authorized participants in law are very careful to maintain a distinction between statements which can be construed to be legal statements (that is, statements from *within* legal discourse) and statements which can be construed as their personal views or opinions. While one often encounters disputes about the quality of a particular scientist's work or interpretation of that work, scientists are not, like lawyers, subject to disbarment.

Political discourses

Significantly contrasting with both law and science are several political discourses which occur in these documents: US national politics, Alaska state politics, world system politics and economics, and Alaska Native politics. These discourses are relatively difficult to treat independently; sometimes it is only the topics under discussion which really distinguish them. It is also important to contrast these political discourses with government-bureaucratic discourse, and this contrast will be taken up below.

Perhaps the most significant contrasts between these political discourses and the more formally and legally constituted discourses of law and science are based on lines of argumentation and authorization for participation. Political discourses are highly varied and versatile in their principles of argumentation. While almost any subject matter can be incorporated within a political discourse, it is rhetorical persuasion which always trumps grammatical precision, rules of evidence and argumentation, or historical precedent. Similarly, authorization to speak within political discourses is fluid; authorization is itself subsumed to the rhetorics of persuasion. A speaker's credentials are often whatever will make him or her credible to the perceived audience. Thus a very significant aspect of Alaska state politics is authorization based on length of residence in Alaska as well as the type of work or lifestyle. 'Bush' residence in the Interior of Alaska or commercial fishing work in the Southeast, for example, are strongly authorizing life experiences. Further, authorization in Alaska state politics is achieved through networks of interpersonal contacts in Alaska. It is also important to show, through one's stance toward both the rest of the US and the world that you 'don't give a damn how it's done outside'. Knowledge and use of words like 'outside' to mean 'anywhere but Alaska' are key semiotic indicators of credibility within Alaska state politics.

The distinction between Alaska state politics and US national politics is mostly cued through adversarial relationships having to do with the recency of statehood and an Alaskan sense of being exceptional through tropes of personal toughness and hardship and of individual agency and independence. Related to Alaska state politics, however, is an important and distinct discourse of Alaska Native politics centered on prior, historical US–American Indian law and legal relationships from early treaties to contemporary legal and political developments arising with ANCSA (Alaska Native Claims Settlement Act, 1971) and ANILCA (Alaska National Interest Land Conservation Act, 1980). Perhaps there is no US state political environment so heavily dominated by such Federal legal determinations. First, early treaties with other indigenous tribes, and then, in the contemporary period, ANCSA, produced a political/legal basis for Alaska Native politics of lands and resources as well as legal conditions for participation in this discourse. While many subsequent legal and political decisions and conditions since 1971 have altered, mitigated, or modified participation in this discourse, as well as the discourse itself, analogous to length of residence or bush experience in Alaska for non-Native Alaskans, whether or not one is a shareholder in an Alaska Native corporation is often what authorizes participation. Like law and science discourses, this can be considered a separate discourse to a considerable extent by these principles of authorization of participation. It is a difference between speaking *within* the discourse and speaking *about* the discourse, between speaking as Alaska Natives and speaking *about* Alaska Natives.

Similarly, related to US national political discourse (as well as the other political discourses) is the discourse of world system politics and economics. Again, in some cases this might be considered to be simply a theme or topical domain within other discourses. In some cases, however, there are constraints on participation as a speaker or writer which produce a somewhat distinct discourse. On the whole, priority is given to individuals who work within or who represent world organizations or institutions such as the WTO, IMF, World Bank, UN, Oxfam, or the Sierra Club. Because these organizations fund research of worldwide scope and claim to work for goals and purposes that transcend national jurisdictions, their employees and representatives speak from a platform that is distinctly different from that of US national politics, Alaska state politics, or Alaska Native politics. The initial call for information and nominations published in the *Federal Register* (0.1) indicates that it is important for those who give testimony in the public hearings or who submit written comments to identify themselves by their institutional membership. The text reads:

> We will make all submissions from organizations or businesses, and from individuals identifying themselves as representatives or officials of organizations or businesses, available for public inspection in their entirety.
>
> (0.1: 48269)

In the hearings themselves speakers are careful, on the whole, to make these identifications as part of placing their comments within a specific discourse. The MMS representatives identify themselves at the outset. As to the others, while it is not always transparent from the name of the organization which of the relevant discourses is the grounding for the organization, in the following list we can see at least Alaska state political, Alaska Native political, and environmental protection discourses are represented.

Native Village of Nuiqsut
North Slope Borough Assembly
North Slope Borough
Alaska NANA Commission
Nanook, Inc./Kuulpik Corporation
Ocean Conservancy
Oil Watch Alaska
Arctic Connections
Northern Alaska Environmental Center
Trustees for Alaska

Alaska Eskimo Whaling Commission
Native Village of Barrow

Government discourse

Concerning the four main discourses present in these documents – politics, law, science, and government – it is important to see a clear distinction between the political discourses, on the one hand, and law and governmental/bureaucratic discourses on the other, as this is a central issue in these documents. The words 'politics' and 'political' are ambiguous both in dictionary definitions and in common usage. In the most general sense they reference everything to do with the practices, procedures, and actions of government, from municipal government to world bodies such as the UN. On the other hand, these words reference actions and practices of particular sides or power groups whose goals are to seek the advantage of their own group in adversarial relations with other groups. The word 'politicize' is located more strongly within this second semantic sphere of adversarial power positioning. This latter sense is the way this analysis uses the term 'political' and makes reference to 'political discourse'. The term 'governmental' or 'bureaucratic' is used to reference the discourse of government management and administration.

Bureaucrats are employees of a government (Federal, Alaska, North Slope Borough, etc.) and, consequently, their participation in this discourse is enabled and constrained by this employment, which includes laws and policies determining the range of activities in which participants can engage. Politics, in the sided, adversarial or advocacy meaning, is often explicitly prohibited for government employees when acting in their official duties. Participants within political discourses, as this term is used here, are elected, appointed, or self-selected by interest and are not constrained except by these elections, appointments, or self-interest. Within the US and Alaska political systems, such figures as the Secretary of the Interior are political appointments (though within constraints of congressional authorization and within the laws binding on the conduct of their appointments) and the Governor of Alaska is a politically elected position, again working within constraints of constitutional authorization and within the laws binding on the conduct of office. Politics is required in these positions.

In practice it is commonplace knowledge that incumbents of political positions such as the Secretary of the Interior may be and usually are considerably under the control and constraints of the bureaucracies which they technically direct, such as the MMS. Similarly, it is also commonplace knowledge that many a political action can be taken under the guise of simply carrying out or failing to carry out legal requirements of one's government position. Further, laws (statutes, policies, rules, and the like) are made by legally constituted bodies of citizens and so the discourse of law is to a considerable extent interlinked with the political and bureaucratic discourses of government.

Nevertheless, this analysis takes law, government, and politics to be separate discourses even in the face of this constant negotiation among the political, the legal, and the governmental because participants in each of the separate discourses are under the conventional requirement to at least give the appearance of participating within the constraints of their authorization in that discourse. Government employees are obliged to always appear to be simply carrying out the directives of their superiors and of the law; politicians are conventionally obliged to appear to be loyal to the political process which has authorized their position in the discourse.

Energy, environment, and traditional knowledge discourses

Finally, three other discourses are crucial within these documents, though as discourses they are more difficult to disentangle: the discourses of energy resources extraction and development, environmental protection, and traditional knowledge. These entanglements are many and complex. The MMS is designated by Congress as the federal agency which, among other things, has responsibility both for outer continental shelf energy resources extraction and for the preparation of environmental impact statements, along with the monitoring and mitigation of any negative impacts. Energy resource corporations, of course, are squarely grounded in the former discourse and mandated by law to comply with the National Environmental Protection Act (NEPA) but, quite naturally, are likely to see the discourse of environmental protection as lying outside their remit or even to be the domain of an adversarial or hostile group of participants. This sense of locating their communications within opposed and adversarial discursive camps is certainly reciprocated by many groups which claim environmental protection as their primary discourse. As a governmental bureaucratic agency with requirements to work within the constraints of law, the MMS is the place where these highly conflictual discourses engage most directly as public policy and as public discourse. On the whole it is best to analyze these two discourses, as they are practiced within the MMS, as blending into the dominant government discourse of the MMS than as independent instantiations.

Almost equally complex are the relations between environmental protection and traditional knowledge discourses. An animal which has been categorized as one of an endangered species has sometimes been the boundary object that links these two discourses in adversarial conflict. Within the first discourse an endangered animal should be protected from hunting as a way of ensuring the survival of the species, while in the second discourse the same animal must be hunted as a crucial activity for the cultural and economic integrity of the traditional knowledge of a cultural group. In yet other cases these two discourses may converge in opposition to some industrial developments and in support of the continued protection of life forms and their environment, including the human environment.

While 'pure' cases are difficult to establish for these three discourses, they are to some extent heuristically distinguished on the basis of participation and agency, and to a lesser extent on lexicogrammar, argumentation, genres, and modes. Participation in the energy resource extraction and development discourse is largely authorized by employment in an energy resources corporation or one of the subsidiary corporations and companies which support these corporations, such as geophysical prospecting companies or contracted advertising companies. As in most corporate activities, agency is corporate, not individual; that is, it is the corporation which is the owner and principal of communications, not the individual employee. As a corollary of this corporate location and authorization of the discourse, lexicogrammar, argumentation, genres and modes are highly varied but are grounded in the economics of profit-making corporations. Arguments are tied to returning profits on investments for shareholders, for example, and so the dominant persuasive rhetoric calls upon a logic of returns on capital investments.

Participation in the discourse of environmental protection is largely authorized by contributions to, membership in, or employment by the boards of NGOs which are committed to environmental protection. As we have seen above, many of those who provided public testimony legitimated their testimony within this environmental protection discourse by claiming representation for such organizations as Oil Watch Alaska, the Ocean Conservancy, or the Northern Alaska Environmental Center. At the same time, speakers within this discourse claim individual and personal agency in their communications. In the public testimony it is common to see the lexicogrammatical sequence: 'My name is X, I represent Y, and I believe that Z.' This contrasts vividly with law, science, and government discourses where the governing formula for communicative agency is: 'I am Dr (or other title) X, my specialization is Y, and the research or findings of my discipline say Z.' This position of agency also contrasts with political discourse, where the governing formula is 'I am X, I represent Y, and Y wants Z'. Finally, the environmental protection discourse references a bottom line of biodiversity and geo-ecological survival which provides the underpinning for the line of argument.

Authority to participate in instantiations of the traditional knowledge discourse are communal and cultural. Credentialization is accomplished through certain actions, in these cases mainly centering on subsistence whaling. Agency is largely individual; a speaker speaks for himself or herself though often referencing others in the community. The dominant line of argument is historical narrative. In some cases this discourse adopts spokespersons who are not in themselves authorized participants in this discourse, as is sometimes the case with anthropologists, linguists, or long-term community members who have achieved relations of trust with more directly authorized participants. Because authorization for participation and agency is mainly individual, this is the one discourse, of the set of seven this analysis has considered, which is specifically not authorized to be 'available for public inspection in their entirety' (0.1: 48269). In this light it is interesting to note that all of the public testimony transcribed for Kaktovik on 26 June 2002 was treated as being within this discourse. None of the speakers claimed organization, business, scientific, or legal credentials to speak. As we saw in Chapter 2, a characteristic claim was given by Isaac Akootchook,

> My name is Isaac Akootchook, raised here in Kaktovik. I've been here 80 years.
>
> (1.3: VII–340)

As we also saw, he might well have claimed political authorization as the Kaktovik member of the North Slope Borough Planning Commission or as President of the Kaktovik Native Village, but did not.

Each of the discourses analyzed here operates within a set of principles which define that discourse and which are binding on legitimate participation. This is not necessarily always the case, in fact, but must always appear to be so. They are, in a word, semiotic. What is important is to signal which discourse one is speaking within, even when one is using that position within that discourse to perform functions that are more properly (or at least more transparently) conducted within a different discourse. As we shall see in the discussion of documents types or genres in Chapter 5, these are the aspects of these documents and of the interdiscursivity found in them which are both most problematical and most likely to provide points of contention in the dialogue among discourses.

PRACTICE

Mutual misunderstanding as well as political and ideological conflict between multiple stakeholders is common within a public consultation process. While this is caused by many factors, including mismatching conceptualizations of nature and conflicting goals, discourse analysis, as an analytical tool, can illuminate some of the complexity involved. The following activities will guide you through an analysis of the interdiscursivity among the documents in your own project.

Activity 1:
Identifying discourses

A public consultation on air quality in Europe was held through 'Your Voice in Europe' (http://europa.eu.int/yourvoice/consultations/index_en.htm). The website concerning this consultation was introduced with the following title and descriptive paragraph:

The CAFE programme
Clean Air for Europe (CAFE) is a programme of technical analysis and policy development which will lead to the adoption of a thematic strategy on air pollution under the Sixth Environmental Action Programme by mid

2005. The major elements of the CAFE programme are outlined in the Communication on CAFE (COM(2001)245). The programme was launched in March 2001. Its aim is to develop a long-term, strategic and integrated policy advice to protect against significant negative effects of air pollution on human health and the environment. The integrated policy advice from the CAFE programme is planned to be ready by the beginning of 2005. The European Commission will present its Thematic Strategy on Air Pollution during the first half year of 2005, outlining the environmental objectives for air quality and measures to be taken to achieve the meet these objectives [sic]. (http://europa.eu.int/comm/environment/air/cafe/index.htm, accessed 18 July 2005, 7:07 AKDT.)

Just at first glance we can see several discourses which are present within these few words. First there is the acronym for 'Clean Air for Europe', CAFE. For many people the word 'café' calls up ideas of leisurely afternoons at a café (Figure 4.1).

The choice of acronym seems clearly designed to capture this discourse of European sidewalk café culture. In addition to this discourse is, of course, a discourse of environmental protection ('Environmental Action Programme', 'human health and the environment'). This is all embedded within a discourse of EU policy development or political discourse. Each of these discourses is relatively transparent in the short segment above.

Figure 4.1

What other discourses might be present here? Is the spelling 'programme' indicative of a discourse of 'British spelling conventions'? What would be the justification for making that argument?

Activity 2:
Analyzing discourse features

ASSIGNMENT

Choose a few documents from your collection, which you consider intuitively to be very different from each other. You may want to continue using the documents you have selected for Activity 3 in Chapter 3 or use new ones. Read through the documents and identify, based on your intuition, how many discourses are circulating through them. Prepare a short list of these discourses and try to arrange them in the order of importance.

Observations

Open up the circumference, you will find more discourses than you might recognize at first. For example, in the Beaufort Sea Sales documents, there are not only the discourses of resource extraction and environment resistance to development, but also the discourses of US national politics and Alaska Native politics. In this assignment you should avoid being overly precise with the labeling or counting of discourses. They are only heuristic notions here, which will be developed in the following activities.

A discourse analysis needs to go beyond just giving an interpretation or a reading of some text or document. Above we 'saw' discourses of European café society, environmental protection, and governmental policy making in the paragraph from the 'Your Voice in Europe' consultation website on the 'CAFE Programme', but what is the justification for these? Certain key terms, phrases, or sentential structures (lexicogrammar) help to identify discourses such as 'café', 'environmental protection', and 'policy'. Can we go further to argue that there are particular authorizations or credentializations for positioning oneself within one or more of these discourses? What kinds of agency are maintained for each of these (or other) discourses in this text? Is this text sufficient for establishing these identifying characteristics or must one bring evidence from other texts into this consultation? Perhaps when it comes down to it 'café society' is not a discourse in the same way that 'EU governmental policy making' is. How are they different? Should further distinctions be made?

Activity 3:
The interdiscursivity of hyperlinks

ASSIGNMENT

Now look at the list of discourses you have made, think about how each of them can be defined in terms of discourse features: participation, agency, lexicogrammar, argumentation, genres, and modes. Make a table which gives the keyword to identify the discourse at the top of each column. Down the side indicate the identifying feature. Then within each cell fill in whatever evidence you have to make that identification.

Extension

Prepare a set of footnotes which support the categorization you have used on your table.

Observations

You will find that some of these cells may be more easily filled than others and this may indicate that some discourses are more clearly identifiable than others. Be sure to consider other sources, such as further documents in the consultation. With this more formally defined set of features you should be able to see the discourses you identified in Activity 1 more clearly. You may also find that this activity leads you to adjust your initial categorizations.

Some of the questions we asked about identifying the discourses in a document or in a consultation process can be answered more clearly by examining other documents in the group. In the CAFE Programme there are two hyperlinks given in the first paragraph. The first one leads to a document called 'Environment 2010: Our Future, Our Choice: The Sixth Environment Action Programme of the European Community'. Landing in this document we see immediately that we are located within a discourse of European environmental policy with the opening paragraph:

> "*Environment policy is one of the success stories of the European Union – thanks to European Union legislation we have made significant improvements such as cleaner air and safer drinking water. But we still face some real problems*" explained Commissioner for the Environment, Margot Wallstrom when she presented the Commission's proposal. The new Environment Action Programme takes a wide-ranging approach to these challenges and gives a

strategic direction to the Commission's environmental policy over the next decade, as the Community prepares to expand its boundaries.

> (http://europa.eu.int/comm/environment/newprg/index.htm,
> accessed 18 July 2005, 8:58 AKDT)

The text is presented as instantiating the EU policy discourse and its pre-eminently authorized spokesperson, the Commissioner for the Environment, is cited in the opening quotation.

If we follow the second hyperlink (Communication on CAFE COM (2001)245) we download a formal policy statement of the Commission of the European Communities which is further given legitimacy with a small graphic in black and white of the flag of the European Union. This location in political/policy discourse is the discourse within which much scientific discourse on air pollution is blended by incorporation as we see in the following selection of text:

> Ground-level ozone is formed in the atmosphere by the reaction of pollut-ants such as nitrogen oxides (NOx) and volatile organic compounds (VOCs) in the presence of sunlight. The severity of its effect on human health depends on the concentration, the duration of exposure, and the level of activity during exposure.

For the assignment that follows you can either use the documents you have downloaded or go back online to follow the hyperlinks available within your consultation process.

ASSIGNMENT

Go back to the web pages from which you downloaded the documents. Are they linked through hyperlinks? If so, how do the hyperlinks contribute to the interdiscursivity in the documents? Write a two- or three-page analysis which illustrates each of the types of interdiscursivity (instantiation, blending, bending, or eclipsing) from your documents. If you cannot illustrate each of these, try to account for why you cannot do this.

Observations

At first sight, hyperlinks may all seem to contribute obviously to the instantiation/independent connection among documents, but that is not always the case. Observe whether the documents are presented as hyperlinks in a separate 'related' or 'links' session or embedded within the text of another document, and note how many times they are linked to other documents.

5　Document types

Who says so? Who do they
think I am?

Figure 5.1
Note: This website was updated in 2005.

THEORY – CASE STUDY

There are many ways in which a communication tells us who is speaking (or
writing) and to whom the message is addressed. In common business or
personal letters this is done by means of a letterhead, an address block, and a
closing signature block. In face-to-face communication we usually convey this
information non-verbally by the projection of our speaking voice, by gesture
and body posture, and by the direction of our gaze, and when we read it wrong
we find ourselves apologizing, 'Oh, I'm sorry; were you speaking to me?'

In Chapter 1 we examined two letterheads for MMS news releases. The news
release in Figure 1.2 uses a complex and highly designed graphic banner with
the US flag positioned at the center to tell us that the news release is coming to

us from the US government. Or that is how we analyzed it there. As it did not contradict the text that followed, which said 'US Department of the Interior', there was no reason to question that analysis. Here, in the epigraph to this chapter (Figure 5.1), we see the banner heading the website of the 'Independent Petroleum Association of America'. The banner for the IPAA is, in fact, strikingly similar to the MMS letterhead we examined in Chapter 1 and again in Chapter 3 (Figure 3.4). Unfurled across most of the banner is the flag of the US. On the left is an offshore oil rig and on the right a common land oil well.

We also see that in the space below the letterhead the largest image, taking up about one-third of the width of the page, is the US Capitol building in Washington. Further, just under the name of the association we see the exact time at which this page was accessed as 'Time in Washington DC'. One cannot help but wonder just how entirely independent the IPAA is from the US government, with such aggressive bending of these iconic images to the branding goals of an organization that claims to be distinct from the US government.

Document (genre/text) types in the multiple sale documents

Between September 2001 and March 2005, from the announcement of the multiple sales to the conclusion of the second sale of leases (Sale 195) there are 26 hyperlinked website entries on the MMS website covering the Beaufort Sea oil and gas lease sales. These are itemized in the Appendix. For the multiple sales and Sale 186, which are grouped together by the MMS, there are 15 numbered website entries. For Sale 195 there are 11. Some of these link to a single page (e.g. 2.4), some link to a sub-directory of multiple attached documents (e.g. 1.12 and 2.8), and four link to the core documents that form the center of gravity of this document/genre complex:

- the draft environmental impact statement (DEIS: 1.2)
- the oil-spill risk analysis (OSRA: 1.4)
- the final environmental impact statement (FEIS: 1.5), and
- the environmental assessment (EA: 2.2.5).

These core documents (DEIS, OSRA, FEIS, and EA) are reports of several volumes which are a genre complex of scientific summaries, charts, maps, responses, and determinations.

The documents range from news releases which are designed for the media to repackage for the general public, to forms for bid submission which are designed for corporate bidders and to be completed and delivered to the US government (MMS) as documents in legal/financial transactions. The most common document type is the 'Leasing Activities Information' memo (of which there are 14 examples). Although these share the same cover sheet format they otherwise vary in length, format, and number of attachments.

The MMS web pages organize this complex of documents into a chronological sequence with many hyperlinks for navigation. The four main scientific documents (DEIS, OSRA, FEIS, and EA) constitute the heart of the environmental analysis. The use of 'scientific' here reflects the position of the Regional Director of the MMS in a news release statement (1.1), but the analysis below raises questions about this designation.

The transcripts of the public hearings (but also the written testimony which is attached to the FEIS) constitute the public responses to the first documents (DEIS/OSRA), and the FEIS and EA include MMS responses to these public responses. The notices in the *Federal Register* constitute the official notices of the full process. These document types are the basis for the analysis which follows, beginning with the official *Federal Register* notices.

A PCDA is a means for the discourse analyst to engage in a particular kind of mediated action, providing testimony in a public consultative process. In order for a document to become a conventional mediational means in an action, including a PCDA, it must somehow fit into an interaction order in which it makes sense for the producer(s) of the document to be engaged in the action of communicating with the receiver(s) of the document. The goal in the analysis of this chapter is to outline how a document sets up production and reception positions so that it will enable or inhibit some actions for some social actors. This will then stand as the basis both for an analysis of a public consultative process and for an analysis of the PCDA itself as an enabling document.

In the analysis below and for a PCDA in general it is heuristically useful to organize around five analytical features:

- function of the document
- framing
- document design
- production/reception (writer/reader) positions
- interdiscursivity.

The first three features – function, framing, and document design – provide the basis for examining writer/reader positions and the interdiscursivity which is present in the documents, and so we will take these up first.

Notices in the Federal Register

The branch of the US government which has responsibility for the publication of the *Federal Register (FR)* is the Government Printing Office (GPO). According to the GPO website, the *FR* is the

> Official daily publication for rules, proposed rules, and notices of Federal agencies and organizations, as well as executive orders and other Presidential documents.
>
> (www.gpoaccess.gov/fr: accessed 16 May 2005, 11:12 am, AKDT)

This function is defined by the US government and carried out by the National Archives and Records Administration (NARA) through the Government Printing Office (GPO). This hierarchy of authority is the basis of the clear framing of the *Federal Register* documents in this series (e.g. 0.1 or 1.13). The document itself is framed by using a consistent format for all notices which are published. Figure 3.1 in Chapter 3 shows this page layout.

The *FR* framing contrasts sharply with news releases, for example 1.1 or 2.8a (see Figures 1.1, 2.2 for an example), in which the MMS is the framing organization for internal contents of the document. The *FR* frame within which the MMS notices appear has a full-page header with a double underscore which sets off the enclosed notices from the *FR* identification (Figure 2.3). The body of the published texts are all given in running columnar format of uniform serifed typeface.

Within that frame the MMS notice itself is framed, like all other notices in the *FR*, by a horizontal line across the column and then a header in a bold sanserif typeface (Figure 2.2) and a closing identification of the government official responsible for the notice; 0.1 is signed by Thomas R. Kitsos, Acting Director of the MMS, 1.13 by Thomas A. Readinger, Acting Director of the MMS. This internal framing is further closed by *FR* filing information and the *FR* billing code (Figure 6.2). Notably, this billing code switches into all small caps in a bold sanserif typeface. Thus responsibility for the contents of notices is clearly framed within the columns, while responsibility for publication is framed through the page header and the overall columnar format.

In these documents writer/reader positions are clearly delineated; it is the government which is officially 'speaking'. The publication authority frame sets these notices within government bureaucratic official discourse. Whatever occurs within the frame is marked as being in an interdiscursive relationship of subordination (Chapter 4). Whatever appears has the authority of the US government. That is, it is a blending relationship of binding incorporation. This sets up a clear reader position as well, though with some complexities to be examined shortly. The reader is set as anybody who has an interest in knowing what the US government's position is on a particular issue as of that day's *FR* publication (6:00 a.m., EST). This producer's position (writer's position) about what kind of action is being enabled with this document is that the reception (reading) of the notice is non-negotiable. It is not an invitation to engage in political discussion, for example.

Having noted this non-negotiable producer–receiver position, it is useful to compare two *FR* notices (0.1 and 1.13) from the point of view of production and reception positions. *FR* 0.1, the notice which initiates the multiple sale process, explicitly marks the notice as originating with 'The Secretary's preliminary decision' and then further explicitly marks the MMS through the pronoun 'we' as the delegated agency which is the principal of this notice.

Goffman (1974, 1981) defined three roles in the production of a communication. Although his attention was directed to spoken discourse, these roles have also been used in the analysis of written-discourse documents. The three production roles are:

- The **principal** of a communication: the person or agency which takes responsibility for the utterance, whether spoken or written. In this case it is the Acting Director of the MMS who has signed the notice. As just noted, this is a formal requirement of publication in the *FR*.
- The **author:** the person or persons who actually craft the wordings of the message.
- The **animator:** the person or persons who produce the communication as a material object.

In the *FR* the author is left to be inferred. From what we know about the conduct of government offices, perhaps we can safely assume that this role or position has been distributed among several MMS employees who have been delegated this responsibility as one aspect of their work. From the point of view of such government discourse it is entirely insignificant to the reader to know just which MMS employee wrote the actual words one is reading. These may well have been partly dictated by law or legal precedent, by bureaucratic precedent or convention, or by careful rewording and editing between the MMS home office in Virginia and the Alaska regional office in Anchorage. From the point of view of the action enabled by this document, how these sentences were actually produced is unimportant. What is finally printed is what the Acting Director has signed, and this stands as the official position of the MMS and, through that agency, the official position of the US government.

This is not to say that authorship (as opposed to principalship) is an unimportant aspect of the production of *FR* notices and other documents in this series. Authorship is extremely important within the office which has prepared this document. Inexact wordings can carry serious consequences in financial, legal, or political terms. A PCDA analysis, however, has no access to the internal authorship process and, therefore, the analyst is in exactly the same position as any other reader. What we know is that the principal is clearly marked, as is the animator (whoever has produced the document as a physical object, in this case the *FR* as an office of the GPO).

Turning to reception positions, there are at least four common receiver (reader or viewer) positions regarding any communication:

- **principal** (takes responsibility for 'reading' or responding to the communication)
- **interpreter** (provides the meaning which is attributed to the communication)
- **handler** (provides the actual material text of the reading in the place where principals or interpreters may act on it), and
- **bystander** or spectator (sees or reads the document but has no role in responding to it).

While Goffman does not theorize these four roles he does suggest them by analogy with the three production format roles. Each of these roles sets up a different class of actions which are enabled for a document. The principal is whoever is required to take action with the document, for example; the bystander or spectator is under no requirement to act, nor is he or she allowed to act. Spectators may watch a game or the construction of a building but they are not allowed to play the game or to pick up tools and work without undergoing some social procedures for changing status.

Document 0.1 defines a wide-open set of principal receivers. It explicitly calls for information and nominations from 'all reviewers', 'the public', from Federal, State, and tribal governments, 'all interested parties', and it uses such open designations as 'respondents' and 'you' which, as these prior designations indicate, is literally anyone who might read this document. Virtually any reader is enabled by this document to act in a specific way – to respond by giving particular kinds of information. In this case, then, there are no bystanders or spectators to the process, as anyone who reads it is invited to respond.

In contrast 1.13, the final notice of sale, is addressed specifically to a progressively narrowing principal (reader/actor). First it is 'bidders', then, given certain conditions, the principal becomes a 'successful bidder', then, if further conditions are satisfied, the principal is termed a 'lessee'. With each successive narrowing of the principal, of course, the role of spectator or bystander to the process expands. Points which are addressed to lessees may be read by anyone who has access to the *FR* but all readers except for the lessees are now spectators, and prohibited from acting.

Two further comments will close this discussion of the writer/reader positions of the *FR* notices. First, just as it is not specified who the authors (crafters of the actual text) are, it is not specified who the interpreters are. Again, our experience with government, corporate, and other bureaucratic organizations tells us that this role is often performed by legal staff within these organizations. This is one significant point at which this government-bureaucratic discourse intersects with the discourse of law, but it is a point which is largely invisible in these documents. This type of social action is enabled elsewhere in the constitution and policies that govern such agencies, as well as in the defining practices of law.

Second, the role of handler is most often simply incorporated as part of the principal and/or interpreter role. One handles the document as one reads, whether that reading is done as principal, interpreter, or bystander. Nevertheless, in cases of translation, for example, the translator performs this role of transforming the message into a material form which can be processed by the receiver. In other cases the role might be performed by secretarial staff who download a document from the MMS website or photocopy the *FR* notice for a company officer to read.

While the handler role is mostly not a significant one, it is important to note that in 1.13 there is clear designation of who in the bidding company is the contact person for the MMS, to whom fax messages should be addressed, to whom Fedex packages should be addressed, and the like. This specific designation of receiver roles right down to the handlers within bidding companies starkly contrasts with the wide-open 'all interested parties' addressed in the initial *FR* notice (0.1). Interestingly, as the documents in this process get more closely honed down to the binding action, that is, to the point where money is bid, bids are evaluated, and contracts between the government and corporations are signed, the specifications of these acting positions of production and reception are more tightly constrained. Only a certain person who is named and registered within the corporation and with the government may sign or even handle the document.

To summarize, then, the production and reception (writer/reader) positions which can be found in the *FR* notices are as follows: the principal (US government > MMS) is fixed for all *FR* notices, the author role is invisible but can be assumed to be distributed within the MMS, likely between home and Alaska regional offices, and the animator role is formally set as the GPO. Reception roles vary, based on the function of the notice itself. The call for information or nominations (0.1) is open to any reader in contrast to the final notice of sale, which specifically designates reception roles right down to handlers who will be responsible for receiving fax messages.

Turning, then, to the discourses which circulate in these *FR* documents, there is variability corresponding to the function of the notice itself. All of the *FR* notices are instantiations of government discourse, that is, they are official statements of a government agency. They also blend in several other discourses to different degrees, as we have observed in Chapter 4. In both document 0.1 and 1.13, for example, the government discourse is subordinated to US laws and policies by reference to the OCS Lands Act or NEPA. In this way environmental protection discourse (NEPA) and science discourse (EIS) are blended through subordination into this discourse. What is most interesting, then, from this point of view, is that no discourses other than government discourse are instantiated in these documents. The others are present through the three forms of blending. The US national political, Alaska state political, and Alaska Native political are blended through referencing. That is, participants in those discourses are invited to respond to 0.1 but this neither subordinates nor incorporates these discourses to the government discourse of the document.

It is of interest, then, in 1.13 to see that the world system political and economic discourse, together with the energy resource extraction and development discourse, are explicitly incorporated (page 50550). Minimum bids, minimum royalty rates and rental rates in Sale 186 are tied directly to oil prices on the world market. This discourse is not simply referenced or mentioned. The actions to which the government is committing itself and which will be binding on bidders are directly tied to factors outside of the bureaucratic control of the MMS or of the US government. This is one of the two cases in these *FR* notices where a discourse is explicitly linked into the government discourse in a mutually negotiated interdiscursivity.

The second discourse which is explicitly linked within an *FR* notice also occurs in 1.13. This is the discourse of US national politics. Under the heading 'Jurisdiction' (p. 50551) it is noted that the four easternmost blocks offered for sale are claimed by Canada. The notice then outlines distinct actions to be taken concerning bidding on these contested blocks. Again, the outcomes of this bidding cannot be exclusively encompassed by the bureaucratic/government/ legal discourse within which the *FR* notice occurs. These actions must not only make reference to this other political discourse, actions taken within the scope of *FR* are linked to actions which lie outside of its scope.

MMS-originated news releases

News releases are the documents in this series which are both most like and yet also most unlike the notices in the *Federal Register*. On the one hand, there is much functional similarity, or at least apparently so. Both types of documents broadcast information concerning MMS activities and actions to readers in a wide band, few of whom ultimately become lessees in contractual relations with the US government. On the other hand they differ strikingly in function, framing, and design and this is reflected in equally striking differences in writer/ reader positions and the discourses which are interdiscursively present in them. The two news releases examined here (1.1 and 2.8a) are parallel to the two *FR* notices we have just examined (0.1 and 1.13). The first two cover the multiple sale process and the second two announce a final notice of sale (Sale 186 (1.13) and Sale 195 (2.8a)). These will also serve both to illustrate the contrast between the *FR* and MMS news releases and to illustrate the differences between the two news releases. The news release for Sale 195 was chosen to illustrate as well the change in MMS news releases between September 2001, the beginning of the multiple sale process, and February 2005, which we have discussed in Chapters 1 and 3.

The essential functional difference between these two document types is that the *FR* notices are official notices of the MMS and as such provide careful and specific coverage of all details which are necessary for the conduct of the MMS vis-à-vis the potential bidders, lessees, and the public. The news releases are constructed as information for the media and for the general public, not for potential lessees. While this statement is true in general, an internet search only turned up one place where the MMS news release was picked up by a media source (*Petroleum News*, Vol. 6., No. 9, Week of 23 September 2001: http:// www.petroleumnews.com/pntruncate/ 328405755.shtml). This poses the question of whether or not the *Petroleum News*, an industry website, is the primary 'media' target for such a news release. The news release in question is almost verbatim but is published under the name Kay Cashman.

Because they are not aimed at potential lessees news releases are very much briefer in the first place. That is, they address mere spectators to the actions which are being enabled by the full process of leasing. And because they are brief, they are much more selective of contents. Paradoxically, the news release addresses a wide and general audience of bystanders and so it is briefer and much narrower than are the *FR* notices in content concerning details about what actions will be taken and how these will be accomplished. More to the point here, they are vague and ambiguous about the discourses and writer/reader positions that are constructed through the design and language of the document.

Both of the news releases examined here follow standard formats for such document types to the letter. The National Education Association, for example, has published a note on 'Writing a News Release' (http://www.nea.org/aew/writingpr.html; accessed 3 June 2005, 3:41 AKDT) which reads, in part, as follows:

> A news release is [sic] statement of facts about an event or issue that affects your community.
>
> It tells readers what the event or issue is, why it is important, when it is pertinent, who is involved or making a statement about the event or issue and how readers can get more information.
>
> Members of the media may use the release word for word as an article, or they may include it in a longer article about a similar event or issue ...
>
> A release should start with the DATE, CONTACT NAME (with phone number) and the RELEASE DATE. Write "FOR IMMEDIATE RELEASE" underneath if the issue or event is that timely.

The NEA's instructions also say that the news release should be written in the 'inverted pyramid' common in journalistic writing, with most important facts in the opening sentences and least significant information at the end.

The design of the document is important for signaling its unusual framing. Unlike the *FR* notices, news release 1.1 is framed as a document produced by the MMS OCS Region. The large sanserif typeface bolded words, 'news release', in the header, along with the details of when it should be released ('immediate') and the contact person with telephone and website details mark this unmistakably as a news release. What is not marked is that all of the text from the headline to the end stands in an ambiguous relationship with the MMS and the readers. The writer/reader positions in all news releases are ambiguous because, as the NEA instructions have noted, it may be used either as information for the media, who will write their own stories, or, perhaps more commonly, the text will be lifted word for word and published as an article under their own header.

This ambiguity leads to the paradoxical situation that these news releases, like news releases generally, are specific about the '5 W's and 1 H' (who, what, when, where, why, and how) of the actions and events within the content frame of the document but the document/publication frame is either vague or contradictory. That is, the news release is clear and specific about the actions it is describing but vague or contradictory about the actions which the news release itself enables or proscribes. Like a good host or a political lobbyist, the news release seeks to make things happen, but to do so without calling attention to itself. Like the Wizard of Oz it pulls strings invisibly from behind a curtain in a puff of smoke.

The header marks the MMS as principal, author, and animator of this document. The text within the content frame marks the MMS in the third person. The text speaks about the MMS as a 'they', not as a 'we'. Note in contrast that the *FR* notice (0.1 which corresponds directly to this news release) has, 'we are issuing this Call/NOI' (p. 48268).

The paradoxical we/they voicing of the news release is further developed in the text by quoting the Alaska Regional Director directly in several places ('he said', 'he added'). This sets up a voicing contrast with the Regional Director, who refers to the MMS in the first person ('we', 'us'). In this way the voice in which the text of the document is written is produced as a voice which is not the MMS but which refers to the MMS as a third person.

Do these voicing or positioning contrasts matter? Within the context of media relations and journalistic writing this is a typical genre, its conventions are clearly prescribed and understood by the participants in journalistic/media relations discourses. There is no confusion in such cases. But the news releases being examined here were not sent to the author as a media organization, they were published as open public documents on the MMS website. In that place they are intertextually embedded, together with *FR* notices, in a matrix set up by the MMS website. In the form of the website, all documents, *FR* notices and news releases alike, are displayed as open to all readers who might have an interest. The conventions may be unknown by many readers who would come across them. In this way there is a higher-level interdiscursivity set up across the documents within the series which may well lead to confusion about basic interpretive issues. To whom are these documents addressed? Who are the producers of the documents (principals, authors, and animators) or the receivers of the documents (principals, interpreters, handlers, and bystanders) when they are posted on the MMS website?

The ambiguities of writer/reader positions which are set up in the news releases by conventions and design are then ramified in the blending of discourses found in the documents. The first of these we have just noted, the blending of government discourse and journalistic/media discourse. The conventions and practices for linguistically indicating responsibility are different in these two discourses. The *FR* notices are signed by the Acting Director of the MMS, a point discussed in Chapter 6. We do not know who is principal of the text we are reading in the media section of the press release. Journalistic/media discourse takes the stance that principalship is always placed on the newsmakers, those who are quoted in the text or whose actions are reported. The journalist is constructed as mere author of the wordings. In the *FR* notices the MMS directly takes responsibility for the statements made. In the news release, then, the MMS is simultaneously presented as taking responsibility (when the Regional Director is quoted) and as denying that responsibility in taking the journalistic, distanced, voice. The government discourse of the MMS bends journalistic discourse to the service of government discourse. While the reader both of this document and of any places where this is printed as a media story sees a different form of discourse blending, the reader sees media discourse blending government discourse into its own discourse through referencing. It is making reference to what the MMS is saying and doing but is not that discourse in itself.

In a few words, then, the main differences in discourse blending between the *FR* notices and the news releases is that the *FR* notices are clear instantiations of government discourse which is also subordinated to law and ultimately to political discourses. The news releases are ambiguous cases of blending and bending of discourses. We do not clearly know who is taking responsibility for saying what is printed in these documents nor what actions this blending enables.

Given this complexity in writer/reader positions in the news releases there are two further issues which are important overall to this analysis; both have to do with what the multiple sale process is all about. Are the sales of oil and gas leases 'about' government matters such as following out the requirements and consequences of congressional law? Are they about scientific matters such as the environmental protection of the Arctic coastal environmental species and habitats? Are they about US national and Alaska state politics, world system politics and economics, or about tribal rights to a subsistence way of life and culture? The analysis of news release 1.1 suggests that the process is about science. This, then, raises the question: where, then, is the political process in relation to the multiple sale process?

Of course the sales are 'about' all of these things in a very complex blend of political, legal, scientific, and government discourses. As a consequence, it is important that the documents covering this process either cover the full ground (as the initial *FR* notice (0.1) actually does quite well) or that they be clear in any particular case about how the document is being selective and why. Again, the *FR* notice (1.13) covering the bidding process does this well. News release 1.1, however, is quite problematical from this point of view. The Regional Director is quoted as saying that the EIS will be 'a complete scientific record on which to base leasing decisions'.

This statement as well as the gist of the rest of the news release sets the entire multiple sale process within a space between government and scientific discourses. If the science is good, and it is promised that it will be, then the decision(s) about the sales will proceed in a straightforward manner. The array of political discourses is conspicuous by their absence. While the news release does say that the MMS is issuing a call for 'public and industry' comments and suggestions, the government discourse subordinates itself not to legal discourse or political discourse but to scientific discourse. Even the environmental protection discourse is subordinated to scientific discourse. The implication is that comments and suggestions are to be made within this scientific discourse.

If the first news release (1.1) is silent about the politics of the multiple sales, the second (2.8a) speaks rather more loudly and in a non-negotiable voice. Attending first to the question of design of the document, as we noted in discussing Figure 1.2, document 2.8a has a striking full-color letterhead which includes an MMS slogan 'Securing Ocean Energy and Economic Value for America'. The letterhead is a collage centered on a cropped image of a portion of the US flag. To the right is the image of an oil drilling platform and on the far right a man who is wearing a white helmet and ear protectors (or earphones), viewed from the back looking at the oil platform from a position above it. On the left is another collage of images which include mesa formations of the Southwestern desert, a person, perhaps a woman, whose activity is unclear, and a US Treasury check. The flag, money, oil rig, desert mountains, man and woman are arrayed in a design configuration which Kress and van Leeuwen have called 'center–margin'.

The center–margin graphic composition configuration conveys through a visual semiotic grammar that what is at the center is, in fact, the main argument or focus, with progressive marginalization outward toward the edges. That is, we have the US national flag at the center. In secondary position, moving outward, are a treasury check and a desert scene on the left side and an oil rig on the right, and in the most marginal positions, left and right sides, are the two human figures. Further, Kress and van Leeuwen note that these are not just positions in a relative hierarchy, but it is the center which mediates these other figures or participants. That is, if we read this letterhead within this grammar of visual design, it is the US flag which mediates relationships among money, the natural environment, and oil development, and these, in turn, mediate relationships among humans.

This letterhead was new to MMS in February 2005. The last news release posted in the old format on the Alaska Region website was dated February 9, 2005, while the first in the new format is dated 24 February 2005. All subsequent news releases are in this new format. This new letterhead is a clear and graphic statement about the discourses to be found under the authority of this principal voice. At the center is US national politics which mediates the natural environment, economics, and ultimately the humans within its scope. This news release (2.8a) sounds a strong note in the discourse of US national politics and with this graphic at least incorporates if not bends all discourses which follow to this political discourse. This visual semiotic display is further ramified both by the presence of the new MMS slogan and by the placement of the slogan. It is both an integral element in the letterhead and it is the marker following the journalistic text at the end of the news release.

The US political discourse instantiated in the letterhead and slogan is further ramified in the text in the quoted statement by MMS Director Johnnie Burton who comments,

> The Beaufort Sea remains the best near-term potential for offshore petroleum reserves on the Alaska OCS that can be vital to our Nation's economy.

(2.8a)

This news release concerns the sale of oil and gas leases and may be compared with the *FR* notice covering this same type of event. The 'facts' covered in the two cases diverge considerably. The *FR* notice focuses very specifically on bidders and the technical processes of bidding. The news release, in contrast, focuses on the political nature of this sale, along with assurances that it is being done with careful consultation among interested parties and with careful attention to the reduction of environmental effects.

In summary, then, by comparison with the *FR* notices, the news releases among these documents present a rather ambiguous array of writer/reader positions as well as important differences in the blends among discourses. *FR* notices are instantiations of government discourse which are, in turn, blended (subordinated) by reference to the laws, rules, and policies of the US government. Other discourses are largely either incorporated (world system economics in 1.14, or environmental protection in both cases, for example) or referenced with neither subordination nor incorporation. In contrast to these, the news releases are much more problematic cases of discourse blending. In the first news release examined (1.1) the government discourse bends journalistic discourse to its purposes and then further subordinates itself to scientific discourse, not law discourse. This genre bending and blending are facilitated by the ambiguous writer/reader positioning that is inherent in the genre of the news release, where text is presented to the media as either facts to be mined for their own uses or as text to be used word for word as their own stories. In news releases it is linguistically problematical to know who is taking responsibility for the statements being made, in contrast to the *FR*, where lines of authority and responsibility are defined by text and design.

Leasing Activities Information memo (LAI)

The Leasing Activities Information (LAI) memo is the most abundant document type in this series of documents. These documents function as memos do in government discourse both to convey information as the full content of the memo and also, in some cases, as a cover sheet to organize enclosures of many other kinds of documents. These enclosures may include not only other document types, such as maps and *FR* notices, they may also include other LAI memos.

The LAI is framed as a document originated by and conveying information from the MMS (Figure 3.2). This is done through a common and unexceptionally designed header with the top-centered words 'Leasing Activities Information' in a large, bold, sanserif typeface. Below this, flush left is the MMS block-letter logo followed by the government hierarchy of agencies: US Department of the Interior, Minerals Management Service, Alaska OCS Region. The text of the memo shifts to a smaller, Times Roman style of serifed typeface which is maintained throughout the memo. The pages are numbered and in some cases the text is closed with a note in a smaller typeface indicating a contact person and information.

Writer/reader (production/reception) positions are relatively uniform and unambiguous, much like those in the *FR* notices. The principal of the memos is the undifferentiated MMS. That is, the LAI memos are not signed, and the person(s) designated as contact are not marked as principals, authors, or animators. Authorship and animation are left unmarked with the presumption that, like the principal roles, these are government tasks accomplished within the MMS, Alaska OCS Region office. Reception positions are marked, as they are in the *FR* notices, through the use of terms such as 'bidders', 'bid submitters', or 'lessees'. That is, they are marked by reference to their function in the actions required by the memo.

An interesting expansion of these receptive roles is seen in LAI 1.12.3, which lists 26 points of information for lessees on Sale 186. In each case a verb form in the passive is given which references the discourse of the information point being noted. For example, under the header '(a) Community Participation in Operations Planning' is the sentence,

> Lessees are encouraged to bring one or more residents of communities in the area of operations into their planning process.
>
> (1.12.3: 2 of 10)

The full paragraph makes it clear that this information point is blending the traditional knowledge discourse into the government discourse of this memo (and consequently of the activities of the leasing process). This reading is further substantiated in point (b), where

> lessees are encouraged to obtain copies of the guide and to incorporate it into their Orientation Program.
>
> (1.12.3:2 of 10)

From this passive verb construction ('lessees are encouraged') we can read both that the discourse is being blended (incorporated) into this discourse and the degree and manner of blending. We can compare with the other 26 points. Altogether there are just three cases in which the lessee 'is encouraged', all of which incorporate the discourse of traditional knowledge into this government discourse. There is one case in which the 'MMS will encourage lessees to use existing pads and islands wherever feasible' (1.12.3:9 of 10). That is, the MMS incorporates the discourses of both traditional knowledge and at least this one instance of environmental protection through encouragement; this encouragement is not binding.

In contrast to these are 12 cases in which 'lessees are advised', one non-passive in which 'MMS advises lessees', and one in which it is only the reader who is passively advised ('Please be advised'). In all of these 14 cases the verb 'advise' indicates a subordination of the leasing process to a legal discourse such as 30 CFR 254 or some other Federal or State requirement. The reader is told of a binding law, rule, or policy that conditions or controls the leasing process.

Other verbs are used but this comparison indicates that an analysis of the verbs used in bringing other documents and references into an LAI memo are crucial because they indicate the kind of blending of discourses which is occurring and whether the blending is binding or not upon the principal being addressed.

The EIS and EA

The documents which constitute the bulk of the multiple sales process up to March 2005 are four: the draft EIS, the Oil-Spill Risk Analysis (OSRA), the final EIS, and then between the first (186) and second sale (195), the EA. Together they constitute thousands of pages of text. In spite of this bulk, these documents provide the fewest problems of discourse blending. This is no doubt because Federal regulations prescribe almost all details of function, purpose, design and format, of authorship, of the manner and appropriateness of incorporation of other texts by reference, and even of writing style and size and scope of the document. It is designed by the NEPA to be an action-forcing document and so roles and actions are quite explicitly made clear.

Working within this highly specified format there is still some small shifting of footing in the identification of writer positions in the EIS, for example. In the opening section 'Overview and General Information' the pronoun 'we' is used to make reference to the MMS:

> Because the draft EIS is somewhat complicated, we in the Minerals Management Service (MMS) urge you to read this first.

This writer-to-reader exchange is further developed in a direct comment concerning the writing itself:

> If you have any suggestions about the format and writing style, we hope you include them in your comments. If you feel any critical references were omitted, please describe them as specifically as possible. Thank you.

This voicing then changes slightly from 'we', that is, the writers of the EIS, to 'The MMS', responsible agency, when the 'Executive Summary' section begins. There is a shift from interpersonal 'you and me' communication to the institutional communication which is then maintained throughout the remainder of the EIS and in the EA to follow a little more than a year later.

The questions of function, framing, design, and production/reception positions are specified, explicitly signaled and unambiguous. This leaves the question of discourse blending: what discourse(s) does this document instantiate, and what discourses does it blend or bend? The Federal regulations specify in Sec. 1501.7 (endnote 10) the following:

Environmental impact statements shall be prepared using an inter-disciplinary approach which will insure the integrated use of the natural and social sciences and the environmental design arts (section 102(2)(A) of the Act). The disciplines of the preparers shall be appropriate to the scope and issues identified in the scoping process.

(Sec. 1501.7)

By regulation, then, the EIS should not be a document which instantiates any single scientific discipline or, for that matter, scientific discourse alone. The 'Overview and General Information' section notes that,

Traditional knowledge information and observations appear throughout the EIS, along with those of Western science.

In keeping with this requirement, the EIS notifies the reader specifically that both traditional knowledge and scientific discourses will be incorporated within the document, though it does not mention 'environmental design arts' or other discourses which might potentially be relevant, for example, political science. It is possible to argue that law and regulations require an EIS to be framed as an instantiation of government discourse which blends in the discourses of science, both natural and social, by incorporation and simultaneously excludes other discourses, notably political discourses.

Given this careful specification of the discursive construction of an EIS (or EA, of course) by NEPA which is binding on MMS, it is important to reflect back on the statement of the Regional Director of MMS in the opening news release (1.1) in which he was quoted as saying that the MMS would be preparing 'a complete scientific record on which to base leasing decisions'. While such a simplification may well be due to the constraints of writing for media release, the statement does narrow this complex of discourse blending to state that the government, and ultimately political, decision would be made on the basis of scientific discourse alone.

Transcript of public testimony in response to the DEIS

Public testimony was taken in four public hearings in late July 2002: Nuiqsut, 24 July; Kaktovik, 2 July; Anchorage, 30 July; and Barrow, 1 August. The function of these hearings is set out in an *FR* notice as being 'on the draft EIS'. The *FR* notice does not further constrain either who may speak or what kind of testimony would be considered acceptable beyond this notice that it should pertain to the draft EIS. In the hearings themselves the function was described by Paul Stang of the MMS as:

(Nuiqsut): We are here this evening to get your testimony and your statements and your expressions about the Beaufort Sea multi-sale EIS, or Environmental Impact Statement.

(1.3: VII–287)

(Kaktovik): The purpose here is to have a meeting to discuss and to hear your testimony on a lease/sale EIS, Environmental Impact Statement, Draft Environmental Impact Statement for three lease/sales.

(1.3: VII–310)

(Anchorage): The purpose of our meeting today is a public hearing on the – what we call the multiple sale EIS for three lease sales in the Beaufort Sea that are proposed for the years 2003, 2005, and 2007.

(1.3: VII–352)

(Barrow): What we're here to talk about is this document here which is the environmental impact statement for multiple sales, three sales.

(1.3: VII–392)

Both the *FR* notice and the MMS representative make it explicitly clear that testimony in the public hearings is to be directed to and a discussion of the draft EIS. This point is made now because the testimony itself often diverges from this discursive restriction to the linked discourses of government–scientific–environmental protection. It is important to note as well that this restriction is specified in the NEPA regulation cited above (see References for this chapter) though it is left to the agency preparing the EIS to decide just which sciences and kinds of analyses will be included.

Taken as a document, these transcripts (1.3) are of a different generic type as compared to all the other documents in this analysis. The transcript function will be discussed first before we briefly take up the embedded genre of spoken public testimony.

As documents, the four transcripts are clearly marked in their function of being written representations of public spoken discourse. Each hearing is set out under a separate cover sheet which identifies the source agency (USDOI/MMS), the purpose 'Official Transcript – Public Hearing', and the title 'Draft Environmental Impact Statement'. The cover sheet further gives the place of the hearing (village and building) and the date. Again, in termination of the transcript frame there are the words '(Off record)' followed by '(END OF THE PROCEEDINGS)'. After this follows a certificate signed by a Notary Public which certifies that the hearing was recorded by whom and when, that it was electronically recorded, transcribed and reduced to print under the direction of the notary, that it is a full, complete and true record, and the notary has no interest in the outcome of this matter. Within this frame lies the transcription itself in which speakers are identified and line numbers are given for referencing the testimony.

While it may seem trivial at first sight, this framing, as well as the design of the transcript with a courier-style typeface, set the language we read apart from the rest of all of these documents as originating as spoken language, not written language. This is important for two reasons: it makes it clear that the speakers are face-to-face with their hearers and so false starts, hesitation phenomena, and overlapping in speaking turns are not failures of editing but naturally occurring adjustments to the needs of multiple speakers to take the floor. Second, the issues we have taken up above of production and reception roles are performed in spoken interaction by other modes such as eye gaze, gesture, and body position, not by letterheads and typefaces.

We note, for example, that in the Anchorage hearing Paul Stang is positioned in the front of the room by his reference to the Regional Director who is together with 'some members of our staff in the back'. As the principal in Alaska regional communications, the Regional Director is set in a position in the room which suggests that he will not be a speaker and testimony should be directed to Paul Stang, who is at the front and who is the lead in making introductions and in responding to questions. Of course, in spoken discourse speakers are most often the authors and animators of their own utterances, though in cases where testimony is read into the record on behalf of a person not present, the speaker is more strictly simply an animator.

While public hearings are hearings of spoken testimony on the whole, it is the transcript which gives them status as part of the public record. This point is treated as a crucial one by the MMS. For example, in Barrow Charlie Hopson asks a question of Paul Stang which the latter hears but suspects has not been recorded. The sequence is as follows (3.1:VII–394,395):

> 9 MR. HOPSON: I don't see after you – if
> 10 something goes wrong, you know, (indiscernible).
> 11 MR. STANG: Could I ask you please to
> 12 come and sit over at that microphone, Charles, because
> 13 that way we can get your question on the record. Would
> 14 you be willing to do that for us? Thank you.
> 15 MR. HOPSON: I was just asking you a
> 16 question.
> 17 MR. STANG: I will answer it, if we can
> 18 get it on the record.
> 19 MR. HOPSON: (Indiscernible)
> 20 MR. STANG: Or, wait a minute. Here.
> 21 Here, she'll bring a microphone right to you.
> 22 UNIDENTIFIED VOICE: We'll get more
> 23 answers if you keep asking.
> 24 MR. STANG: You can sit down, that's
> 25 easiest. Okay. The question was can we encourage

00007

> 1 companies to drill. I guess we could verbally, but we
> 2 have no legal mechanism to encourage them to drill. The

Such cases make it clear that the MMS representative is concerned to give the recorded speech and the subsequent transcription we read the authorization of the MMS as 'the' public hearing. Whatever else might be said in and around such a speech event is produced as not part of the hearing. That is, there are definite, though not always explicitly stated, criteria of what counts as legitimate public testimony. The *FR* as well as the MMS introduction at each hearing sets this out as discussion of the draft EIS.

This observation is further supported in the Anchorage transcript when a member of the public goes on at considerable length on the topic of nepotism in the State of Alaska, a topic which all but the most generous of interpretations would consider off topic and irrelevant to the issue of discussion of the EIS and of the proposed plan for oil and gas leases. After more than five pages of recorded testimony the speaker concludes (3.1: VII–381),

8 And so I'd really like for you to read
9 this over and look at it, and understand it, and then I
10 would be glad to field questions. You're probably tired
11 and want to go. And would you forgive me for coming
12 late? I should have come earlier, and I wanted to, but I
13 just didn't get over here until right now. So I'm sorry
14 to – I hope I'm not keeping you.
15 Did anyone have a question about anything
16 I've said?
17 MR. STANG: Maybe after we go off the
18 record. I just had something to ask about the school
19 board, but …
20 MS. OBERMEYER: Oh, sure.
21 MR. STANG: … maybe separate.
22 MS. OBERMEYER: Would you want to go off
23 the record?
24 MR. STANG: Are you done?
25 MS. OBERMEYER: Yes, of course. Unless

00060

1 you have – any of you have a question. I'd be glad to
2 field questions.
3 MR. STANG: Okay.

While Paul Stang appears to recognize that this testimony lies outside the scope of the public hearing, he is careful to allow the speaker a very generous amount of time to come around to the topic if this should be her way of speaking. When the speaker gives the opening for a turn exchange in line 15, Stang suggests that he would discuss the matter with her personally, that is, not as a representative of the MMS and not as part of the public record concerning the draft EIS.

In another place (Nuiqsut) Paul Stang makes a comment while on record which he marks clearly as being his personal opinion, not that of the MMS. He says,

> Now, personally, and this is not Department of Interior speaking or MMS, but myself, personally …
>
> (3.1: VII–296)

Finally, on the point of relevance to the discussion of the EIS, normally, throughout the transcripts, when a speaker concludes she or he is thanked, much as occurs in this example from Nuiqsut, 24 July 2002:

> 13 MR. STANG: Thank you. Frank. Would you
> 14 like to translate?
> 15 INTERPRETER: In Native.
> 16 MR. STANG: Good. Thank you. Would anyone
> 17 else like to testify now, please. Eli?
>
> (3.1: VII–290)

In a few cases, however, there is a clear evaluation given, as in the example below from Kaktovik, 26 July 2002:

> 17 MR. STANG: Thank you, Robert. Your
> 18 questions were very appropriate. Yes, Albert.
>
> (VII–335)

It would be incautious to over-interpret these several ways of closing out a speaker's turn at giving testimony in an analysis of this limited scope. A fuller analysis might indicate, however, that such closings do suggest to other potential speakers and to those in the audience that their testimony is being evaluated for its relevance and so in this way is being shaped toward specific MMS goals.

As documents, these transcripts present an objective record of public testimony. Thus, as documents, they highlight the important distinction between written and spoken discourse. Written discourse is given primacy over spoken discourse throughout this series of documents. Spoken discourse is accepted into the process only to the extent it may be converted into written discourse, at least where public discourse is concerned. Because this analysis is confined to the written documents published by the MMS on its website as the public record of the Beaufort Sea multiple sale process, this analysis cannot examine any instances of the presumably very large spoken, off-record communication that takes place among members of the public in the audience, among government bureaucrats in their offices or in traveling, among politicians, NGO representatives, and corporate officers who are seeking to shape the outcomes, or among the scientists who have been given formal discursive ascendancy in the aspects of the process which concern environmental protection. Thus, this analysis is blinded to much of the discourse which is crucial to the development of the multiple sale process.

Nevertheless, much can be inferred about what is not visible to this analysis from what is visible in the discourse captured in these public hearings. This testimony and the responses from the MMS which are published in the FEIS, as well as later in the EA, are sufficient to grasp at least one crucial bending of discourses: with very minor exceptions, all public testimony recorded here in these 148 pages of transcript expresses an opposition to proceeding with the first Sale 186 and also with the multiple sale process itself. This opposition is stated directly in some cases, in others it is stated as supporting 'Alternative II', the 'no sale' option, and in still others it is stated as supporting a moratorium on OCS oil and gas leases. In the majority of cases, however, opposition to the sale(s) is stated through the discourses of science or through the discourses of traditional knowledge (that is, statements about the subsistence and cultural way of life of the people who live in the three most-affected North Slope communities).

This bending of scientific and of traditional knowledge discourses to serve the political discourse of opposition to the sale of these leases is central to the analysis of this sale process. Here in these transcripts we read many pages of what is, in essence, political public discourse, shaped into the terms and conditions of scientific analysis and traditional knowledge. The questions to be resolved concerning these members of the public and the representatives of several local and tribal governments and environmental NGOs are these:

- Are they speaking in ignorance of the published constraints on what constitutes acceptable responses to the EIS?
- Are they intentionally ignoring these constraints in their interest in pursuing a political debate at an inappropriate point in the policy development process?
- Are they intentionally bending the scientific discourse and the traditional knowledge discourse for political purposes?
- Are they naive in believing that straightforward science and traditional knowledge is all that is needed to protect their own interests?
- Are they working with an assessment of full trust, lack of ambivalence, and certainty concerning either the scientific research surrounding the multiple sales or the work of the MMS in managing them?

On the other side of this dialogue we are faced with the corresponding questions about the MMS and the scientific, government discourses they represent:

- Are they naive in thinking that the only relevant or appropriate public testimony is scientific or traditional knowledge directed toward the analysis found in the draft EIS?
- Are they eclipsing what is essentially a US national political discourse with an environmental, scientific discourse?

- Are they taking a position which is duplicitous or are they being positioned in that way by the government/legal discourses within which they operate due to their employment and its restrictions on their activities in public conduct of their office?

This analysis cannot provide any direct answers to these questions, simply because here we are dealing with a large number of people who have worked largely anonymously as authors of a large number of written documents and who have also engaged in many hours of public spoken discourse. Certainly these questions might be answered positively in some cases and negatively in others, whether we are considering individuals, agencies, or events. What this analysis does show us, however, is that these public, on-record statements of many different interested parties are far from clear, unambiguous, non-ambivalent statements. They reflect an absence of public–government trust. They work towards political ends through complex blending and bending of discourses which include all of the forms this analysis has outlined above.

MMS website

Finally, there remains one type of document to be examined briefly, the pages of the MMS website. It is, of course, problematical to refer to a web page or a website as a document but, for the purposes of this analysis, it is considered a document because it sheds light on the questions raised above on how individual documents in the series, as well as the series itself, may be interpreted.

The function of the website as a whole is to provide publicly available information to all interested parties concerning the MMS and its activities. This is not the only source of that information. It is also available from the MMS in other forms, including in writing or by telephone. For example, the FEIS may be downloaded from the MMS website or, alternatively, requested in CD format from the regional office. Next to a visit in person to the MMS regional office in Anchorage, however, the website provides and organizes for access the fullest view of the MMS and its activities, as well as a large number of documents which may be viewed online or downloaded in several different formats.

The function of providing access to the series of documents covering the Beaufort Sea multiple sales is organized within a conventional web page design, as is the series covering the Cook Inlet sales. The header information identifying the principal as well as the chain of command is at the top of the page. A column on the left side of the page provides a navigation index of areas of the website which provide different kinds of information (Figure 3.5). The bottom provides a second index, which largely reiterates the sidebar index. While some MMS web pages give names for 'content' and the 'pagemaster', these web pages do not indicate authorship or animation. The contents of the page are set within this 'C' shaped page frame, set off by white space.

The page which lists and provides links to the documents considered in this analysis carries the title 'Beaufort Sea – Multiple Sales 186, 195, and 202'. There are two sub-headers, one for Sale 195 and another for Sale 186. The documents are listed in reverse chronological order by date. The Appendix gives the URL for this page, which is updated as new documents are posted.

As this analysis has noted above, the functions of documents in this series are to some considerable extent coordinated with their design features. Official notices directed to all interested parties in the general public are published in the *FR*. News releases, which provide information to the news media, have a common design format and embody common ambiguities of writer/reader positions. The design and possibly the accompanying writer/reader positions underwent a sea change in February 2005 with a new full-color letterhead. Similarly, Leasing Activities Information memos and transcripts of public hearings occur in a standard format across all Beaufort Sea and Cook Inlet documents. Because of the overlay of NEPA requirements for the production and presentation of EISs and EAs is it not surprising that these too display very similar formats. Thus, is it in keeping with this documentary design standardization that the web pages of not just the Regional Office in Anchorage but the MMS nationally are presented within a common design with only relatively minor variations. In a few words, one can 'read' simply from the document design the function, framing, writer/reader positions, and to some extent make assumptions about the discourse blending which is operating.

Taken together, the hypertext structure of the web pages, along with the layout and color of the design, signal the government discourse which organizes the documents which are linked within the web pages. This indexing function stands in stark contrast with the black and white text-dominated documents which occur as further downloaded documents. In making this stark contrast the web page is set off as a neutral, organizing government discourse which blends all of the discourses thus contained within it as incorporated discourses.

The incorporation of all of the hyperlinked documents obscures two discourse blendings that this analysis highlights. First, the documents are of different legal statuses, address different reader positions, and require or anticipate different responses. In other words, the website links and creates interdiscursivities among documents and participants which otherwise would have no direct connection with each other.

Second, there are two means by which hyperlinks can be made: those links which occur within the frame of the website – these are often marked with a common color and design scheme – and those which are external links. This difference in linking conventionally signals a shift in principalship for the communication. The hosting or sponsoring website takes responsibility for the content (etc.) of internal links but disclaims responsibility for external links. Such external links are very rare in these pages.

There is such an external link as the top entry on the page 'Cook Inlet Lease Sales 191 and 199 (http://www.mms.gov/alaska/cproject/Cook_Inlet/ Cook%20Inlet%20Sale.htm) which first gives the link in the same format as all other links on the page but below which are the words 'External Link Disclaimer' in smaller and contrasting green lettering. That link takes the user to a website of 'Cook Inlet Oil and Gas' (http://www.cookinletoilandgas.org) which carries the logo identification of the Kenai Peninsula Borough, a borough organized within the State of Alaska.

This contrast between internal and external links then sets up an ambiguity with such documents as the *FR* notices (e.g. 0.1, 1.13) or, perhaps more importantly, the guide (1.12) prepared by the people of Kaktovik for those who want to work in their region. These documents are incorporated into the MMS website and so, by the implication of internal linkage, the MMS takes responsibility for the contents of those documents. This is done quite differently in these two cases, however. In the case of the *FR* notices (and also news releases, EIS, and EA) these are documents originally produced by the MMS itself. The principalship entailed in internal linkage parallels or even absorbs the principalship constructed in the documents themselves, as noted in the analysis above. In the case of the Kaktovik guide, however, the document is incorporated, but in only a limited way. As noted above, the lease stipulations only 'encourage' lessees to pay attention to this guide, they are not 'advised' that it is binding on them. It is an ambiguous incorporation that on the one hand blends the guide into the government process while on the other hand only referencing it.

While the Kaktovik guide may not be available elsewhere for access through the web, the *FR* is fully accessible through the same technology that is used to arrive at the MMS website. It is a matter of choice, then, whether the *FR* notices should be accessed through an external link to the *FR* website or included on the multiple sale website as internal links. It is not clear whether these notices are included as internal links for the convenience of the user or because they are considered more integral to the sale process. In any case, there is also further ambiguity in the incorporation of *FR* notices that points to a more general ambiguity of the MMS document postings.

Some *FR* notices are listed at the top level of the tree structure with a dated link on this website (e.g. 1.13, 2.2, 2.6) and others are incorporated within other documents, such as when *FR* notice 1.12.1 is incorporated under the LAI memo in the Final Notice of Sale Package (1.12). Interestingly, 1.13 and 1.12.1 are the same *FR* notice. This might argue that the MMS was simply making sure that this notice was available redundantly where it might be most easily accessed. One wonders, then, about the failure to include the *FR* notice which officially launched this multiple sale process (0.1) in this document series. One also notes the absence of the news release covering the actual sale (2.8a), which was, in fact, listed elsewhere on the MMS website.

This analysis assumes that these inconsistencies are minor oversights which are the consequence of a busy office staff working with a very large number of complex documents under both government time pressures and legal regulations. While a discourse analysis is not in itself competent to probe the intentions of the producers of documents, there can be little doubt that the guiding intention of the MMS is to provide wide public access in multiple formats to the documents which constitute the public, written record of information and actions involved in their activities such as these multiple sales. As will be suggested below in conclusion, it could be argued that, paradoxically, it is exactly this wide public access which produces some of these ambiguities. Highly complex engagements among multiple discourses must inevitably lead to misrepresentations when the complexities are simplified and understated and to ambiguities when multiple communicative windows are opened upon the processes and its documents.

To summarize, the common format of the web pages ties them clearly to the government discourse of the MMS but, perhaps in the interest of succinct presentation, the format and design give no clues about the documents to which links are made. All documents are presented in a chronological sequence, but this may not necessarily be the sequence in which the actions have occurred or the texts have been produced. The transcripts of the Barrow public hearing, for example, are posted as 30 July 2002, but the transcript says that the hearing took place the following day (1 August 2002).

The website gives few clues overall about the nature of the documents being listed, whether concerning their size, their significance in the process, their status within the several discourses which circulate through this process, or of their authorship and the degree to which the MMS claims principal productive authority. It is at least possible for a user who is a less than cautious interpreter to misinterpret such matters as these in reading the documents placed on the website because of this neutral presentation, as if they were all of equal status.

Dialogue among multiple stakeholders

There is a running and changing weave of discourses among the discourses of politics, law, science, and government in the multiple sale process for oil and gas leases managed by the MMS. Each of these discourses is driven by its own set of organizing principles based on participation, agency, lexicogrammar, argumentation, genres, and modes; and, further, the document text types themselves necessarily blend and bend these discourses together in different mixes which depend on function, framing, document design, and production/ reception roles. Complex and difficult blends are the inevitable outcome in the series of documents analyzed here.

The analysis shows that there is a tendency for formal, legally binding documents such as the *FR* notices or the EIS and EA to be the clearest and the least ambiguous. This is largely because both the discourses which are present and the document functions, frames, and designs are highly specified and must be responsive to binding legal requirements of laws and regulations. Unfortunately, while these documents are the least problematical from the point of view of this analysis of interdiscursivity, they are not easily interpreted and read by non-specialists. This is precisely because their structure and contents are constrained within the specialized discourses of government and law. Participants in other discourses who lack this specialized knowledge and the enabling training and credentialization may find these formal notices opaque and difficult to incorporate into their own enabling discourses.

On the other side of the coin, the documents in this series which are functionally aimed at a readership of members of the general public, such as the news
releases, or which are designed to be neutral to the specific uses to be made of the
documents, such as the web pages, tend to be the most ambiguous and, consequently, potentially misleading. The necessary simplifications of content and the
structurally ambiguous language of text which might be appropriated directly for
use in another author's text which are required by the genre of the news release,
for example, present two quite separable problems for interpretation. The simplification tends to exaggerate the role of certain discourses and to blend or even
eclipse other discourses which the more formally specified documents keep
distinct. Further, readers who do not know the formatting conventions of journalism and public relations genres can be forgiven for their difficulties in
processing the ambiguous positions of those genres.

The public hearings on the DEIS tend toward political discourse carried out
by the discursive means of scientific discourse. Environmental protection
incorporates scientific discourse, while both are incorporated by government
discourse. All are subordinated to legal discourse, which is itself incorporated
by national political discourse. Such blending, bending, and eclipsing occur
throughout the documents in the sale process. An analysis of discourse and of
the relationships across discourses must be understood as a phenomenon of
rhetorical strategizing, not as simple instantiations of separate discourses.

These discourse problems do not arise only in these documents or in this
process of the sale of oil and gas leases. The interdiscursivity we have seen in
these documents is not exceptional but the nature of discourse in general. What
is exceptional is the relatively small number of discourses – science and law are
among them – in which a kind of firewall is built around the discourse to isolate
it from common usages and the widespread mixing, weaving, and blending
which we have seen in these documents.

There is an irony that at least some of the ambiguities and conflicts among the
discourses found in the MMS multiple oil and gas lease sales are a direct
outcome of the laudable goal of maintaining a full and very accessible public
record of the sale process and of calling for input from all interested parties. It is
the successful achievement of the communication goal itself which enables
these complex interdiscursivities to flourish.

These problems can be succinctly summarized as the following five:

1   Interdiscursivities are not general relations between discourses, but specific
    to particular documents and events.
2   Official, legally binding texts are unambiguous but difficult to read for non-
    specialists; simplified texts are more generally readable but are inherently
    ambiguous.
3   Discourse blending, bending, and eclipsing are used as strategies to achieve
    the ends of one discourse through the means of another:.

4   Interdiscursive processes are inherent in the nature of discourse, not isolable features of these documents or this sale process.
5   Commitment to a full public record and public involvement exacerbates these complexities.

The complexity of these problems, as well as the fact that they are inherently part of natural processes of communication, is the central problem faced by stakeholders in this example of public discourse. As the major producer of these documents, the MMS is the entity which can make changes to some of the documents and to the ways in which they are made available for the public as part of the public record and consultation. Nevertheless, the MMS is under legal and government constraints set by the US Department of the Interior on the one hand and by NEPA on the other. Further, the scholarly and professional constraints within which scientists work are essential to the function of science to provide cautious, carefully argued, and empirically tested findings. Moreover, the fundamental ambiguity of the political process in the US within which struggles for ideological ascendancy and group positions of power are carried out through democratic debate and then through the legal constraints of laws, rules, and regulations places the MMS in an inherently ambiguous position in juggling political, government, and legal discourses, largely through the means of the discourse(s) of science.

While this analysis does not constitute a critical discourse analysis as commonly practiced, it does suggest, however, that there is considerable confusion at the level of the purpose or goals of both the documents in this analysis and the goals and purposes of the participants in the intersecting discourses. There is apparently a strong public need to engage in the political discourses implied by this multiple sale process which is equally apparently not being met by the process as it is now constituted. There is also an urgent need for discourse analysts to bring these complexities of the democratic processes of public discourse to public attention.

When science is used to further political goals, that is a common aspect of the discourse of politics. On the other hand, when political discourse usurps the practices of scientific discourse to then turn around and undermine the science, we arrive at a point where it is necessary to examine how truth and reality are established within such a complex weave of multiple discourses. This is the problem of modality to which we turn in Chapter 6.

PRACTICE

By now you will have found documents from different sources. However, what counts as a different source? Does this mean that the documents are from different organizations, different websites, or located via a different communication channel, e.g. posters you requested from an organization? In this practice session, you will examine these differences in the light of document types.

Activity 1:
Who is the writer? Who is the reader?

In March 2001, the European Commission adopted Directive 2001/18/EC on the deliberate release into the environment of genetically modified organisms (GMOs), creating a legal framework for the commercialization of genetically modified crops across Europe. In July the same year, the Commission proposed further regulations concerning the traceability and labeling of GMOs and the traceability of food and feed produced from GMOs. In Wales, public comments on both the directive and the proposals were sought by the Food Standards Agency and the Welsh Assembly, before 'The Genetically Modified Organisms (Deliberate Release) (Wales) Regulations 2002' was made.

A few major document types can be summarized from the documents accessed via the internet:

- Directives
- Explanatory notes
- Invitation letters for public comments
- Response papers from the public
- Consultation papers
- Press releases
- Consultation web pages.

The function of the directives is to order actions to be taken. A fine line separates the header from the body text in the Directive of the European Parliament and the Council. The header states the date of publication '17.4.2001', the name of the publication 'Journal of the European Communities', and the record number 'L106/1'. This outer framing places the directive inside an official discourse of the European Union. Internally, the text is set in two columns, almost every paragraph is hierarchically numbered and grouped in one directive, 38 articles and 10 annexes. Such document design points to the legal discourse within the official framing. The principal was clearly stated in the opening sentence of the directive, in serif capital letters 'THE EUROPEAN PARLIAMENT AND THE COUNCIL OF THE EUROPEAN UNION'. We learn from Article 38 that the directive was 'done at Brussels, 12 March 2001', but the author remains unknown. Instead, the principals were reiterated and specified at the end of the body text before the annexes:

For the European Parliament	For the Council
N. FONTAINEL.	PAGROTSKY
The President	The President

The designated principal reader can be gleaned from the 38th article: 'This Directive is addressed to the Member States', which implies the governments in member states are responsible for transposing the directive into state regulations.

However, distributing the directive to public stakeholders during public consultations also expanded the range of principal readers. The readers of non-member states could, like the researcher, take on the reception roles of 'bystanders' or 'spectators'.

In contrast, in the response papers by organizations, such as Friends of the Earth Cymru and Organic Strategy Group (OSG), the principals were the organizations and the designated reader was the National Assembly of Wales. However, exactly who would read the response papers was uncertain, as reflected in FoE's use of 'the Minister/officials' as their addressees.

ASSIGNMENT

One feature of a certain document type is the production/reception positions. Draw a table, and list all document types you have collected in the top row and put *principal, author, animator, interpreter, handler,* and *bystander/spectator* in the left-most column. Write down in each cell the name of the responsible organization or person. Put a question mark in that cell if the producer or receiver cannot be identified.

Observations

Observe which document type has the most diversified distribution among the production/reception positions, which document type has the most consistent distribution, and which document type has the most question marks. How does this feature affect the interdiscursivity of the document type and the ambiguity or clarity of its messages?

Activity 2:
News releases (press releases)

A press release (http://europa.eu.int/comm/dgs/health_consumer/library/press/press 172_en.pdf, accessed 1 August 2005, PDT) from the European Commission starts with the following sentences:

> The European Commission adopted today an important legislative package on genetically modified organisms (GMOs) which establishes a sound community system to trace and label GMOs and to regulate the placing on the market and labeling of food and feed products derived from GMOs. The new legislation is intended to provide a trustworthy and environmentally safe approach to GMOs, GM food and GM feed. The package consists of a proposal for traceability and labeling of GMOs and products produced from GMOs and a proposal on regulating GM food and feed. It will require the traceability of GMOs throughout the chain from farm to table and provide

consumers with information by labeling all food and feed consisting of, containing or produced from a GMO ....

'The European Commission' was represented in the first sentence as the agent of action. However, the complex actions of enforcing a new law across Europe were packed into one single verb 'adopt'. It appears that both the principal and author positions were of a journalist, but excessive complimentary adjectives, such as 'important', 'sound', 'trustworthy', 'environmentally safe', would signal to the reader that the principal was really the European Commission. Starting from the second sentence, the 'package' became the agent of the actions of law enforcement.

In the following paragraphs, it quotes officials of the European Commission commenting on the new legislation:

> Commenting on the proposals, Environment Commissioner Margot Wallström said: 'The provisions for traceability ensure a high level of environmental and health protection and pave the way for a proper labeling system. Certainly, there is a cost for the producers and for trade, but what is at stake is our ability to build public confidence. European companies will only be able to seize the opportunities provided by biotechnology if this confidence is established'.

By quoting, the authors of the document make newsmakers take up the role of the principal and the original animator of the words. Then, they return to the combined positions of the principal and the author. The bulk part of the press release consists of explanations of key terms in the newly devised legislation, grouped under bold, sans-serif subheadings, such as 'traceability', which is uncommon journalist practice and reinforces the principalship of the Commission. The names of the authors, with their phone numbers, were revealed at the end of the main text, before the appendix.

Beate GMINDER: 02/296.56.94
Pia AHRENKILDE: 02/299.12.23
Thorsten MUENCH: 02/296.10.63
Catherine BUNYAN: 02/299.65.12

ASSIGNMENT

Find a news release in your project and observe how the production positions shift. Imagine you are to rewrite it to facilitate more effective communication with stakeholders. What would you change? Prepare a mock-up of the re-written and re-formatted news release.

Observations

You may find that writing a news release is no easy task. One of the difficulties lies in the wide range of potential readers of this message, including journalists who may want to adapt the news release into a news story. However, precisely because of this, it is more important to keep the production positions consistent and clear, so there is little room left for manipulation.

6 Modes and modality

The multimodal shaping of reality in public discourse

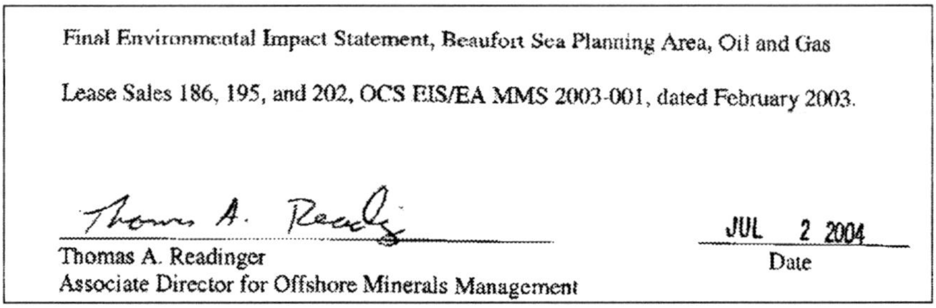

Final Environmental Impact Statement, Beaufort Sea Planning Area, Oil and Gas

Lease Sales 186, 195, and 202, OCS EIS/EA MMS 2003-001, dated February 2003.

Thomas A. Readinger
Associate Director for Offshore Minerals Management

JUL   2 2004
Date

Figure 6.1 Minerals Management Service, US Department of the Interior

THEORY – CASE STUDY

Communicative modes: form and action

We communicate in many different modes: we talk, write, gesture, pose, gaze, and dress ourselves in particular ways. And we make drawings, photos, films, or videos, or buildings and other artifacts. And we never do just one of these and only one of these at a time: we talk while we are gazing at the person we are speaking to or, perhaps, looking over their shoulder. In the morning before an important meeting we dress in a way that we feel will suit the tenor of the meeting and as we speak we sit or stand in particular ways and gesture in accompaniment of our speech.

Some of the modes we use are embodied modes – ways of communicating which are performed through our own bodies and which are perceived by others who are together with us face to face as we communicate. Other modes transform actions of our body into more or less permanent records of those actions and these work at greater or lesser distance from our bodies.

The signature of Thomas A. Readinger along with the rubber-stamped date, 2 July 2004, makes it legal to undertake the second sale of oil and gas leases in the Beaufort Sea (Sale 195). The 'Finding of No Significant Impacts' (2.4) is the official document which enables the second sale (195) to go ahead. After the first sale (186) a call was issued for new information, an EA was prepared to evaluate any changes which might have occurred since the EIS; this was reviewed by the MMS, and this finding was declared, signed, and dated. The signature tells us that it was the Associate Director himself who authorized this document as a legally binding document. Perhaps he did not put the rubber-stamped date on himself and he quite certainly did not type the letter. But the signature tells us that this real-world, identifiable historical body took an action with his own hand for which he claims and accepts the responsibility within his official government authority. The signature inscription on this letter leaves a permanent trace in which we see the movements of the Associate Director's hand, but the typography of the letter which he has signed is so distant that we cannot tell whose body did the word processing and printing.

Whether communicative modes are embodied ones or distant, disembodied ones, to a great extent we make conventional judgments about truth and reality, reliability or official status or the binding nature of communications on the basis of the modes which are used to perform the action of communication. If the 'Finding of No Significant Impacts' appeared, for example, as in the photographically doctored image in Figure 6.2, with a different font and a printed date, we might assume that it was designed as a copy of some original with a signature which was being held elsewhere, but not that it was a copy of the signed document itself.

In pre-photocopying days this is, in fact, how legal copies of documents were made. They were typed 'exactly' and then an affidavit swearing the exactness of the copy was signed by the animator of the document, the typist. This was, in fact, one of my jobs in the army – to be a human 'photocopier'.

This is what occurs in notices which appear in the *Federal Register*, such as in Figure 6.3, which is the 'signature block' for the Final Notice of Sale (1.13). In this case the bolded name of the Acting Director and the italicized title under the name indicate by contrast with the other typefaces that these are facsimiles of what has been registered and archived elsewhere as the official, authorizing letter.

There is no very clear or widely agreed upon definition of the word 'mode' among researchers on communicative modes, whether in communication,

Figure 6.2

Provisions, Sale 186" included in the
FNOS 186 package.

Dated: August 15, 2003.

Thomas A. Readinger,

*Acting Director, Minerals Management
Service.*

[FR Doc. 03–21472 Filed 8–20–03; 8:45 am]

BILLING CODE 4310–MR–P

Figure 6.3

psychology, or linguistics, but in most cases a distinction is made between mode
and medium. A mode is a configuration of expressions that is conventionally
recognized as being a symbolic system. A medium is the physical or material
substance (paper, ink, pixels on a screen, clothing or even parts of the body such
as the hands, arms, trunk, tongue, teeth, and larynx) in which a mode is formed.
Generally we recognize the distinction, for example, between writing as the
physical process of making marks (the medium) and writing as the semiotic
process of making shapes within an alphabet (mode).

Of course these relate to the production/reception roles which we discussed
in Chapter 5. The principal and the author of a document are concerned with
the mode (written expression of ideas in a language or other semiotic code –
English and Iñupiaq in this case study) and the animator is concerned with the
medium (typeface, paper choice, digital format of HTML or PDF). A signature
is, then, an interesting case in which we take it as legally binding when the
animator and the principal are the same person or social actor; that is, the person
who takes ultimate responsibility must be the same person who animates the
text 'Thomas A. Readinger' with his own handwriting.

Our concern in this chapter, then, is to discuss several ways in which
communications may take on different statuses in relationship to the real world
of social action through the mechanisms not only of lexicogrammar and
discourse, as we have studied in previous chapters, but now also through the
modes and media in which they are physically produced as objects in the world.

For PCDA we are mostly concerned with the modes and media of documentation and these are mostly print/text modes, though as we have seen in Figure
1.2 (3.4), the use of images has increasingly entered into consideration through
such letterheads and through the use of color and images on websites. Even
public testimony which is produced in the mode of speech is normally transformed into the mode of written text as part of making it a legitimate part of the
public consultative process.

Truth and reality in public discourse: modality

It is unfortunate that the words 'mode', 'modality', and 'multimodality' have come to mean quite different things across disciplines and research fields, because in an interdisciplinary project such as this one it is important to be clear about just how these words are being used. What is common to all of these modes, however, is the basic meaning of 'mode' (or also 'mood'). In all cases the meaning of 'mode' suggests ideas of 'manner' or 'the way things are done' in a particular case or situation.

In communication the word 'mode' means a semiotic configuration or code in which a meaning is expressed such as writing, speech, gesture, posture, gaze, painting, architecture, interior design, or urban design, as we have noted above. That is, in communication the focus is on the manner of communicating. In linguistics the word 'mode' means the logical truth or reality status of a statement or sentence, as indicated by such means as modal verb auxiliaries like 'would', 'could, 'should'. For our purposes here it may help to use the term 'mode' as it is used in communication and the term 'modality' for the linguistic use of the term.

We can make this clearer by looking at several statements which were made in public hearings concerning the multiple oil and gas lease sales in the Beaufort Sea (1.3).

Anchorage, 30 July 2002
   These comments that we get here at this public hearing and the other public hearings will be used by the Secretary of Interior in making her decision on the proposed sale, on each of these three proposed sales.

Barrow, 1 August 2002
   I doubt if the Secretary of Interior or the Director of the Minerals Management Service would sign a contract between you and them ...

Nuiqsut, 24 July 2002
   The first sale is in 2003. The second sale is in 2005. The third sale is in 2007. These are proposed sales.

Kaktovik, 26 July 2002
   What we mean by deferral is these are alternatives that are in the EIS that could be selected by the Secretary of Interior where leasing would not occur.

We will, this fall, produce a – or I guess it's in February, will produce a Final Environmental Impact Statement, and then there will ultimately be a decision by the Secretary and the sale will occur a little more than a year from now.

Let's say as a hypothetical, the Secretary decided to pick one of the alternatives. Let's just say hypothetically the Secretary decided to pick the Kaktovik green deferral and say I won't have leasing there.

Will the sale occur or won't it? Will these comments be used by the Secretary or won't they? Will the Secretary sign or won't she? Will the alternatives be selected or not? Will there be a sale in a year, in 2005, and in 2007? The verbs which tell us these things are modal verbs (or auxiliaries) like 'would', 'could', 'should', 'might', 'ought'. These verbs do not assert what we can observe to have happened; they present an imagined or alternate reality – usually one somewhere in the future, sometimes conditional on other events or occurrences.

'I will go to the store after a while,' conveys the idea that it is definite that I plan to go to the store. 'I would go to the store after a while,' conveys the more tentative notion that this action requires certain conditions to be met for it to happen – 'If you would do the dishes, I would go to the store.' 'I could go to the store after a while,' focuses on the speaker's ability to do the action. It is possible but no commitment is made. 'I should go to the store after a while,' suggests that the speaker thinks it would be right for that action to happen, but he or she remains doubtful that it will happen. 'Modality' is the word linguists use to talk about these varying states of projected reality or truth status. As we shall see below, these are far from being trivial grammatical matters of choice of words as we might have thought from our experiences of grammar in school; they are the material out of which political discourse and ideology are crafted.

Of course, it is not always the verb that tells us the truth or reality of what someone is saying, because we can also say, 'These are proposed', or 'Let's say as a hypothetical', but often the way we set up the truth or reality status of what we are saying is through the use of these verbs. This whole process of making the metacommunication about how we are to take a statement is called modality.

The central distinction in modality is between *realis* and *irrealis*. *Realis* is something that is 'real', 'definite', 'perceived by the person speaking' (or, of course, assumed to be perceived by the listener or a third person). *Irrealis* is 'imagined', 'unreal', 'indefinite', 'unknown', or 'unknowable'. And the modality might not just be located in the view or position of the speaker. It can be attributed to the hearer or even some other third person. 'I should go to the store this afternoon,' 'You ought to go to the store this afternoon,' 'He might go to the store this afternoon.'

Sometimes the modality distinction between *realis* 'real' and *irrealis* 'unreal' is not directly visible. If we have just the sentence, 'I need to buy a book,' we don't know precisely whether this is *realis* or *irrealis*. We can compare two fuller sentences,

I need to buy a book which I read about in a review yesterday (*realis*),

and

I need to buy a book because it's a long flight to Hong Kong (*irrealis*).

In the first case the speaker is talking about a concrete, specific book and so it is known (at least to her or him) exactly which book is being referred to, but in the second case it is just some book or any book, and so linguistically it is categorized as *irrealis*. In common conversations these are just the kinds of things that we respond to for clarifications, 'Does it matter what kind of book, or is there a particular book you are looking for?' In conversation we don't ask: is that a *realis* or an *irrealis* statement you are making? Wherever modality is placed interactionally, or whether it is marked in the verb or elsewhere in the lexicogrammatical system, we must successfully interpret the modality of communications in order to be able to respond or to act upon them appropriately.

Our sense of truth and reality lie at the very heart of our ability to undertake action in the world. And because public discourse on social policy is our major guide to sociopolitical actions in the future, modality, both lexicogrammatical modality and the modality that comes from multiple communicative modes, is central in public discourse.

Knowledge and agency in anticipatory discourse

Future national energy needs are not a fact (*realis*); they are a theory (*irrealis*). This is simply for the logical reason that the future is not known to us; it is a constructed world. It is constructed out of language, images, memories, stories, our artifacts, the objects we buy, treasure and discard, and the built and natural environment we move around in. Linguistically speaking, truth and reality are always from a point of view; the point of view of someone who makes a claim about reality or who attributes it to someone else. In the public hearing in Anchorage Jim Sykes says,

The oil is not needed.

(3.1: VII–358)

This is a simple, declarative *realis* statement about the oil to be extracted from the Beaufort Sea. He did not say, '*The oil may not be needed,*' '*The oil should not be needed,*' '*The oil would not be needed.*' He did not even say, '*The oil will not be needed.*' He took a clear, declarative, *realis* stand in the present: it is not needed. This is a reality for Sykes, a truth that he is willing to directly assert and to stand behind.

The statement in the EA of July 2004 contrasts very strongly with the statement of Sykes:

Oil from the adjacent Beaufort Sea shelf can help to reduce the Nation's need for oil imports.

(2.5: EA Page 1, 2)

The modal is can, not *will*. The verb phrase is 'help to reduce', not 'reduce'. It is the 'need' that may be reduced, not necessarily the oil imports themselves. Hedged in this way, and cast in the *irrealis* modality with 'can', the EA takes an anticipatory stance which is somewhat agnostic, that is, the EA is not ready to assert, at least within the scope of that statement, that the oil from the Beaufort Sea will either be needed or, more finely put, reduce the need for oil imports.

Work in the area of linguistics and discourse analysis which is sometimes discussed as anticipatory discourse focuses on such future-oriented statements (as well as other semiotic communications). There are many different stances which can be taken about the future which then shape the way we speak about actions yet to come. These can be plotted along two axes, one is a knowledge axis and the other is an agency axis as diagrammed in Figure 6.4.

The range on the knowledge axis is from oracular to agnostic, from claims of certainty to the profession of ignorance. At the oracular end, at the top of the graph, one takes the stance that what one is talking about is absolutely certain; though it has not yet happened one is certain that it will. Most of us, in talking about tomorrow's sunrise, are likely to take an oracular stance toward this event. We would be shocked if it did not happen. In the quotation above, Jim Sykes takes an oracular stance. There is no doubt left; he feels he *knows* with certainty that the oil is not needed.

Whether we are talking about the sunrise tomorrow or about the need for oil from the Beaufort Sea over the next decade or two, this oracular position is based on making many assumptions about the world which are so deeply buried in our historical bodies that we are not able to make ourselves aware of them, or we are strategically hiding those assumptions from others in a rhetorical move to be persuasive. Needless to say, much political discourse would be plotted at the top end of this knowledge axis, as political discourse frequently takes a stance of certainty toward future events and actions.

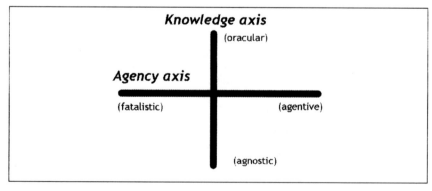

Figure 6.4

At the other end of this knowledge axis is the agnostic position. Here the person takes the position that he or she does not know at all what might happen. In Nuiqsut Paul Stang comments on a question concerning environmental justice in two parts. The first part of the question is whether or not there would be adverse effects on a minority population (the people of Nuiqsut) and the second part is whether or not those would be highly adverse effects. He answers by saying that the MMS recognizes that there would be some effects, but concerning the second issue of whether these would be highly adverse, he says,

> No one really knows until any development proceeds.
>
> (3.1: VII–295)

This statement would be plotted at the far bottom end of the knowledge axis, the agnostic end. Paul Stang does not claim any knowledge about this and goes so far as to suggest that nobody else could have that knowledge either. Of course such an agnostic position, like the extreme opposite oracular position, is based on many assumptions about the world, perhaps never articulated and, like the oracular position, it can be used for strategic purposes. It might indicate a bureaucratic dodge of responsibility or it might indicate a careful assessment of a scientifically supportable conclusion.

In responding to a question in Kaktovik concerning the distance from an oil spill at which negative effects could be measured, the same speaker, Paul Stang, comments,

> Our analysts look at those specific issues and they make their best judgment based on the data that they've got available.
>
> (3.1: VII–326)

Here he takes a much more mitigated and intermediate position, perhaps somewhat toward the middle of the knowledge axis: there is knowledge concerning effects; it is partial; analysts need to use their judgment to make predictions based on this partial knowledge. It is fair to say that the bulk of scientific discourse is positioned about where this statement is positioned. It asserts neither oracular knowledge about the future nor agnostic ignorance of what might occur. It is a 'best informed guess' position.

The modality involved in anticipating the future in discourse is not, however, governed solely by knowledge. The second dimension which is represented by the agency axis represents whether or not it is believed that social actors have the power to influence the outcomes of actions. Again, this varies quite a lot across discourses, persons, and situations. When we go into a restaurant we most likely take a relatively high agentive position – we will decide what we will order – but along with this we take a relatively low knowledge position – we do not know what is possible and so ask for the menu. When we are guests at a formal dinner we are likely to be considerably more fatalistic and assume that it will be a set meal with only the option of eating a prepared dish or leaving it untouched. Concerning the rising of the sun tomorrow, perhaps most humans would take a fatalistic position: whether we do anything or not, or even whether we know for certain that it will rise or not, the sun will do what it is going to do.

The people of Kaktovik prepared what they have called *In this place: A guide for those who would work in the country of the Kaktovikmiut. An unfinished and ongoing work of the people of Kaktovik, Alaska*, which is available on the MMS website as document 1.12.3,b. As part of their general position statement they write,

> Outsiders constantly ask us if we are 'for' or 'against' oil development. These are outsider positions, commitments by outside interests, to be for or against whatever the industry does. Neither makes any sense to us, and we reject them both. How can anybody be for or against something that remains to be defined? Surely oil development is yet to be defined here, its impact on us yet unclear. Nobody else knows and neither do we. Instead, we choose a third path, our own, one that makes sense to us.
>
> This third path, the one we choose, is to be responsible, as we have always been, for the well being of our people and the well being of this country to which we are attached. We expect to control what is done here and how it is done. We also expect to be accountable for our decisions. This is our country, and we cannot allow anyone to come here who would damage it. We shall not permit the country to be harmed nor will we permit our use of it or responsibility for it to be questioned or restricted. Our position is that there will be no damages to our country nor to us but instead that we will control and gain from whatever activity we permit here. We propose in other documents our plans for maintaining that control.
>
> (1.12.3,b:10)

The Kaktovik people set out their position on the knowledge axis in the first paragraph. It is agnostic. They do not know what the impact of these developments on them will be. But then, in the second paragraph, they turn to the agency axis. Here they express no doubt about their agency; they will control their country and what is done in that country. This position would be located at the far right end of the agency axis, but, because of the agnostic view of the future, in the lower right quadrant. It is a position of agnostic agency. 'We do not know but we assert our agency,' summarizes this position.

Perhaps it is obvious that political discourse makes ample use of the agency axis in strategizing positions. As Fairclough and other critical discourse analysts have observed, a rhetorical strategy within neo–liberal discourse is to assert that globalization is absolutely inevitable; there is nothing anyone can do about it other than to position oneself in relationship to it. This neo–liberal discourse achieves its power to persuade through adopting a fatalistic–oracular position, a position in the upper, left hand quadrant in Figure 6.4. 'We know with certainty and there is nothing to be done about it,' summarizes this position. Thus there is a stark contrast between these two positions: globalization is inevitable and there is nothing you can do about it; the impacts of oil development cannot be known in advance but we will control those impacts.

The discursive means for talking about the future and for positioning ourselves as social actors in that future can be located anywhere on this graph. A strong upper left position (fatalistic-oracular) would be expressed as: 'We are certain X will happen, but there is nothing we can do about it.' A strong lower left position (fatalistic-agnostic) would be expressed as: 'We have no idea what will happen, and anyway there is nothing we can do about it.' A strong upper right position (agentive-oracular) would be expressed as: 'We are certain X will happen, and we will do Y about the consequences of that.' A strong lower right position (agentive-agnostic) would be expressed as: 'We have no idea what will happen, but we will be ready to act as soon as we find out.' A PCDA analysis needs to examine where participants and documents position themselves when they make statements in anticipation of future actions.

The concern of this book follows from this: social actors who are located in different discourses as they speak and as they act may profoundly disagree with the actions and motives of others at this level of modality. Both individuals and discourses may take up positions of modality. While the public discourse may be carried out on a surface level of scientific (or bureaucratic or legal) discourse, underlying this discourse is a rock-solid ideological position about the nature of the world, the nature of our knowledge about the world, and the degree of human agency which is thought to be possible in having impacts on the world.

A PCDA may not be able to move social actors from their ideological positions concerning the basis of human actions, but it can and should make it clear how and where different positions are being taken up as part of the process of opening public discourse to a fuller examination of social actions.

Modality in science and politics: global warming

Linguistic modality can be used as a potent tool of political discourse. Scientific discourse, as we noted in Chapters 4 and 5, is cautious in drawing conclusions from experimental data. Conclusions are built on an extended series of studies, each of which more closely refines our understanding of a phenomenon. Scientists insist on cross-checking findings through replication studies and through closely examining research results in review by peers before publication. At the same time, scientists are also very unlikely to make statements that are simply fatalistic or agnostic. Scientists would not be scientists if they took the position that there is nothing we can know and nothing we can do about our world. Science is a discourse within which participants are schooled and credentialed in an ideology of accumulated human knowledge as the basis for careful human action. In terms of modality, then, only when most of the ramifications of a theory have been followed out by experimental data do scientists feel comfortable making either very oracular or very agentive statements.

Our contemporary knowledge of global warming is based on a large body of scientific studies carried out throughout the world by scientists who themselves conduct their research within very different socio-cultural or political environments. It is therefore striking when they come to the widespread agreement they have expressed concerning the imminent danger to life on the earth which global warming threatens. They have further expressed widespread agreement that a major cause of this global warming is under the control of human agency. In a few words the scientific consensus is that, taken together, we are burning too much fossil fuel for the survival of life as we now know it. The position of scientists on global warming is, for science, surprisingly oracular and agentive. Rarely do scientists agree to such a great extent that we actually do know enough about the phenomenon to do something and also that there is something we can and should do.

There are political interests, however, which see the issue from a different ideological position. That position holds a considerably more agnostic and non-agentive position concerning global warming. The position taken is that we do not know much about what causes global warming or even if there is such a phenomenon at all. Further, that position asserts that even if there is some evidence of global warming, it is a purely natural phenomenon about which humans can do nothing. It is not surprising that this is the position taken by a substantial segment of the petroleum industry.

New York Times articles by Andrew C. Revkin in June 2005 tell the story of the whistleblower Rick S. Piltz, Senior Associate, Climate Change Science Program Office of the US government and editor of 'Our Changing Planet', a regular government publication concerning global warming. According to the *New York Times*, as well as subsequent interviews with Piltz, scientific reports made by his agency were regularly edited by a White House staffer, Philip A. Cooney, chief of staff for the White House Council on Environmental Quality. Before joining the White House staff Cooney was a leader in the petroleum industry's aggressive campaign to debunk the concept of global warming through greenhouse gases, gases which result in part from the burning of petroleum products.

An example cited by Revkin shows how Cooney edited Piltz's report 'Our Changing Planet' over time with a steady remodalization that drew the statements into line with Cooney's, the White House's, and the petroleum industry's political ideology concerning global warming.

For example, the following paragraph first appeared in the draft text of October 2002 as follows:

> Warming will also cause reductions in mountain glaciers and advance the timing of the melt of mountain snow packs in polar regions. In turn runoff rates will change and flood potential will be altered in ways that are currently not well understood. There will be significant shifts in the seasonality of runoff that will have serious impacts on native populations that rely on fishing and hunting for their livelihood. These changes will be further

complicated by shifts in precipitation regimes and possible intensification and increased frequency of extreme hydrologic events.

In response to this draft the White House editor, Cooney, made the suggestions to this draft which are indicated below in bold type.

> Warming **would** also cause reductions in mountain glaciers and advance the timing of the melt of mountain snow packs in polar regions. In turn runoff rates **would** change and flood potential **would** be altered in ways that are currently not well understood. There will be significant shifts in the seasonality of runoff that will have serious impacts on native populations that rely on fishing and hunting for their livelihood. These changes will be further complicated by shifts in precipitation regimes and possible intensification and increased frequency of extreme hydrologic events.

The *realis* 'will' was changed to the *irrealis* 'would'. The modal auxiliary 'would' is a conditional. 'If X occurs then Y would occur.' The changes suggested by Cooney leave hanging the 'if' question. Since there is no suggestion of this precondition, the change of *realis* to *irrealis* is a direct shift from a scientific statement of cause and effect – 'Global warming will cause X' – to a non-scientific *irrealis* – 'Global warming would cause X (under unspecified conditions).'

When the public review draft was made available in November of 2002, the lead sentence read,

> Warming **could** also **lead to changes in the water cycle in polar regions. Etc.**

The implied conditional of 'would' is reduced still further to the merely probabilistic 'could'. 'Cause reductions' is reduced to 'lead to changes'. Still further changes occurred throughout the paragraph.

Finally, when the report was published in July of 2003 the entire paragraph was simply deleted. Next to the paragraph had appeared Mr Cooney's comment:

> straying from research strategy into speculative findings/musings here.

'Warming will cause reductions,' becomes 'Warming would cause reductions.' This, then, becomes 'Warming could lead to changes.' That is ultimately followed by full deletion.

Here we can note two things: first, over successive stages this remodalization moves the scientific statement from certainty to a conditional reality, *realis* to *irrealis*. Then, once it is posed as an *irrealis* 'truth' – something that might be true under some unspecific conditions – it is further shifted to merely probable 'truth'. The political discourse can take over at this point by arguing that there is no basis for administration policy to be set on merely probable statements. More studies are needed, stronger scientific evidence is required, the political process of taking action is conveniently deferred. That is the first point.

The second point is important for a PCDA. The editor requiring these revisions in a scientific document is not doing so on the basis of any scientific knowledge or credentials by which he could make a scientific judgment about the *realis/irrealis* status of the scientific statements. His editing is based, rather, on political ideology. But, having said that, Cooney used a common feature of scientific discourse for political purposes. Cooney used the propensity of science to avoid strongly oracular or agentive statements as major political weapon against scientific discourse itself.

Modes and modality

This is where we come to the crucial point: different modes from speaking and writing to gesture and images handle modality (the questions of truth and reality we have just discussed) in different ways. When different constellations of modes come together, as they always do and as we saw so strikingly in the case of the new letterhead for the MMS news releases, the result is a complex kaleidoscope of modality in which the boundaries between truth and reality can be obscured. Whereas in Chapters 4 and 5 we discussed the problem of interdiscursivity – when discourses collide, are woven together, blend, bend, and eclipse each other – here we focus on the problem of multimodality. The problem in discourse is that the use of multiple modes in all communicative expressions gives rise to multiple positions on the truth and reality of what is being communicated. Multimodality as it is used in this book refers both to the fact that all communications occur simultaneously in multiple modes and to the fact that this multimodality produces multiple stances toward truth and reality. Scientists, logicians, and some linguists and lawyers deplore this; politicians, bureaucrats, marketers, and advertisers exploit it to the fullest advantage.

Much of what is needed to analyze the multimodality of the documents of the Beaufort Sea Sale has been said in passing in the preceding chapters. In Chapter 1 we saw that the typeface which is used may differentiate types of documents; a large sanserif typeface is used for the words 'News Release', but a different one may also indicate different portions of a single document. *Federal Register* notices are printed in a serifed typeface but bolded sanserif type is used to segment the document into header, content section, and the concluding *FR* authority for printing. This does not just display the structure of the document, along with the header at the top of the page and the columnar text formatting, it also cues the production format roles of principal, author, and animator as an official US government publication. It is only through these modes of framing (Chapter 3) that we see the binding actional status of these documents.

As we also have observed in Chapter 3, the framing of the discourses which are relevant to the interpretation of a document may be accomplished through different modal configurations. There we noted that the full-color news release header (Figures 1.2, 3.4) framed the contents of the news release within the hegemonic political discourse of the current governmental administration. The common document layout of header and text/content sections can be seen as a visual display of the ideal–real dimension discussed by Kress and van Leeuwen (1996). The upper discourse of US national politics is set up as the 'ideal', while the substance of the news release is presented in the lower 'real' section of the display through which the ideal is realized.

In Chapter 5 we noted that within this upper, 'ideal' graphic banner the organization was what Kress and van Leeuwen call the 'center-margin' composition in which what lies at the very center mediates whatever lies outward toward the margins. In this case it is the US national flag which mediates first relationships among money, the natural environment, and oil development discourses which, in turn, mediate relationships among humans. From this point of view it is worth extending our analysis here by looking at this graphic banner letterhead from the point of view of modality as we have discussed it here in this chapter.

Full-color images tend to be used within discourses where there is a naturalistic orientation to the world as commonly seen by human beings. Naturalistic photography is widely used in discourses such as travel marketing as a way of evoking the sense of personal experience that the viewer is being promised. The photography in this letterhead, while it is in full color, is anything but naturalistic. The US flag which stands in the prominent central position is not the US flag as we ever see it in the day-to-day world. We see it at an angle that exposes only ten or eleven of the stars and just three of the stripes. The margins all around fade under the other images of the collage. Those images themselves are more suggestive than distinct. And, of course, because it is a collage, we are not surprised to see a US Treasury check fully the size of a New Mexico mountain butte. What is important for this analysis is that this is not one or several naturalistic images but an *irrealis* collage that suggests but never states the ideal world of US national politics. Thus, this letterhead doubly suggests an *irrealis* condition, once through the positioning at the top of the page as the 'ideal', not the 'real' portion of the document, and again through the *irrealis* images of the designed collage.

In Chapter 3 we noted that even in 'purely' textual documents, the way a text is laid out on the page produces strikingly different modes for visual images. There we noted the contrast between the running prose text of the *Federal Register* notices and the bullet-pointed text of the Leasing Activities Information memos. When we compared these with the bidding forms and other legally binding documents of the bidding process which are among the most *realis* documents in this process, we saw that while high graphic design might signal the expenditure of a marketing budget, when it comes to actions that value millions of dollars, engage the parties for a minimum period of a decade, and commit national energy and wildlife resources to specific lines of development and exploitation, this is done through a very low level of design with templates, word-processed documents which are to be simply photocopied, the blanks filled in, and delivered to the appropriate person at a specific address.

One might be forgiven for thinking that across the entire set of documents the conclusion would be that in more binding and financially encumbering documents less attention is likely to be paid to questions of mode and design. Conversely, one might come to the conclusion that careful design with full-color decoration signals full-blown *irrealis*; a world of unknown, hypothetical, indefinite or unreal expectations for action.

Modalities of discourse

Modality in communicative modes other than lexicogrammar is not conventionally fixed but varies depending on the discourses within which the modes are used. In this, modality in non-grammatical modes is not so much like the modal auxiliaries ('could', 'should', 'ought') as it is like the example of the two sentences given earlier in this chapter in which 'book' may either be a general, non-specific book ('some book', 'any book') or a specific book ('the one I read a review of' or *War and Peace*) depending on how it is used within a sentence.

We also noted in Chapter 4 that in scientific discourse careful argumentation and careful statement of conclusions means that statements are cautious and hedged. Scientific discourse does not easily or frequently say 'We know that ...', but rather, 'Scientific studies indicate that ...'. Likewise, scientific discourse is primarily presented in the printed textual mode. This mode includes, of course, much use of charts, maps, graphs, and other images, but these decontextualized semiotic modes in scientific discourse are pared down to the highly abstract lines and symbols of an analytical presentation.

To give an illustration of this difference, Figure 6.5 is a photograph taken by the author from the mountain above his hometown of Haines, Alaska. Photos much like this one, shot from exactly this place, appear in full-color travel brochures which advertise vacationing and hiking in this town. As travel advertisements we see them as being 'natural' and 'true' photos of the place.

In this published version the same photo is reproduced in black and white to reduce printing costs which, of course, translate into cover price for the book. Already this change from the mode of color photography to the mode of black and white printing signals a shift in reality status from 'the real place' to 'an image used in academic argument'. It is no less true or false a photograph, but by the same measure that the photograph loses *realis* value as a travel image it gains *realis* status as textbook illustration.

At a much higher degree of abstraction is the image of Haines that one gets from a topographical map of 'the same' view. Here in Figure 6.6 are the same mountains, the same town site, and the same ocean channel and river channel along the sides of the Chilkat Peninsula.

The scientific configuration of topographical cartography has translated the view of the mountain across the horizon into closed, irregular looping lines at fixed elevations. Land forms and sea are separated by outlines of the land forms

Figure 6.5

and different shadings of gray. Further, the entire viewpoint is oriented so that north is squared to the top of the page, in contrast to the photography, which takes the point of view of the hiker on the mountain who is looking south, down the Chilkat Peninsula. This, of course, is again very different from the perspective one would get from a bullet-pointed textual description you might find in a Chamber of Commerce fact sheet:

Haines and the Chilkat Peninsula

- Small, compact townsite (pop. 1811)
- High, relatively trackless mountains
- Glaciers
- Ocean
- Deep river valley

Like the difference between color and black and white modes, these differences among photographic, cartographic, and textual modes are not inherently tied to modality; that is, we cannot say independently of the discourse within which it is used that any one of these images is *realis* or any of them is *irrealis*. This can only be determined within a specific discourse and within its organizing purposes. The discourse of travel advertising generally works within the

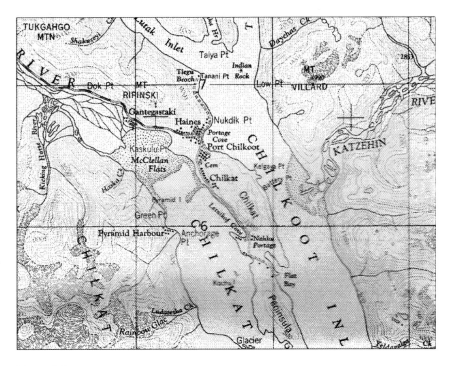

Figure 6.6

purpose of enticing the viewer to want to think in terms of the personal experience he or she will enjoy, and so full-color images taken on nice days have a
realis status within this discourse and for this purpose. Within cartographic
discourse the very different goal is to factor out all kinds of irrelevant detail so
that the view can focus on land forms and elevations (among other things).
Within that discourse and for that purpose the topographical sheet of Haines in
Figure 6.6 has *realis* status.

Modes, modality, and interdiscursivity

No mode of communication can automatically convert knowledge or information
from another mode. Consequently, if there is a predominance of one or very few
modes in a discourse or in a sequence of documents, it must be asked what modes
are missing and what knowledge or information or even whole discourses this is
obscuring. The public record of the multiple sale process for oil and gas leases is an
extended series of documents that runs to thousands of pages, as we have noted.
Among those thousands of pages relatively few modes beyond text and the corresponding scientific/bureaucratic modes of graphs, charts, and tables are found.
What's missing?

The public hearing that was held in Barrow on 1 August 2002 was held in the Iñupiaq Heritage Center in Barrow. The MMS has posted no photographs of the public hearings, though perhaps some are available in its archives. As far as the process of public consultation is concerned, only the written transcripts are considered relevant to the process. The photos in Figure 6.7 were taken in the same room in the Iñupiaq Heritage Center a year or so before the hearing, but these are not public hearings. We see a birthday party for a one-year-old boy, a college graduation ceremony, visiting Eskimo dancers at the State Library Conference, and a student art display.

In the documents and in the transcript of the Barrow hearing itself we have seen there is much blending of the discourses of science, energy development, and traditional knowledge as well as other interdiscursivities, but this interdiscursivity is presented largely in the form of print-text statements. In this photograph we also see some of these same blends. For example, the baby's grandfather is a whaler, an artist, and a teacher of carving. His grandmother is a mathematics teacher in the elementary school. His father is a counselor in the high school and a hunter.

While it is almost invisible to the eyes of people who do not live there, the most striking blend, perhaps, is lodged in the room itself and the building which encloses it. The Iñupiat Heritage Center was opened in 1999 after ten years of planning. It both houses permanent installations ranging from traditional whaling to global warming and is used constantly for activities from dances, conferences, and graduations to birthday parties, as shown in Figure 6.7. While the discourse of oil extraction is backgrounded in all of this – there are no exhibitions about the role of the oil industry in shaping traditional and

Figure 6.7

contemporary life in Barrow or on the North Slope – both the North Slope Borough itself and this building are direct outcomes of the fossil fuel industry. The North Slope Borough arose in 1972 as part of a complex political response to Alaska statehood and to the development of the oil field at Prudhoe Bay. Its area of 88,000 square miles makes it the largest municipal government in the world – slightly smaller than the UK, larger than Austria and Hungary combined, about the same size as the Korean Peninsula or the US State of Minnesota – even though there are just 6,290 or so residents.

Now the majority of the residents live in homes of a style imported from the temperate zone of the south but which have been adapted to Arctic conditions. Meeting the vision of Eben Hopson for the North Slope Borough that its residents have the same basic services and infrastructure as other Americans, the Iñupiat Heritage Center is a large, centrally heated building with large open spaces which, like the homes and other buildings of Barrow, is enabled both by the burning of fossil fuels (mostly natural gas) as its source of heat but also by the oil-fueled transportation system which has brought these materials to the Arctic Coast of Alaska by plane. As the website of the North Slope Borough notes, the borough is

> home to resources like oil and gas, which have enabled our people, the Iñupiat, to enter the cash economy of the modern world with self-determination and an enduring respect for the survival skills taught to us by our ancestors.
>
> (http://www.north-slope.org/nsb/default.htm)

In a sense one could say that the discourse of oil extraction underwrites pretty much all of the infrastructure of the North Slope Borough and of Barrow, including the Iñupiat Heritage Center. This profound underwriting interdiscursivity of the discourse of oil and gas extraction with the support and sustenance of traditional whaling, as well as many other community discourses of schooling, and even religion, is visible wherever one might go in the community.

This interdiscursivity is captured in a photo such as that in Figure 6.7. We can compare, then, two views of these interdiscursivities. The first is the view of these discourses and how they relate to each other that we might get by reading the documents of the Beaufort Sea Sales. This has been the view that has been discussed at length in Chapters 4 and 5. The second is the view, really just a glimpse, that we get through a photographic collage of events in the community center in Barrow. This shift in modes makes it clear that whatever else might be said about the substance of the proposal to sell oil and gas leases in this particular way at this particular time, it is said against a background of not just dependence but active community support and ratification of the role of the petroleum industry in the development of the community, its political structure, and even its traditional whaling culture.

There is a large and rapidly growing research literature on multimodality covering face-to-face communication, visual images, objects and the built environment. This example shows that while a linguistic basis for discourse analysis can be very fruitful, it should never be assumed to be showing us the whole picture. The documents of the Beaufort Sea Sale give us a particular view of the process of the sale which includes the texts of the public hearing. But the documents themselves present us with a distinctively text-based view of this process. As we have noted first in Chapters 4 and 5, and now here, such a text-based modality is a view of reality that can be located in the discourses of science, law, and government. Presenting the multiple sale process as a matter of texts produces an eclipsing modality, a version of *realis* that claims that only text does or can present the reality of that sale. This *realis* eclipses all other views of the process which might be achieved by viewing the process through other modes, including images, face-to-face communication, song, or actional experience.

A PCDA cannot do everything, of course. By the definition that has been adopted in this book a PCDA deals with an analysis of what are mostly texts. A PCDA probably cannot and should not try to move beyond this remit. Still, one needs to do mostly as we have done here – conduct a sub-analysis within the analysis of framing, discourses and interdiscursivity, and document types. Special attention needs to be given, however, to the likelihood of interdiscursive blending, bending, and eclipsing that occurs with the text-based mode of a documentary analysis. One essential aspect of any analysis is to ask: what are we not seeing or hearing or otherwise perceiving in the documents under analysis? What modes are not present in the documents? How is our analytical perception of *realis/irrealis* being bent through transporting other discourses or other modal presentations of discourses into text-based documentation?

The ways in which a PCDA can make use of multimodal discourse analysis can be summarized with four points:

- Modality is conveyed differently within the 'grammar' of each mode,.
- The modality of a particular mode is not fixed or inherent but varies with the discourse and the communicative purpose.
- When communications occur across discourses, the modality (*realis/irrealis* status) of communication may become distorted either unwittingly or as a strategy to achieve political ascendancy.
- The guiding analytical question is: what's missing? What is absent from the analysis because that knowledge or information is predominantly available in a different mode, and what might we see if it were presented in another way?

PRACTICE

The activities of previous chapters have been mainly concerned with the analyses of texts in your public consultation documents. Our concern here is somewhat more difficult to prepare activities for because when we deal with modality we are more often focused on what is *not* said, what is *not* pictured, or what is *not* presupposed so that we can see the modality of what the documents actually say and do.

Activity 1:
Document types, discourses and images

ASSIGNMENT

Collect all images you can find in your documents, including image-dominant documents such as brochures and website mastheads, and illustrations in text-dominant documents. It is recommended that you take screenshots of each image using the method described in the practice section of Chapter 3 and gather all images in one folder.

Draw a table with the document types you have identified in Chapter 5 in the top row and the discourses you have identified in the left-most column. In the cells of the table, write down the number and types of images.

Observations

By drawing a table like the one above you should be able to notice how images weave multiple discourses into a type of document and how the status of discourses shifts across different documents. Note which documents or document types favor images over text or which blend images and text. Note also which discourses favor which kinds of multimodal configurations.

Activity 2:
Placing images on the knowledge–agency axes

Images, like lexicogrammatical features, can also convey statements oriented towards events in the future. A brochure concerning genetically modified food products may show international aid workers distributing food to victims of a natural catastrophe such as an earthquake or a tidal wave and thus suggest through the *realis* mode of color photography that this is the future outcome toward which the science is directed.

ASSIGNMENT

In each of the images you have found in your documents examine where you would place the image on the knowledge–agency axes.

Write a short analysis of several of the images, giving your reasons for the placement you have made.

Observations

It may be important in doing this activity to also analyze any contrasts between the graphic images and the texts which they accompany. It is often the case that images will establish one position but the text will establish a different one.

Activity 3:
Looking for the missing

As pointed out at the end of this chapter, the central question is to ask what is missing from the public consultative documents under analysis – what is being obscured.

ASSIGNMENT

Take your camera out or look around on the internet. Some of the missing parts of the process can be found from other sources. If you are lucky enough to be in the vicinity where the public consultation of the issue takes place, take your camera out onto the streets or even attend some of the public hearings, if there are any. Take pictures of anything related to the public consultation process you are studying.

If you are not able to shoot the photos yourself, you can try asking friends living in the region to help you to take some pictures. The internet is, again, another good source for this task. You may be able to find pictures of the consultation process on the official website or in the related news stories

Write a two-page analysis of what is missing from the official documents concerning the consultation. Be sure to include practical suggestions as to how these absences could be remedied.

Observations

It is relatively easy to point to absences since, in a way, everything that is not in the official documents is missing. But it is important also to think of practical considerations. Color photography greatly increases the cost of published documents. Color on the internet is not a problem but the many images or larger images increase the bandwidth required and increase download times for many users.

7   Documents to mediate action (PCDA)

Tips on taking part in consultations

Be brief
Focus on what is really important to you
Provide evidence
Send your response as soon as possible
Reply to the questions
Say who you are

(www.consultations.gov.uk)

Doing a PCDA

The 'Tips on taking part in consultations' posted on the UK Government Public Consultations website say to 'be brief'. This is always good advice, but how to do it? The six chapters which make up the bulk of this book have given an analysis of the documents for just the first two sales of the Beaufort Sea Multiple Sales process. At the time of writing, a further 'Call for Information and Notice of Intent (NOI) to prepare an Environmental Assessment' was just issued for Sale 202. Where does the discourse analyst draw the line? How many documents need to be analyzed? How much of the analysis needs to be presented within the consultation? The amount of analysis will almost always exceed the space allowed for commentary, so how can the analysis be summarized to fit the Procrustean bed of the public consultation process?

Not surprisingly, the answers to these questions will depend upon the specific consultation in which your PCDA is taking part. This chapter will cover four points which will help you focus your PCDA as a mediational means for taking the specific action of providing written testimony or comments within the consultative process.

First, this chapter gives a section on consultations and contacts which will show you where to go to begin finding a consultation for your own PCDA as well as steps you can take in the process of starting up your own study. The second section is an outline of questions which might be used in guiding a

PCDA. This outline includes suggestions for aspects of a discourse analysis which were not covered in this case but which might be very important in other cases. The third section of this chapter presents suggestions, along the lines of those given on the UK Public Consultations website for actually preparing a submission in a public consultation. Finally, in the fourth section the chapter comments on the dialectic and unfinalizable nature of PCDA.

Consultations and contacts for your own PCDA

Finding a public consultation

Public consultations are conducted in many countries or regions of the world. These cover a vast range of topics you can choose from. The list below gives just some of the regular consultation websites you could review for finding a project to work on. The URL addresses have been checked and are valid at the time of publication, but of course it is possible that they may change.

> Canada: Consulting with Canadians
> http://www.consultingcanadians.gc.ca/

> Europe: Your Voice in Europe
> http://europa.eu.int/yourvoice/

> Hong Kong: Consultation Papers
> http://www.info.gov.hk/policy_f.htm

> New Zealand: Submissions to Select Committees in the Parliament
> http://www. clerk.parliament.govt.nz/Programme/ Committees/
> Submissions/

> Singapore: Feedback Unit, Government Consultation Portal
> http://app.feedback.gov.sg/asp/

> South Africa: Documents for Public Comment
> http://www.info.gov.za/documents/comment.htm

> UK: UK Government Public Consultation Documents
> http://www.consultations.gov.uk/

> US: Your One-Stop Site to Comment on Federal Regulations
> http://www.regulations.gov/

A number of countries and regions, such as those listed above, have web portals containing links to current and past public consultations, arranged according to dates, subjects, and/or government agencies. For other countries, such as Australia, consultation documents can usually be found on the website of the directly involved department. For example, the Department of Education and Training of Victoria, Australia, hosts its own consultation documents at http://www.det. vic.gov.au/det/ consultation/default.htm.

The term 'public consultation' has been used in this book to cover all types of dialogues between agencies, mostly government agencies, and the public on issues and policies of the agency. This term is used in Canada, Europe, the United Kingdom, Hong Kong and the United States. In the US, however, 'public hearing' is also often used. A very similar process is referred to as 'public comment' in South Africa. In Singapore, the feedback unit is responsible for 'government consultations'. 'Public comment', 'public hearings' and 'public consultations' are used in Australia. In New Zealand, 'public input' and 'public hearings' are used. If you are looking for a project in some other political jurisdiction you should try searching on several of these terms until you discover the most common term for that jurisdiction.

You should always check to see that you are using the appropriate terminology for the jurisdiction you are researching. For example, in the US, an EIS is an 'environmental impact statement', an EA an 'environmental assessment'. An EIS is mandated by the NEPA (National Environmental Protection Act). The law which corresponds to NEPA in Australia is the EPBC Act (the Environment Protection and Biodiversity Conservation Act). Canada has CEPA (Canadian Environmental Protection Act). Japan has the Basic Environment Law and the Environmental Impact Assessment Law. In South Africa, there is the ECA (Environment Conservation Act). India has the Environment Impact Assessment Notification. China has the People's Republic of China Environmental Protection Law and also the People's Republic of China Environmental Impact Assessment Law. The European Union has the Environmental Law implemented and enforced by IMPEL (Implementation and Enforcement of the Environmental Law).

Locating an issue for your PCDA

To start collecting information for your PCDA project you will first need to identify the issue you are interested in. The best place to start is with your own interests and concerns. If you have a clear idea in mind, you can move directly to your topic by conducting an internet or library search using keywords such as 'global warming', or 'genetically modified foods'. If you do not yet have a clear idea of what you want to study, you can browse the public consultation sites listed above. This can be done in any of the following ways:

- Start from general internet search engines, such as Google. It is recommended that you use the 'advanced search' option. This allows you to combine several keywords using Boolean logic, for example, 'public consultations' and 'Thailand', or 'environment' and 'India' and 'public consultations'. Browse through the results and locate a key website which contains the most essential information on the issue intriguing you.

- If you know which country or region you are interested in, you can also start from a government portal website, such as one of those in the above list. Browse through the topics and find the issue you will be focusing on.
- If you are looking for a case which has garnered much media attention, you can start by searching in the archives of newspapers. Most major newspapers have online archives available, although some may charge for past articles. Again, if you have a specific place in mind, look for the local newspaper. For example, if you are interested in a certain public consultation process in New Zealand, you are more likely to find information in the *New Zealand Herald* than in the *Washington Post*.
- The websites of NGOs are also good starting points. Many NGOs play an active role in public consultation processes and have their 'stories' available online.

Two technical notes might be helpful in this searching:

- Bookmark every web page you come across in which y听证会ave even a small interest. Some may not show up again during your next search. Before settling down on a specific issue, you can put all bookmarks under a bookmark folder named, for example, 'PCDA'. After picking the case of your choice, that is, from the next step on, you may find it easier to put all bookmarks related to the issue under a sub-bookmark folder named according to the topic, for example, 'Seattle Monorail'.
- Also try searching for keywords using the language used in the country or region, which you are interested in. For example, searching for '   ' ('public hearing' in Chinese) will give you more results than searching for 'public hearings in China'.

Identifying the stakeholders

After locating the issue, you can focus on the information provided by the key website and make a list of the multiple stakeholders involved in the issue. Then look for the websites or other publications of these other stakeholders and read how they represent the issue online. For example, the public consultation about a proposal to host the V8 Street Car Race in Wellington, New Zealand, not only involves the City Council, but also the Australian company AVESCO, which is behind the race, residents in Wellington, competing cities, and V8 fans in New Zealand. Hot issues are also often reported in local newspapers.

Collecting documents

Once you have bookmarked almost all of the web pages related to the issue, the next step is to download any document (in .pdf, .doc, or other formats) you can find from those web pages. This step is necessary because, although you have bookmarked the web pages, you have not saved them onto your computer. Documents have often disappeared when you visit the website the next time, or they may have been modified. That process of modification may in itself be useful for your analysis in order to see how the producing agency is altering its perspective on the issue or its participants over time. For newspaper articles, you may find it easier to copy and paste the article into a word-processing document than to download the entire web page. Also remember to copy and paste the URL as well as the date and time of access along with the article, for future reference. Conventional citation practices are just developing for citing online research but most publishers' formats require these three elements.

A few examples

A stunning variety of consultations is available throughout the world at almost any time. Here are just a few which were going on at the time of writing. They are listed by topic and URL.

London Congestion Charge
http://www.tfl.gov.uk/tfl/cc-ex/index.shtml

Seattle Monorail
http://www.monorailontrack.org/

Hong Kong 2030
http://www.info.gov.hk/hk2030/

Kemess North Copper-Gold Mine Project, British Columbia, Canada
http://www.ceaa-acee.gc.ca/050/DocHTML
container_e.cfm?DocumentID=9079

Water Allocation Reform in South Africa
http://www.info.gov.za/documents/comment.htm

*scape in Singapore
http://app.feedback.gov.sg/scape/

Australia's Demographic Challenges
http://demographics.treasury.gov.au/content/
consultations.asp?NavID=7

Once you have reached this stage you will have identified an issue, and a public consultation which involves that issue. You will also now have a fairly full set of documents you can work with for your analysis. You should be especially focused on the deadline and the means of submitting your response and be certain to complete your analysis and submit it within the deadline. As the UK 'Tips on taking part in consultations' notes, and as we will discuss below on writing your PCDA, it is not a good idea to submit at the very last minute. There is a much better chance of your analysis being examined carefully if the receiving agency has had the time to read it.

Outline guide for conducting a PCDA

Focus on action

Your analysis should focus on two kinds of action: their actions and your own. What actions are considered in this consultation? Is it holding a car race, drilling an oil well, selling a GMO product in a national market, or opening up a gold mine? How will your action of analyzing the documents and submitting a PCDA impact those actions? An analysis that makes many interesting points as a discourse analysis would not qualify as a PCDA if it was not clear to all participants what actions it would require or enable or inhibit.

The discourse analyses presented in this book have worked, in a sense, from the inside outward. We began with a focus on theory and defined the terms 'historical body', 'interaction order', and 'discourses in place' in Chapter 2. In Chapter 3 the focus then moved to the representation of action in discourse, summarization, framing, and synchronization. In that analysis we did not take up a number of areas that are commonly examined in discourse analysis. We did not, for example, look into the representation of social actors, which has been a highly productive area of critical discourse analysis. We also did not take up a number of other themes such as are treated in Fairclough's (2003) book on textual analysis in social research. Further, we paid scant attention to central topics in discourse analysis such as how cohesion (what holds a text together) and coherence (unity, topic, and message) are accomplished in texts or how narrative texts differ from descriptive ones.

The choice of topics and the kind of analyses used in the case study of the MMS Beaufort Sea Multiple Sales emerged out of the documents and out of the needs of that consultation itself. In many cases it would be very useful, indeed necessary, for your analysis to examine the inner workings of the language of the documents themselves. Because such discourse analysis is so excellently represented in the literature and journals on discourse analysis, here it has seemed unnecessary to reiterate that literature.

While this book has presented the analysis as an unfolding outward from language to discourses, to document structures, to modality, in many ways this is the opposite direction from that in which the work actually took place. In what follows, then, it is suggested that you work in the opposite direction in your analysis. You should always be guided by your focus on action, as this gives you the test of relevance for your analysis.

Begin with the issue and the documents

What is the issue upon which you are focused? Who are the participants/stake-holders? How are they identified? Is it the same issue for all stakeholders? If not, how is the issue treated differently? For example, for the communities of the North Slope of Alaska the issue is exploration, drilling, and development *offshore* in the ocean. For the environmental opposition to the sales the issue is *any drilling at all* in the region, either offshore or onshore. For the MMS the issue is following out their mandate to explore and develop US internal energy resources on the outer continental shelf surrounding the US. In almost all cases 'an issue' will really be a nexus of related issues and much of the discourse of the consultation will be bending and blending discourses to try to shift the definition of 'the issue' to suit the goals and purposes of the participant or stakeholder. Modality is a central issue as stakeholders try to assert what is 'really' at issue from their own point of view.

Your initial explorations in setting up your study, which we outlined in the previous section, will have already answered many of these questions and so your analysis has already begun. The crucial questions from a discourse analysis perspective are: how are these differences among stakeholders expressed? How do differences on the definition of the issue place different participants in different positions for action? As we have seen, the MMS is restricted by Federal law concerning the EIS process to take public testimony only on matters having to do with the EIS, not with the broad sociopolitical issue of US energy resources. Framing the issue in this way enables them to limit political discourse to only the discourse of science. This leads to the bending of science to political purposes. This is the sort of concern you should have in mind as you analyze the different stakeholders and their positions concerning the nexus of issues you have identified.

What are the documents? You should already have an extended list of documents. You will already have seen that they are quite different in purpose, in design, in audience and so they are also different in the actions they enable or inhibit. The surest guide to these functional differences in the documents is the design of the document. Put quite roughly, the ones that look the same are probably also functionally very much in the same category. This must be tested, of course, but you probably already have a fairly good idea of which documents fall into which categories.

Once the documents are categorized, pick a typical example of each to analyze. Of course you want to be certain the document you are analyzing is typical, so be sure to cross-check and contrast among documents that appear to be similar or have similar functions. Here, as always, the concern is with the actions that can be carried out with the documents and the participants for whom this enabling of action occurs.

When you have a fairly clear analysis of *what* the documents are doing you need to then ask yourself *how* the documents do this. In the case study examined in this book, we saw that *what documents do* mostly had to do with the participant structure of the production and reception roles of the document. This was often, but not always, done through a combination of language and document design. In any case you will need to know about each document type how author, animator, and principal are established and also what reception roles (principal, interpreter, handler, or bystander) are indicated.

By the time you have worked through these typical document types you will have seen the main discourses which are circulating in the documents. For each of these discourses lay out a chart which indicates who is an authorized or credentialized participant and how this participation is accomplished (university courses or lifetime experiences, for example). Examine how agency works within this discourse. Critical discourse analysis is particularly important for this analysis, especially studies in the representation of social actors. What specific lexicogrammatical forms are characteristic of each discourse? Are there special buzzwords that are used by participants but not very well known to outsiders? Are there technical terms or grammatical structures that only participants feel comfortable using? That is, do participants 'sound' like proper participants? You also want to examine argument structures. These will range from the hypothetico-deductive logical structure of science to the wide-open structures of rhetorical argument in political discourse. Here the large literature on English (and other languages) for Special Purposes is very helpful.

Finally, it is important to see if there are specific genres or modes which are characteristic of any of the discourses you have identified. In the MMS documents there were no examples at all of any use of or reference to music. In a PCDA concerning world poverty, in contrast, it would be difficult not to include the role of world-famous musicians and their music in publicizing this issue.

It will be impossible to distinguish and analyze the discourses involved in your documents without analyzing how they might be instantiated in 'pure' cases – a very rare occurrence – and how they are blended, bent, or eclipsed. Of course, as we have seen, this bending or blending of discourses cannot be analyzed without also examining the participants who are doing this and their overall purposes. Specific tools for mixing discourses or for accomplishing other goals in discourse are summarization, framing, and synchronization. The public hearings on the EIS which we have looked at in this book, for example, were synchronized by the MMS as 'being about' (and only being about) the science of the EIS. For other participants other cycles such as annual cultural subsistence hunting cycles were central to their understanding of the process.

Finally, a public consultative process is inherently focused on future actions. This makes it useful to examine the positions of stakeholders as anticipatory discourse. What are the stakeholder positions on human agency? Are they highly fatalistic or highly agentive or, perhaps, located in a moderate position? What is their position concerning the action at the heart of the issue you are studying? Is this importantly different from their position in other cases. What are stakeholder positions on human knowledge – oracular or agnostic? Do they treat the future of this issue as known with certainty or do they approach it with doubt? Each stakeholder can be positioned on the chart given in Figure 6.3 and this will provide much insight about ways in which participants will disagree or even fail to communicate with each other.

Keeping the focus on action throughout your analysis will make sure you are not drifting too far from your goal of producing a timely PCDA that can be entered into the public consultative process. Using the tripartite structure of participants (historical bodies), social interactions (interaction order), and documents (discourses in place) will give you a framework for asking the basic questions about human action: who is doing what and how is this process enabling them to do it?

Writing a PCDA

The 'Tips on taking part in consultations' posted on the UK Government Public Consultations website (www.consultations.gov.uk) could hardly be improved upon in general terms:

- Be brief
- Focus on what is really important to you
- Provide evidence
- Send your response as soon as possible
- Reply to the questions
- Say who you are

On that website each of these points is expanded with further clarifications and you would do well to consult that source and other similar ones for ideas on how to prepare a statement.

Public consultations vary widely in the responses which are expected or acceptable. Some of them are little more than public opinion polls in which the only responses which will be accepted are ticks in one of two boxes. Some have a small online form in addition to this which allows a little more commentary but still this is just a paragraph or so. And then others at the opposite extreme, such as the MMS public hearings on the EIS, are open-ended, stating only that in spoken public testimony a limit of ten minutes may be set if it appears that there are many people wishing to speak.

Most public consultations allow or even prefer written testimony. That seems advisable wherever it is allowed for two reasons: written testimony usually requires more careful thought about the line of argument and this guarantees that you will have your own copy of your contribution which is identical to what you have submitted. This could be crucial in evaluating the responses of the agency to your submission.

A written submission also has the advantage of allowing you more space (usually) than spoken testimony or online submissions. It is also common to allow written submissions to include enclosures. As the 'Tips' website suggests, it is best to actually send hard copy of any documentary evidence or elaborations on your analysis rather than to simply give a URL or reference to where it can be found. It is to your advantage to make it as easy as possible for the over-worked office personnel and officials who need to see your contribution to have everything in hand that they need to make sense of your submission.

When you actually write up the analysis, remember to focus your attention on your reader. What does someone need to know in order to make sense of your argument? You should never assume knowledge of your field of expertise, but at the same time you should not try to give a mini-dissertation in your field before getting to your main point. It is always a useful learning experience to restate an analysis which has been made within a discipline for readers or listeners who come to it without knowing the jargon and argument structures of your field.

Perhaps the most common error in writing an analysis is to simply write a narrative of your own path of discovery. First I did X, then I did Y, and finally discovered that Z. Tell them your conclusion, your Z, right at the start. The reader may go no further because of constraints on time or interest but at least will have read your main point.

A response of about 1,000–1,500 words in length will fit on three sheets of common printer paper. With a cover letter of one more page, this submission would take four sheets. This should be considered a maximum length in most cases. The sections given below can serve as a guide for your own PCDA:

- Summary: state your conclusions in this section. While the rest may be read, it will be this summary to which readers will return when they summarize responses for their own actions within the agency.
- Background: state what you actually did to make your analysis. Be sure to make it clear just how much (or how little) coverage your analysis gives.
- Analysis: state your analysis as succinctly as possible. Here you want to be sure that another reader who had your same data in its extended form would come to these same conclusions. To put this another way, avoid simply ideological statements of your own position on the issue. This is a PCDA and should limit itself to what a discourse analysis allows you to say. Part of that is to say what you are not able to support or substantiate with your analysis.
- Recommendations: state the actions which you believe stakeholders should take, based upon your analysis. These actions could focus on your analysis and recommend that a further analysis should be done (and what questions should be addressed) or focus on the central action(s) of the consultation.
- Documentation: state any places where this analysis, especially in fuller form, is published. Attach any of these documents which you have available.

Your analysis should be submitted with a cover letter – no more than one page – in which you identify yourself and give full contact details. Here it is important to make it clear what stakeholder constituency you belong in, if any.

You can also use the cover letter to clarify the status of your submission. You should say whether you are submitting your contribution as a private citizen or as the representative of a group. Some consultations will summarize individual contributions and only give responses to contributions from established organizations. If your submission is from such an organization, be sure it is clear what kind of group this is and, preferably, give the contact information such as a postal address or the URL for the organization's website. You should also make clear what kind of a contribution you are making. It is a discourse analysis and since this term is quite unlikely to be well known to readers in the agency to which you are sending your contribution, it might be well not to specifically call it a discourse analysis but rather an analysis of the language of the documents or an analysis of communication among stakeholders. You should also state your qualifications for making such an analysis.

You will have chosen the issue and the consultation you are involved in because of your own interests and your own sociopolitical positions and ideology. In that sense you are deploying the tools of a discourse analysis for a specific purpose. You want to affect the outcomes of the consultation toward accomplishing some action(s) and restricting other action(s). The first task, then, before doing any of the rest of this is to examine your own position and your own ideology. What actions do you want to see as an outcome of the process and why do you want to see them? Critical discourse analysis and mediated discourse analysis are not value-free academic exercises. They take the position that it is not only appropriate but necessary to use discourse analysis to address issues of social importance to our society. They further take the position that we seek social change toward democratic social justice. From the beginning and throughout your PCDA you should continue to examine your own position, know how it is developing and changing as a result of your analysis, and when you prepare your PCDA for submission you should be clear in your own mind what outcomes you are seeking to achieve. It is this knowledge which will enable you to focus your contribution to the public discourse.

An alternative route

This book is directed toward building a direct engagement with the public consultation process. Now, at the point of concluding, there are two final suggestions that may also be useful to you in developing a PCDA along an alternative route that runs outside of but parallel to a formal public consultation:

1   Begin a blog for your PCDA.
2   Make a website for the issue you are concerned with.

Neither of these suggestions necessarily excludes direct engagement in the process of public consultation, of course. As I have noted above, many agencies which conduct public consultations prefer representations to come from organizations rather than from individuals. In that case an established website gives a certain degree of organizational status to your submission. From there it is quite a natural step to use that website as a springboard for multiple users to engage in several related consultations.

By the same token, some agencies prefer individual submissions. Among current media possibilities the blog is one of the richest means for carrying on a continuing discussion of ideas, testing out your thoughts and analysis, and getting feedback on them. Whether your blog results in a direct engagement as a PCDA as described here or runs a separate course, it is quite likely that whatever agency you are responding to will find it useful to visit your blog to see the range of commentary.

Unfinalizability in PCDA

A PCDA is not the 'last word' but rather the beginning of an active dialogue. As a new stakeholder in the process you are seeking to become engaged with the other stakeholders. You will have in mind that your contribution may change their anticipated actions. You should remain acutely aware as well that their contributions may also change your actions and your position. This is the nature of democratic public discourse: positions are stated, positions are argued, positions are negotiated, and the actions which are taken and which become policy and practice are the outcome of this dialectic. As a public consultative discourse analyst you do not stand outside of and away from this process. You are part of the dialectic.

Appendix

Document type listing for Beaufort Sea – Multiple Sales 186, 195, and 202
http://www.mms.gov/alaska/cproject/beaufortsale/index.htm.

Date	Number	Document name	Genre/text type
19 Sep 2001	0.1*	Outer Continental Shelf (OCS), Alaska Region, Beaufort Sea, Oil and Gas Lease Sales 186, 195, 202 for Years 2003, 2005, 2007	*Federal Register* notice★★★
19 Sep 2001	1.1	News Release – MMS Announces Multiple Sale Process – Alaska's Beaufort Sea	News release
11 Mar 2005	Periodic update	Beaufort Sea – Multiple Sales 186, 195, and 202	Web page
8 Mar 2005	Periodic update	Alaska Lease Sales Schedule	Web page
Jun 2002	1.2	Executive Summary – Beaufort Sea Planning Area, Sales 186, 195, and 202 (DEIS) – Inupiaaq Translation	Executive summary
30 Jul 2002	1.3	Beaufort Sea Public Hearings on the Draft Environmental Impact Statement for Sales 186, 195, and 202	Transcript of spoken discourse
Sep 2002	1.4	Oil-Spill Risk Analysis: Beaufort Sea Planning Area, Sales 186, 195, and 202	OSRA (scientific analysis, complex of genres)
Feb 2003	1.5	Beaufort Sea Multiple Sale Final Environmental Impact Statement OCS EIS/EA MMS 2003-001	FEIS (scientific analysis, complex of genres); PDF file
20 Feb 2003	1.6	Royalty Suspension Provisions – Beaufort Sea Oil and Gas Lease Sale 186	Leasing Activities Information memo

Date	Number	Document name	Genre/text type
20 Feb 2003	1.7	Proposed Notice of Sale – Beaufort Sea Oil and Gas Lease Sale 186	Leasing Activities Information memo
20 Feb 2003	1.8	Executive Summary, Final Environmental Impact Statement – Beaufort Sea Planning Area, Sales 186, 195, and 202 – Inupiaaq Translation	Executive summary
13 May 2003	1.9	Official Protraction Diagrams and Block List included in Proposed Notice of Sale – Beaufort Sea Oil and Gas Sale 186	Leasing Activities Information memo with charts, maps
17 Jul 2003	1.10	Notice of Proposed Intent to Reduce Minimum Bid Requirements and Set Sliding-Scale Rentals for Proposed Beaufort Sea OCS Oil and Gas Lease Sale 186	*Federal Register* notice
21 Aug 2003	1.11	Area Map Beaufort Sea Sale 186	Map
21 Aug 2003	1.12	Final Notice of Sale 186 Package	Web package directory
	1.12.1	Notice of Sale – Beaufort Sea Oil and Gas Lease Sale 186	Leasing Activities Information memo: includes *Federal Register* notice, map
	1.12.2	Lease Stipulations for Oil and Gas Lease Sale 186 – Beaufort Sea, 24 September 2003	Leasing Activities Information memo
	1.12.3	Information to Lessees for Oil and Gas Lease Sale 186 – Beaufort Sea, 24 September 2003	Leasing Activities Information memo: 26 attachments
	1.12.4	Royalty Suspension Provisions, Sale 186	Leasing Activities Information memo
	1.12.5	Blocks Available for Leasing Oil and Gas Lease Sale 1: Beaufort Sea – 24 September 2003	Leasing Activities Information memo
	1.12.6	Debarment Certification Information and Form	Leasing Activities Information memo
	1.12.7	Bid Form and Envelope	Leasing Activities Information memo
	1.12.8	Bid Submission Form	Bid submission form
	1.12.9	Instructions for Making EFT Bonus Payments	Leasing Activities Information memo
21 Aug 2003	1.13	Final Notice of Sale – Beaufort Sea Oil and Gas Lease Sale 186	*Federal Register* notice

Date	Number	Document name	Genre/text type
8 Sep 2003	1.14	Changes to Final Notice of Sale – Beaufort Sea Oil and Gas Lease Sale 186	Leasing Activities Information memo
24 Sep 2003	1.15	Sale 186 Bid Recap, Statistics, Analysis	Summary charts
16 Dec 2003	2.1	News Release – MMS Announces Request for Information	News release
16 Dec 2003	2.2	Request for Information – Beaufort Sea Oil and Gas Lease Sale 195, March 2005	*Federal Register* notice
30 Jan 2004	2.3	Beaufort Sea Current Leased Blocks	Map
26 Jul 2004	2.4	Finding of No Significant Impacts	Letter with signature
26 Jul 2004	2.5	Environmental Assessment – Proposed Oil and Gas Lease Sale 195 Beaufort Sea Planning Area	EA (scientific analysis, complex of genres)
26 Jul 2004	2.6	Notice of Availability of an Environmental Assessment (EA) and Finding of No Significant Impact (FONSI)	*Federal Register* notice
18 Oct 2004	2.7	Proposed Notice of Sale – Beaufort Sea Oil and Gas Lease Sale 196	Leasing Activities Information memo: many attachments (cf. 1.12)
24 Feb 2005	2.8a★★	MMS Announces March 30 Date for Beaufort Sea Sale 195	News release
24 Feb 2005	2.8	Final Notice of Sale 195	Web package directory: many attachments (cf. 1.12)
10 Mar 2005	2.9	Changes to the Final Notice of Sale – Beaufort Sea Oil and Gas Lease Sale 195	Leasing Activities Information memo
17 Mar 2005	2.10	Changes to the Final Notice of Sale – Beaufort Sea Oil and Gas Lease Sale 195	Leasing Activities Information memo
30 Mar 2005	2.11	Sale 195 Bid Recap, Statistics, Analysis, Map	Summary charts

Notes
★   The number given has been assigned by the author chronologically from the beginning of the sequence for Sales 186, 195, and 202 for ease of cross-referencing. The items are listed according to their sequence at the time of the first access.
★★   Posted under News Releases on MMS website but not with Sale documents.
★★★ All items are in English except where otherwise noted (e.g. 1.2, 1.8).

Notes

This section contains notes on the main sources I have used in writing this book. In order to avoid excessive footnoting and citation in the main text of the book, general comments on those sources is provided here. The actual citations for all sources used in the main text as well as in these notes are provided in the References.

Preface

Earlier work in Alaska done together with Suzie Wong Scollon is summarized within the newer framework of nexus analysis in Scollon and Scollon (2004) which also contains a bibliography of earlier publications concerning Alaska. The project to which I make reference can be examined at the following URL: http://www.mms.gov/ eppd/sciences/esp/profiles/ak/AK-04-09.htm.

1 Alaskan oil, Scottish scallops, and German paints

Kress and van Leeuwen (1996, 2001; van Leeuwen 2005) have established a very workable grammar of visual design and a theory of multimodal discourse analysis which are the basis for the analyses of images and of document layout and design in this book. These frameworks have been further developed in Scollon and Scollon (2003) as part of mediated discourse analysis (see Notes for Chapter 2) with a special focus on the geosemiotics of moments of action. The argument is that all actions take place in concrete times and places in the material world and that meanings of actions function by reference to those specific times and places.

The display of the US national flag works within what Billig (1995) calls 'banal nationalism', that is, it is implicit that 'the' nation is the United States by virtue of the representation of 'the' flag. This banal signaling of nationalism works strongly through non-textual representations, hence the importance of multimodal discourse analysis in reading such meanings.

Schiffrin (1994) gives a comprehensive list of largely linguistic approaches to discourse analysis: conversational analysis, pragmatics, speech act theory, the ethnography of communication, interactional sociolinguistics, variation analysis. Schiffrin, Tannen, and Hamilton (2001) include many contemporary discourse analysts which extend this listing considerably to also include semantics, relevance theory, computer-assisted text and corpus analysis, critical discourse analysis, political discourse analysis, media studies, intercultural communication, computer-mediated communication, and social psychology. More recently Bhatia, Flowerdew, and Jones (f2007) add to this list multimodal discourse analysis, mediated discourse analysis, and ethnographic approaches to discourse analysis, especially with a focus on discourse in organizations and in education. Wodak (2001a; Wodak and Meyer 2001) makes it clear that fields such as political science and sociology should be included in more social-theoretical approaches to discourse as does Fairclough (2006). Blommaert (2005) elucidates the extended resonance between work in anthropological linguistics often connected with Hymes (1996) and then Silverstein and Urban (1996) and work in critical discourse analysis. Norris (2004a) opens up the field of non-verbal communication as multimodal discourse analysis and Norris and Jones (2005) include within mediated discourse analysis some aspects of neo-Vygotskian (1978) sociocultural psychology (e.g. Wertsch 1991, 1998). Further, much work in cultural geography and urban development (Crang 1998; Harvey 1989, 1996; Jensen and Richardson 2004; Macnaghten and Urry 1998) shares the goals, theoretical orientation, and methodologies of discourse analysis, even where it is not always referenced by that term.

Discourse analysis which addresses crucial social issues is often, but not necessarily, done under the rubric of critical discourse analysis such as Fairclough's (2000) study of the language of New Labour in the UK, the perceptive ethnographic study done by Wodak and her colleagues (Wodak 2000; Muntigl, Weiss, and Wodak 2002) of policy development in the European Union, or the study of racism in parliamentary discourse in six European states done by Wodak and Van Dijk (2000). Though perhaps not thought of as critical discourse analysis, Flowerdew's (1998) study of the final days of British administration in Hong Kong included an extended analysis of public consultations which the British governor, Chris Patten, conducted as part of his British withdrawal strategy. Smart's (2006) ethnographic study of the writing of the global economy through the internal workings of the Bank of Canada, like Hensel's (1996) ethnographic comparison of public testimony concerning subsistence rights for Alaska Natives, which comes closest to the case study reported in this book, would fall more solidly within the framework of the ethnography of communication.

Comments on corporate social responsibility (CSR) are based on Conley (2005), who notes that CSR is inherently a linguistic activity.

2 Action in critical discourse analysis

Austin (1962) and Searle (1969) are basic sources for the beginnings of speech act theory. Owen Barfield (1967) in literary criticism and the philosopher Ludwig Wittgenstein (1990 [1953]) focused on the crucial distinction between the meaning of the sentence and the meaning of the person who is using the sentence. Anthropologists and linguistic anthropologists who have focused on language as it is used to do things include Boas (1966 [1911]), Sapir (Mandelbaum 1958), Hymes (1996) and Gumperz (Gumperz and Hymes 1972).

Social interactional analysis is based to a considerable extent on the writing of Schutz (1962). Directly consequent on his writing is the focus on the moment-by-moment construction of the social world in research now done as social interactional analysis (Sacks 1984; Goffman 1959) and conversational analysis (Schegloff 1972; Drew and Heritage 1991).

Norris and Jones (2005) is a useful introduction to the basic concepts of mediated discourse analysis (MDA) which also includes some of the newest work done within this approach to social action. Habitus is a term that Bourdieu (1977, 1985, 1998) developed and elaborated within a practice theory of social activity. He was influenced in this development, as was Goffman (1959, 1963, 1971, 1974, 1983) in a quite different way, by the earlier work of Elias (2000 [1994]). Quite separately, and much earlier than Bourdieu, Nishida (1958) used historical body as it is being used here and in other works of mediated discourse analysis (R. Scollon 1998, 2001a; Scollon and Scollon 2005a; S. Scollon 2001, 2002). The centrality of the concept of discourses in place is elaborated in the book of that name (Scollon and Scollon 2003), while Norris (2004a, 2004b) has theorized the background–foreground continuum in the analysis of multimodal discourse analysis which is crucial to this concept. Schmidt (2001) provides a cogent analysis of the complex literature concerning attention in face-to-face communication.

Bakhtin (1981) introduced the idea of social languages, that is, customary or conventional ways of speaking that are recognized as the common ways of speaking in particular social groups. This book refers to such social languages as discourses as in 'the discourse of science' or 'the discourse of government/bureaucracy'. The term 'intertextuality' was first introduced in English by Kristeva (1986), based on this work of Bakhtin. Fairclough (1992) extended the idea of intertextuality to encompass whole discourses with the term 'interdiscursivity', which is discussed in more detail in Chapter 4.

Distributed cognition theory is often taken to have begun with Hutchins (1994) as a development of activity theory (Engeström 1999). More recent work such as that of Al Zidjaly (2005) and Jocuns (2005) has emphasized that the (historical) bodies of other social actors are integrated interactionally in joint social actions. Cultural geographers who have considered material objects and artifacts in both the built and 'natural' environment to be expressions of discourses are Crang (1998), Jensen (2004; Jensen and Richardson 2004; Richardson and Jensen 2003), Macnaghten and Urry (1998), and Mitchell (2000). The concepts of resemiotization (or recontextualization or revoicing) are from Bernstein (1990), Iedema (2003), Latour (1996), Lemke (2003), Silverstein and Urban (1996), and Thibault (2004).

The discourse-historical approach to CDA is elaborated in Wodak (2001b). Scollon and Scollon (2004) is an extended nexus analysis as well as an explication of how to do such research in practice. The book includes a fieldguide as an appendix for doing a nexus analysis.

Cole (1995) is a concise explication of the intellectual roots of both activity theory and practice theory in Marxist social theory. MDA draws on both of these, often separate, intellectual traditions. For neo-Vygotskian sociocultural psychology see Vygotsky (1978), Lantolf (1999), Wertsch (1991, 1998). Chouliaraki and Fairclough (1999) and Fairclough (1992) are clear explications of the relationships between discourse and social change.

Examples of MDA studies which have used insider ethnographic analysis to good effect are Castillo-Ayometzi (2003), de Saint-Georges (2003), Disler (2003), Dunne (2003), Johnston (2003), and Jones (1997, 1999). See also the studies in Norris and Jones (2005). Fairclough (1995, 2001, 2003) and Wodak (2001a, 2001b) are excellent treatments of the place of CDA within the broader sphere of contemporary social theory. R. Scollon (2001b) argues for locating MDA solidly within CDA as well.

The full designation for the Beaufort Sea sales was given in the *Federal Register* as: Outer Continental Shelf (OCS), Alaska Region, Beaufort Sea, Oil and Gas Lease Sales 186, 195, 202 for Years 2003, 2005, 2007 (http://www.mms.gov/alaska/cproject/beaufortsale/ index.htm).

The Minerals Management Service (MMS) of the US Department of the Interior has published the full transcript of this hearing, the transcripts of the other three hearings concerning this planned sale, and all of the transcripts covering the preceding 25 years of such sales on their website. These are available for public examination (http://www.mms.gov/ alaska/cproject/ beaufortsale index.htm). The full transcript of the 1997 Barrow public hearing may be found on the MMS website at: http://www.mms.gov/alaska/ref/Public HearingsArctic/1997%20Sale% 20170%20Barrow.pdf.

The full EIS which is also published on this website includes MMS responses to the public testimony given at the hearing. The name of the place in which the hearings were held is misspelled 'Quargi' on the MMS transcript and in the *Federal Register* notice announcing this hearing. In Iñupiaq the letter 'q' represents a 'back velar' (a stop articulated with base of the tongue against the velum) which contrasts with the 'front velar' 'k'. Thus 'Qu' in the transcription represents an intrusion of English orthography into Iñupiaq. 'Qargi' quite appropriately means 'Gathering Place' in Iñupiaq.

See Darnell (1988) on Native American patterns of interaction.

The reference to funerals and other events in small-town gymnasiums and community centers is Lende (2005).

3 The representation of action

Public statements concerning the Beaufort Sea oil and gas leases are all taken from transcripts of the public hearings held in conjunction with this process. Citations of documents reference the website of the Alaska OCS Region, Minerals Management Service, US Department of the Interior, by the date of the chronological posting of documents, http://www.mms.gov/alaska/cproject/beaufortsale/index.htm. The Appendix of this book gives a full list of the documents as well as the reference numbers used in this book. The transcripts are document 1.3.

As noted in Chapter 2, backgrounding and foregrounding are treated by Goffman (1959) and Norris (2004a, 2004b). The term 'recontextualization' is Bernstein's (1990). Studies of unemployment policy making in European Union committees are from Wodak (2000, 2002); of decision making in meetings in China from Gu (1999, 2001); the development and design of museums from Star and Griesemer (1989); hospital planning and design from Iedema (2003); the introduction of technological innovations from Latour (1996) and Scollon and Scollon (2004); disability testing and tracking in education from Mehan (1993); personal identity construction from Norris (2004a, 2004b); and linguistic anthropological fieldwork from Silverstein and Urban (1996).

Sociolinguistic research on discourse markers such as 'well' or 'ok' are richly analyzed in Schiffrin (1987).

Hensel (1996) presents a cogent study of the dialectic between subsistence practices and public testimony concerning the subsistence way of life. Halliday and Hasan (1976) is the major source on adversatives and other conjunctions in English lexicogrammar.

Bateson's article of the 1950s (republished in Bateson 1972) on what he called 'frame' or 'metacommunication' is the source reference. The concept was further developed by Gumperz (1977a, 1977b, 1978) and Tannen (1993) as well as by Goffman (1974) within social interaction studies and interactional sociolinguistics. The term 'framing' is also widely used in mass communication and media research (McCombs 1972; McCombs and Weaver 1985; McCombs, Shaw, and Weaver 1997) in association with what is also called agenda-setting theory. While there are important areas of mutual interest and overlap between these two theoretical positions, this book uses the concept of framing to reference the social interactional, sociolinguistic literature. Kress and van Leeuwen (1996, 2001; van Leeuwen 2005) are the primary sources on framing in visual semiotic or multimodal discourse analysis.

Observations on the role of smiling as a contextualization cue are from Scollon and Scollon (2001). Tannen (1984) discusses 'machine gun questions' and rapid turnover of turns among New Yorkers, while Scollon and Scollon (1981, 2001) and Lehtonen and Sajavaara (1985) examine interpretations which arise from such differences for Alaska Native people and for Finns, respectively.

Cook (2004) has examined Fairclough's (1992; Chouliaraki and Fairclough 1999) concept of synthetic personalization in websites and other sources of information and policy concerning the development, marketing, and sale of genetically modified organisms. This strategy for obscuring relevant information could also be referred to as strategic multimodality (R. Scollon 2006; Scollon and Scollon 2005b).

In the United States the sequential process of drafting an EIS, holding a public hearing, preparing the final EIS, and taking an action followed by an EA to determine if further action should be taken is called a tiered analysis. That is, each subsequent action or analysis incorporates the preceding ones by reference and then attends just to the portions which are considered relevant to the new action or analysis because of new information or changed conditions. The goal is to achieve a higher degree of efficiency while maintaining sensitivity to changing conditions. An early example is US Navy (1994), and the policy governing the tiered analysis which constitutes the Beaufort Sea oil and gas lease sale is covered in US Department of the Interior (2004).

Blommaert (2005) is the source of the term 'layered simultaneity', based on Braudel's (1981) earlier concepts of the tripartite layering of history as epochs (*longue durée*), intermediate cycles, and events (*événement*). This layered understanding of human action has been further developed by Wallerstein (1983, 2004). Hägerstrand (1975, 1978; Carlstein, Parkes, and Thrift 1978) anticipated this concept in the Lund School of human geography. 'Synchronization', the fallacy of not accounting for layered simultaneity is also Blommaert's term. Lemke (2000a, 2000b, 2002) is the source on the construction of semiotics (meanings) across the layers of timescales.

4 When discourses collide

A portion of Van Edwardsen's testimony was quoted in Chapter 2 and is requoted here as the chapter epigraph. The full testimony can be found on the MMS website at: http://www.mms. gov/alaska/ref/PublicHearingsArctic/ 1997%20Sale%20170%20Barrow.pdf.

Macnaghten and Urry (1998) are the primary source used here on miscommunication among the public, policy makers in the government, and scientists. They, in turn, make much use of Wynne (1992, 1996) and Yearley (1991).

The analysis of discourse in this chapter is principally informed by work in critical discourse analysis (Fairclough 1992, 1995, 2003; Gee 1990, 1999; R. Scollon 1998, 2001a, 2001b; Scollon and Scollon 1981, 2001). Van Leeuwen (1996) is the primary source on the representation of social actors.

The series of documents covering Cook Inlet multiple Sales 191 and 199 have also been analyzed for comparison. This analysis does not discuss the Cook Inlet documents beyond noting that in the generic/discourse matters of function, framing, design, discourses and participants there are no contrasts with these documents. Specific contents and lexicogrammatical differences have not been analyzed. The documents are also available on the MMS website (http:// www.mms.gov/alaska).

Discourse is used in this chapter primarily in the sense characterized by Gee (1990, 1999) as 'capital D' discourses, that is, as ways of speaking and being which organize participant identities such as 'the discourse of law' or 'the discourse of medicine'. This corresponds closely to the notion of orders of discourse (Fairclough 1992; Foucault 1973, 1976, 1977).

'Interdiscursivity' was introduced by Fairclough (1992, 1995, 2003; Chouliaraki and Fairclough 1999) as an extension of the term 'intertextuality', which entered into discourse analysis from Bakhtin (1981). The term itself is Kristeva's (1986) and Fairclough has generally preferred to use 'discourse representation'.

Lemke (1995) gives a penetrating analysis of the discourse of science and its linguistic means of achieving hegemonic power in our society. Scollon (2004) is an analysis of intertextuality in three discourses: academic, journalistic, and advertising. The terms 'blending' and 'bending' as well as the spirit of this analysis are influenced by genre analysis (Swales 1990, 1998; Bhatia 1993, 2004), though the discussion in this chapter identifies more strongly with critical discourse analysis.

Both Burke (1969) and Goffman (1974) argue that it is not only heuristically useful but also necessary to base the analysis of discourse on common-sense categories used by participants, because for them the central question is not what the analyst believes is occurring in discourse but what the participants themselves believe is going on.

Star and Griesemer (1989) developed the concept of the boundary object.

5 Document types

Goffman (1974, 1981) is the source for the analysis of principal, author, and animator roles. His treatment of these framing roles in his first publication on the subject (1974) is somewhat different from his later analysis (1981), which is the basis of the analysis in this chapter. See R. Scollon 2004 for an analysis of how the different distribution of these roles characterizes journalistic, academic, and advertising discourse.

Kress and van Leeuwen (1996) is the primary source on the grammar of visual design; see also Scollon and Scollon (2003), van Leeuwen (2005) and further discussion in Chapter 6.

Regulations governing EIS format and writing are set out at the following URL: http://ceq.eh.doe.gov/nepa/regs/ceq/1502.htm. Authority: NEPA, the Environmental Quality Improvement Act of 1970, as amended (42 U.S.C. 4371 et seq.), sec. 309 of the Clean Air Act, as amended (42 U.S.C. 7609), and E.O. 11514 (5 March 1970, as amended by E.O. 11991, 24 May 1977). Source: 43 *FR* 55994, 29 Nov 1978, unless otherwise noted.

The notice announcing the public hearings is in *Federal Register*/ Vol. 67, No. 118/ Wednesday, 19 June 2002/ Notices: 41731. This notice was not posted on the MMS website as part of this set of documents.

6 Modes and modality

The primary sources used here on visual semiotics and multimodality in images are Kress and van Leeuwen (1996, 2001), van Leeuwen (2005); and on multimodality in face-to-face interaction Norris (2004a, 2004b). Scollon and Scollon (1995) is the source for embodied and distant modes although in that case the term 'somatic' and 'extra-somatic' were used.

Linguistic sources for the concepts of modality (also referred to as mood) such as *realis* and *irrealis* are Bybee and Fleischman (1995), Chafe (1995), Finnegan (2002), Harvey (1996), Kress and van Leeuwen (1996), Lemke (1990, 1995, 2000b, 2003), Palmer (2001), and van Leeuwen (2005). Halliday's (1978) systemic-functional linguistics makes central use of modality in grammatical analysis because of the importance of this process in human social life and social interaction.

Anticipatory discourse was outlined in S. Scollon (2001) and more fully developed through an ethnographic study of long-term unemployed people in Belgium by de Saint-Georges (2003). Fairclough (2000, 2003, 2006) sets out the argument concerning the strategy in neo-liberal discourse of taking a fatalistic/oracular position concerning globalization.

The details on the political doctoring of scientific reports on global warming are from Mooney (2005), Novak (2005), Piltz (2005a, 2005b), Reid (2005), Revkin (2005a, 2005b, 2005c), Thacker (2005).

Multimodal analyses of objects and of the built environment are discussed in the cultural geographic references given as sources for Chapter 2.

Details concerning the North Slope Borough of Alaska are from the borough government website at http://www.north-slope.org/nsb/default.htm.

References

Al Zidjaly, Najma (2005) *Communication across Ability-Status: A Nexus Analysis of the Co-construction of Agency and Disability in Oman*. Georgetown University, doctoral dissertation.

Austin, John (1962) *How to Do Things with Words*. Oxford: Clarendon Press.

Bakhtin, M. M. (1981 [1934–5]) *The Dialogic Imagination*. Austin: University of Texas Press.

Barfield, Owen (1967) *Speaker's Meaning*. Middletown, CT: Wesleyan University Press.

Bateson, Gregory (1972) *Steps to an Ecology of Mind*. New York: Ballantine.

Bernstein, Basil (1990) *The Structure of Pedagogic Discourse: Class, Codes and Control*, Vol. 6. London: Routledge.

Bhatia, Vijay (1993) *Analyzing Genre: Language Use in Professional Settings*. London: Longman.

—— (2004) *Worlds of Written Discourse: A Genre-Based View*. London: Continuum.

——, John Flowerdew and Rodney H. Jones (2007) *Advances in Discourse Studies*. Abingdon, Oxon: Routledge, pp. 402–24.

Billig, Michael (1995) *Banal Nationalism*. London: Sage.

Blommaert, Jan (2005) *Discourse: A Critical Introduction*. Cambridge: Cambridge University Press.

Boas, Franz (1966 [1911]) *Introduction to the Handbook of American Indian Languages*. Lincoln: University of Nebraska Press.

Bourdieu, Pierre (1977) *Outline of a Theory of Practice*. Richard Nice (tr.) Cambridge: Cambridge University Press.

—— (1985) The genesis of the concepts of habitus and of field. *Sociocriticism*, 2 (December 1985): 11–24.

—— (1998) *Practical Reason: On the Theory of Action*. Stanford: Stanford University Press.

Braudel, Fernand (1981) *The Structures of Everyday Life: The Limits of the Possible. (Civilization and Capitalism)*, Vol. 1. New York: Harper and Row.

Burke, Kenneth (1950) *A Rhetoric of Motives*. Englewood Cliffs, NJ: Prentice-Hall.

—— (1969 [1945]) *A Grammar of Motives*. Englewood Cliffs, NJ: Prentice-Hall.

Bybee, Joan and Suzanne Fleischman (1995) Modality in grammar and discourse: An introductory essay. In Joan Bybee and Suzanne Fleischman (eds.) *Modality in Grammar and Discourse*. Amsterdam, Philadelphia: John Benjamins, pp. 1–14.

Carlstein, Tommy, Don Parkes and Nigel Thrift (1978) *Human Activity and Time Geography*. New York: John Wiley and Sons.

Castillo-Ayometzi, Cecilia (2003) *Discourse, Practice, and Identity Transformation: An Immigrant Experience of Religious Conversion*. Georgetown University, doctoral dissertation.

Chafe, Wallace (1995) The realis-irrealis distinction in Caddo, the Northern Iroquoian languages and English. In Joan Bybee and Suzanne Fleischman (eds.) *Modality in Grammar and Discourse*. Amsterdam, Philadelphia: John Benjamins, pp. 349–65.

Chouliaraki, Lilie and Norman Fairclough (1999) *Discourse in Late Modernity: Rethinking Critical Discourse Analysis*. Edinburgh: Edinburgh University Press.

Cole, Michael (1995) The supra-individual envelope of development: Activity and practice, situation and context. *New Directions for Child Development*, 67 (Spring 1995): 105–18.

Conley, John (2005) A responsibility to talk the talk. *Guardian Weekly*, 25 May 2005, http://education.guardian.co.uk/tefl/story/0,5500,1492743,00.html. Accessed 15 June 2005, 4:53 pm AKDT.

Cook, Guy (2004) *Genetically Modified Language: The Discourse of Arguments for GM Crops and Food*. London: Routledge.

Crang, Mike (1998) *Cultural Geography*. London: Routledge.

Darnell, Regna (1988) The implications of Cree interactional etiquette. In Regna Darnell and Michael K. Foster (eds.) *Native North American Interaction Patterns*. Hull, Quebec: Canadian Museum of Civilization, National Museums Canada, pp. 69–77.

de Saint-Georges, Ingrid (2003) *Anticipatory Discourse: Producing Futures of Action in a Vocational Program for Long-Term Unemployed*. Georgetown University, doctoral dissertation.

Disler, Edith (2003) Words and weapons: The power of discourse. *Air and Space Power Journal*, Fall 2003, http://www.airpower.maxwell.af.mil/airchronicles/apj/apj03/fal03/ disler. html. Accessed 22 June 2007, 9:27 am AKDT.

Drew, Paul and John Heritage (1991) *Talk at Work*. New York: Cambridge University Press.

Dunne, Michele Durocher (2003) *Democracy in Contemporary Egyptian Political Discourse*. Amsterdam, Philadelphia: John Benjamins Publishing Company.

Elias, Norbert (2000 [1994]) *The Civilizing Process: Sociogenetic and Psychogenetic Investigations*. Edmund Jephcott, tr. with some notes and corrections by the author. Revised edition: Eric Dunning, Johan Goudsblom and Stephen Mennell (eds.) Oxford: Blackwell.

Engeström, Yrjo (1999) Activity theory and individual and social transformation. In Yrjo Engeström, R. Miettenen and R.-L. Punamake (eds.) *Perspectives on Activity Theory*. Cambridge: Cambridge University Press, pp. 19–38.

Fairclough, Norman (1992) *Discourse and Social Change*. Cambridge: Polity Press.

—— (1995) *Critical Discourse Analysis: The Critical Study of Language*. London, New York: Longman.

—— (2000) *New Labour, New Language?* London: Routledge.

—— (2001) Critical discourse analysis as a method in social scientific research. In Ruth Wodak and Michael Meyer (eds.) *Methods in Critical Discourse Analysis*. London: Sage, pp. 121–38.

—— (2003) *Analysing Discourse: Textual Analysis for Social Research*. London: Routledge.

—— (2006) *Language and Globalization*. Abingdon: Routledge.

Finnegan, Ruth (2002) *Communicating*. London: Routledge.

Flowerdew, John (1998) *The Final Years of British Hong Kong: The Discourse of Colonial Withdrawal*. London: Macmillan.

Foucault, Michel (1973) *The Order of Things*. New York: Random House.

—— (1976) *The Archeology of Knowledge*. New York: Harper and Row.

Foucault, Michel (1977) *Discipline and Punish*. New York: Pantheon Books.

Gee, James Paul (1990) *Social Linguistics and Literacies*. London: The Falmer Press.

—— (1999) *An Introduction to Discourse Analysis: Theory and Method*. London: Routledge.

Goffman, Erving (1959) *The Presentation of Self in Everyday Life*. New York: Doubleday.

—— (1963) *Behavior in Public Places: Notes on the Social Organization of Gatherings*. New York: Free Press.

—— (1971) *Relations in Public*. New York: Harper and Row.

—— (1974) *Frame Analysis*. New York: Harper and Row.

—— (1981) *Forms of Talk*. Philadelphia: University of Pennsylvania Press.

—— (1983) The interaction ritual. *American Sociological Review*, 48: 1–19.

Gu, Yueguo (1999) Towards a model of situated discourse analysis. In Ken Turner (ed.) *The Semantics/Pragmatics Interface from Different Points of View*. Elsevier Science.

—— (2001) Towards an understanding of workplace discourse. In Christopher Candlin (ed.) *Theory and Practice in Professional Discourse*. Hong Kong: The City University of Hong Kong Press.

Gumperz, John (1977a) Sociocultural knowledge in conversational inference. In Muriel Saville-Troike (ed.) *28th Annual Roundtable on Language and Linguistics*. Washington, DC: Georgetown University Press. Revised version published in John J. Gumperz (1982) *Discourse Strategies*. New York: Cambridge University Press.

—— (1977b) The conversational analysis of interethnic communication. In E. Lamar Ross (ed.) *Interethnic Communication: Proceedings of the Southern Anthropological Society.* University of Georgia: University of Georgia Press.

—— (1978) The retrieval of sociocultural knowledge in conversation. Paper presented at the American Anthropological Association, November 1978. Revised version published in John J. Gumperz (1982) *Discourse Strategies.* New York: Cambridge University Press.

—— and Dell Hymes (1972) *Directions in Sociolinguistics: The Ethnography of Communication.* New York: Holt, Rinehart and Winston, Inc.

Hägerstrand, Torsten (1975) Space, time and human conditions. In A. Karlqvist, L. Lundqvist, and F. Snickars (eds.) *Dynamic Allocation of Urban Space.* Farnborough: Saxon House, pp. 3–12.

—— (1978) Survival and arena. In Tommy Carlstein, Don Parkes and Nigel Thrift (eds.) *Human Activity and Time Geography.* New York: John Wiley and Sons, pp. 122–45.

Halliday, M. A. K. (1978) *Language as Social Semiotic.* London: Edward Arnold.

—— and Ruquiya Hasan (1976) *Cohesion in English.* London: Longman.

Harvey, David (1989) *The Condition of Postmodernity.* Oxford: Blackwell.

—— (1996) *Justice, Nature and the Geography of Difference.* Oxford: Blackwell.

Hensel, Chase (1996) *Telling Our Selves: Ethnicity and Discourse in Southwestern Alaska.* New York, Oxford: Oxford University Press.

Hutchins, Edwin (1994) *Cognition in the Wild Cambridge.* Cambridge, MA: MIT Press.

Hymes, Dell (1996) *Ethnography, Linguistics, Narrative Inequality: Toward an Understanding of Voice.* London: Taylor and Francis.

Iedema, Rick (2003) Multimodality, resemiotisation: Extending the analysis of discourse as multi-semiotic practice. *Visual Communication*, 2(1): 29–57.

Jensen, Ole B. (2004) The BID's [sic] of New York: Power, place and the role of business improvement districts. Paper presented at the XVIII AESOP Congress, 1–3 July 2004. Grenoble: France.

Jensen, Ole B. and Tim Richardson (2004) *Making European Space: Mobility, Power and Territorial Identity.* London: Routledge.

Jocuns, Andrew A. (2005) *Knowledge and Discourse: A Study of Knowledge in Social Interaction using the Theories of Mediated Discourse and Distributed Cognition.* Georgetown University, doctoral dissertation.

Johnston, Alexandra (2003) *A Mediated Discourse Analysis of Immigration Gatekeeping Interviews.* Georgetown University, doctoral dissertation.

Jones, Rodney Hale (1997) Marketing the damaged self: The construction of identity in advertisements directed towards people with HIV/AIDS. *Journal of Sociolinguistics*, 1: 393–419.

—— (1999) Mediated action and sexual risk: Searching for 'culture' in discourses of homosexuality and AIDS prevention in China. *Culture, Health and Sexuality*, 1(2): 161–80.

Kress, Gunther and Theo van Leeuwen (1996) *Reading Images: The Grammar of Visual Design*. London: Routledge.

—— (2001) *Multimodal Discourse: The Modes and Media of Contemporary Communication*. London: Edward Arnold.

Kristeva, Julia (1986) Word, dialogue and novel. In T. Moi (ed.) *The Kristeva Reader*. Oxford: Basil Blackwell, pp. 34–61.

Lantolf, James P. (1999) Second culture acquisition: Cognitive considerations. In Eli Hinkel (ed.) *Culture in Second Language Teaching and Learning*. Cambridge: Cambridge University Press, pp. 28–46.

Latour, Bruno (1996) On interobjectivity. *Mind, Culture, and Activity*, 3(4): 228–45.

Lehtonen, Jaakko and Kari Sajavaara (1985) The silent Finn. In Deborah Tannen and Muriel Saville-Troike (eds.) *Perspectives on Silence*. Norwood, NJ: Ablex Publishing Corporation, pp. 193–201.

Lemke, Jay L. (1990) Technical discourse and technocratic ideology. In M. A. K. Halliday, John Gibbons and Howard Nicholas (eds.) *Learning, Keeping and Using Language*. Selected papers from the 8th AILA World Congress of Applied Linguistics, Sydney 1987. Vol. 2, pp. 435–60. Amsterdam: John Benjamins.

—— (1995) *Textual Politics*. London: Taylor and Francis.

—— (2000a) Across the scales of time: Artifacts, activities and meanings in ecosocial systems. *Mind, Culture, and Activity*, 7(4): 273–90.

—— (2000b) Opening up closure: Semiotics across scales. In Jerry L. R. Chandler and Gertrudis Van de Vijver (eds.) *Closure: Emergent Organizations and their Dynamics*. Vol. 901. New York: Annals of the New York Academy of Sciences, pp. 100–11.

—— (2002) Travels in hypermodality. *Visual Communication*, 1(3): 299–325.

—— (2003) Texts and discourses in the technologies of social organization. In Ruth Wodak and Gilbert Weiss (eds.) *Critical Discourse Analysis: Interdisciplinary Theory and Applications*. London: Palgrave.

Lende, Heather (2005) *If You Lived Here, I'd Know Your Name: News from Small-Town Alaska*. Chapel Hill, NC: Algonquin Books of Chapel Hill.

Macnaghten, Phil and John Urry (1998) *Contested Natures*. London: Sage.

Mandelbaum, David G. (1958) *Selected Writings of Edward Sapir*. Berkeley, Los Angeles: University of California Press.

McCombs, Maxwell E. (1972) Mass communication in political campaigns: Information, gratification and persuasion. In F. Kline and P. J. Tichenor (eds.) *Current Perspectives in Mass Communication Research*. Beverly Hills, CA: Sage.

—— and David Weaver (1985) Toward a merger of gratifications and agenda-setting research. In K. E. Rosengren, L. A. Wenner and P. Palmgreen (eds.) *Media Gratifications Research: Current Perspectives*. Beverly Hills, CA: Sage.

McCombs, Maxwell E., Donald L. Shaw and David L. Weaver (1997) *Communication and Democracy: Exploring the Intellectual Frontiers in Agenda-Setting Theory*. Mahwah, NJ: Lawrence Erlbaum.

Mehan, Hugh (1993) Beneath the skin and between the ears: A case study in the politics of representation. In Seth Chaiklin and Jean Lave (eds.) *Understanding Practice: Perspectives on Activity and Context*. Cambridge: Cambridge University Press, pp. 241–68.

Mitchell, Don (2000) *Cultural Geography: A Critical Introduction*. Oxford: Blackwell.

Mooney, Chris (2005) Low-ball warming: There should be a special circle in hell for people who mess with scientific data. *American Prospect*, 20 June 2005, http://www.prospect.org/web/page.ww?section=root&name=ViewWeb &articleId=9884. Accessed 22 June 2007, 9:30 am AKDT.

Muntigl, Peter, Gilbert Weiss and Ruth Wodak (2002) *European Union Discourses on Un/employment: An Interdisciplinary Approach to Employment Policy-Making and Organizational Change*. Amsterdam: John Benjamins.

Nishida, Kitaroo (1958) *Intelligibility and the Philosophy of Nothingness*. Tokyo: Maruzen Co. Ltd.

Norris, Sigrid (2004a) *Analyzing Multimodal Interaction: A Methodological Framework*. London: Routledge.

—— (2004b) Multimodal discourse analysis: A conceptual framework. In Philip Le Vine and Ron Scollon (eds.) *Discourse and Technology: Multimodal Discourse Analysis*. Washington, DC: Georgetown University Press.

—— and Rodney Jones (2005) *Discourse and Action: Introduction to Mediated Discourse Analysis*. London: Routledge.

Novak, Robert (2005) Blair turns up global warming heat. *Washington Post*, 13 June 2005.

Palmer, Frank Robert (2001) *Mood and Modality*. 2nd edn. Cambridge: Cambridge University Press.

Piltz, Rick S. (2005a) On issues of concern about the governance and direction of the climate change science program. Memo to US climate change science program agency principals, 1 June 2005. US Government Accountability Project: www.whistleblower.org.

—— (2005b) Censorship and secrecy: Politicizing the US climate change science program. Memo to US climate change science program agency principals, 8 June 2005. US Government Accountability Project: www.whistleblower.org.

Reid, Harry (2005) Democrats unveil initiative to keep science out of politics: Senators join whistleblower in unveiling amendment to put science first. Press release, Senator Harry Reid, 20 June 2005. Washington, DC: Senate Democratic Communications Center.

Revkin, Andrew C. (2005a) Bush aide edited climate reports: Ex-oil lobbyist softened greenhouse gas links. *New York Times*, 8 June 2005.

—— (2005b) Editor of climate report resigns. *New York Times*, 11 June 2005.

—— (2005c) Former Bush aide who edited climate reports is hired by Exxon. *New York Times*, 15 June 2005.

Richardson, Tim and Ole B. Jensen (2003) Linking discourse and space: Towards a cultural sociology of space in analysing spatial policy discourses. *Urban Studies*, Vol. 40, no. 1 March 2003: 7–22.

Sacks, Harvey (1984) On doing 'being ordinary'. In J. M. Atkinson and J. Heritage (eds.) *Structure of Social Action: Studies in Conversational Analysis.* Cambridge: Cambridge University Press.

Schegloff, Emanuel (1972) Sequencing in conversational openings. In John Gumperz and Dell Hymes (eds.) *Directions in Sociolinguistics.* New York: Holt, Rinehart and Winston.

Schiffrin, Deborah (1987) *Discourse Markers.* Cambridge: Cambridge University Press.

—— (1994) *Approaches to Discourse.* Oxford: Basil Blackwell.

——, Deborah Tannen and Heidi Hamilton (2001) *The Handbook of Discourse Analysis.* Oxford: Basil Blackwell.

Schmidt, Richard (2001) Attention. In Peter J. Robinson (ed.) *Cognition and Second Language Instruction.* Cambridge: Cambridge University Press.

Schutz, Alfred (1962) *Collected Papers.* The Hague: Nijhoff.

Scollon, Ron (1998) *Mediated Discourse as Social Interaction: The Study of News Discourse.* London: Longman.

—— (2001a) *Mediated Discourse: The Nexus of Practice.* London: Routledge.

—— (2001b) Action and text: Toward an integrated understanding of the place of text in social (inter)action. In Ruth Wodak and Michael Meyer (eds.) *Methods in Critical Discourse Analysis.* London: Sage, pp. 139–83.

—— (2004) Intertextuality across communities of practice: Academics, journalism and advertising. In Carol Lynn Moder and Aida Martinovic-Zic (eds.) *Discourse across Languages and Cultures.* Philadelphia: John Benjamins.

—— (2006) Food and behavior: A Burkean motive analysis of a quasi-medical text. *Text and Talk,* 26(1): 105–26.

—— and Suzanne Wong Scollon (1981) *Narrative, Literacy and Face in Interethnic Communication.* Norwood, NJ: Ablex Publishing Corporation.

—— (1995) Somatic communication: How useful is 'orality' for the characterization of speech events and cultures? In Uta M. Quasthoff (ed.) *Aspects of Oral Communication.* Berlin: DeGruyter, pp. 19–29.

—— (2001) *Intercultural Communication: A Discourse Approach.* Second edition. Oxford: Basil Blackwell.

—— (2003) *Discourses in Place: Language in the Material World.* London: Routledge.

—— (2004) *Nexus Analysis: Discourse and the Emerging Internet.* London: Routledge.

—— (2005a) Lighting the stove: Why habitus isn't enough for critical discourse analysis. In Ruth Wodak and Paul Chilton (eds.) *A New Agenda in (Critical) Discourse Analysis.* Amsterdam: John Benjamins, pp. 101–17.

—— (2005b) Strategic multimodality: Ingredients of power. Lecture presented at the Department of Linguistics, Hong Kong University, 20 April 2005.

Scollon, Suzanne (2001) Habitus, consciousness, agency and the problem of intention: How we carry and are carried by political discourses. *Folia Linguistica,* XXXV/1–2: 97–129.

—— (2002) Political and somatic alignment: Habitus, ideology and social practice. In Ruth Wodak and Gilbert Weiss (eds.) *Theory and Interdisciplinarity in Critical Discourse Analysis*. London: Palgrave.

Searle, John R. (1969) *Speech Acts*. New York: Cambridge University Press.

Silverstein, Michael and Greg Urban (1996) The natural history of discourse. In Michael Silverstein and Greg Urban (eds.) *Natural Histories of Discourse*. Chicago, London: The University of Chicago Press, pp. 1–17.

Smart, Graham (2006) *Writing the Economy: Activity, Genre and Technology in the World of Banking*. London: Equinox Press.

Star, Susan Leigh and James R. Griesemer (1989) Institutional ecology, 'translations' and boundary objects: Amateurs and professionals in Berkeley's Museum of Vertebrate Zoology, 1907–39. *Social Studies of Science*, 19: 387–420.

Swales, John M. (1990) *Genre Analysis: English in Academic and Research Settings*. Cambridge: Cambridge University Press.

—— (1998) *Other Floors, Other Voices: A Textography of a Small University Building*. Mahway, NJ: Lawrence Erlbaum Associates.

Tannen, Deborah (1984) *Conversational Style*. Norwood, NJ: Ablex Publishing Corporation.

—— (1993) *Framing in Discourse*. New York: Oxford University Press.

Thacker, Paul (2005) Blowing the whistle on climage change: Interview with Rick Piltz. *Environmental Science and Technology*, 22 June 2005, http://pubs.acs.org/subscribe/journals/esthag-w/2005/jun/policy/pt_piltz.html. Accessed 22 June 2007, 9:33 am AKDT.

Thibault, Paul J. (2004) *Agency and Consciousness in Discourse: Self–Other Dynamics as a Complex System*. London: Continuum.

US Department of the Interior (2004) Interior department announces modernized procedures implementing the National Environmental Policy Act (NEPA), http://www.doi.gov/news/949308a. Accessed 28 November 2004, 10:25am EST.

US Navy (1994) Appendix E, Environmental effects abroad of major Navy actions, OPNAVINST 5090.1B, 1 November 1994.

Van Leeuwen, Theo (1996) The representation of social actors. In Carmen Rosa Caldas-Coulthard and Malcolm Coulthard (eds.) *Texts and Practices: Readings in Critical Discourse Analysis*. London, New York: Routledge, pp. 32–70.

—— (2005) *Introducing Social Semiotics*. Abingdon: Routledge.

Vygotsky, L. S. (1978) *Mind in Society: The Development of Higher Psychological Processes*. Cambridge: Harvard University Press.

Wallerstein, Immanuel (1983) *Historical Capitalism*. London: Verso.

—— (2004) *The Uncertainties of Knowledge*. Philadelphia: Temple University Press.

Wertsch, James V. (1991) *Voices of the Mind: A Sociocultural Approach to Mediated Action*. Cambridge, MA: Harvard University Press.

Wertsch, James V. (1998) *Mind as Action.* New York: Oxford University Press.

Wittgenstein, Ludwig (1980) Remarks on the philosophy of psychology, Vol. 1, no. 78, cited in John Shotter, *Cultural Politics of Everyday Life: Social Constructionism, Rhetoric and Knowing of the Third Kind.* Toronto, Buffalo: University of Toronto Press 1993, p. 83.

—— (1990 [1953]) *Philosophical Investigations.* Encyclopaedia Britannica Great Books series. Chicago: Encyclopaedia Britannica, Inc., pp. 311–440.

Wodak, Ruth (2000) Recontextualization and the transformation of meanings: A critical discourse analysis of decision making in EU meetings about employment policies. In Srikant Sarangi and Malcolm Coulthard (eds.) *Discourse and Social Life.* Harlow: Pearson Education, pp. 185–206.

Wodak, Ruth (2001a) What CDA is about – a summary of its history, important concepts and its developments. In Ruth Wodak and Michael Meyer (eds.) *Methods in Critical Discourse Analysis.* London: Sage, pp. 1–13.

—— (2001b) The discourse-historical approach. In Ruth Wodak and Michael Meyer (eds.) *Methods in Critical Discourse Analysis.* London: Sage.

—— (2002) From conflict to consensus? The co-construction of a policy paper. In Peter Muntigl, Gilbert Weiss and Ruth Wodak (eds.) *European Union Discourses on Un/employment: An Interdisciplinary Approach to Employment Policy-Making and Organizational Change.* Amsterdam: John Benjamins, pp. 73–114.

—— and Michael Meyer (2001) *Methods in Critical Discourse Analysis.* London: Sage.

—— and Teun Van Dijk (2000) *Racism at the Top: Parliamentary Discourse on Ethnic Issues in Six European States.* Klagenfurt: Drava.

Wynne, Brian (1992) Risk and social learning: Reification to engagement. In Sue Golding and Dominic Golding (eds.) *Theories of Risk.* New York: Praeger.

—— (1996) May the sheep graze safely. In Scott M. Lash, Bronislaw Szerszynski and Brian Wynne (eds.) *Risk, Environment and Modernity: Towards a New Ecology.* London: Sage.

Yearley, S. (1991) *The Green Case: A Sociology of Environmental Issues, Arguments and Politics.* London: HarperCollins.

Index

action: language about 42–43
'action-intuition' 18
actions 14–15, 18
activism 2
agency 78, 91
agency axis 134–7
Al Zidjaly, Najma 168
ambivalence 75–6
animators 4, 101
anticipatory discourses 133–7, 172
argumentation 78, 91
Austin, John 167
authors 4, 101, 102

Bakhtin, M. M. 79, 168, 171
Barfield, Owen 167
Bateson, Gregory 53–4, 169
Beaufort Sea case study 24–36
bending 84, 106–7, 117, 171
Bernstein, Basil 168, 169
Bhatia, Vijay 167
bid form example 61, 62
Billig, Michael 166
binding referential incorporation
    (subordination) 83
blending 83, 106–7, 111–12, 118,
    119, 171
Blommaert, Jan 64, 65, 66, 167, 170
Boas, Franz 167
Bordieu, Pierre 18, 22, 167–8
Braudel, Fernand 170
Burke, Kenneth 54, 171

Bybee, Joan 171
bystanders 101, 102, 105

case studies: sale of oil and gas leases
    24–36
Castillo-Ayometzi, Cecilia 168
CDA (critical discourse analysis) 15,
    24
Chafe, Wallace 171
Chouliaraki, Lili 168
Cole, Michael 168
communicative modes 128–30
Conley, John 167
consultation websites 152–3
consultations 155
contextualization 53–63
Cook, Guy 170
corporate social responsibility (CSR)
    9
Crang, Mike 168
critical discourse analysis (CDA) 15,
    24
CSR (corporate social responsibility)
    9

Darnell, Regna 169
de Saint-Georges, Ingrid 168, 172
design 55–8, 60–1, 99, 105, 107–8
discourse analysis: news release
    example 3–7
discourse blending 79–84, 106–7,
    111–12, 118, 119

discourses: anticipatory 133–7; categorization 84–5; energy resources extraction 90–2; environmental protection 90–2; features 77–9; government 89–90, 103, 106–7, 119; journalistic/media 106–7; legal 85–6; political 87–9, 103–4, 107–9, 137–40; science 85–6, 137–40, 171; traditional knowledge 90–2
discourses in place 19–20, 21–2, 34–6
Disler, Edith 168
document design *see* design
document types: general 98–9; Leasing Activities Information memos (LAI) 109–11; letterheads 97–8; MMS website 98–9, 118–21; news releases 104–9; public testimony 112–18
documents: as action 43–5
draft environmental impact statements (DEIS) 9
Dunne, Michele Durocher 168

EA (Environmental Assessment) 111
eclipsing 84
EIS (environmental impact statements) 8–9, 111–12, 169
Elias, Norbert 168
energy resources extraction discourses 90–2
Environmental Assessment (EA) 111
environmental idealism 75
environmental impact statements (EIS) *see* EIS (environmental impact statements)
environmental protection discourses 90–2
environmental realism 75
extended discourses 20

Fairclough, Norman 24, 79, 136, 167, 168, 171, 172

Federal Register notices example 14, 15–16, 17, 99–104, 120
FEIS (Final environmental impact statements) 9
Finnegan, Ruth 171
Fleischman, Suzanne 171
Flowerdew, John 167
FR notices example *see Federal Register* notices example
framing 53–63, 66–7, 99–100, 105, 109–10, 169
function: of documents 99

Gee, James Paul 171
'genesis amnesia' 22
genres 78, 91, 171
global warming example: and modality 138–40
Goffman, Erving 19, 100, 102, 168, 169, 171
government discourses 89–90, 103, 106–7, 119
graphic design 55–58, 60–61, 107–108
Griesemer, James R. 169, 171
Gu, Yueguo 169
Gumperz, John 167, 169

habitus 18–19, 167–168
Hägerstrand, Torsten 65, 170
Halliday, M. A. K. 169, 172
Hamilton, Heidi 166
handlers 101, 102–103
Harvey, David 171
Hasan, Ruquiya 169
Hensel, Chase 167, 169
historical body 18–19, 21, 22, 24, 32, 168
Hutchins, Edwin 168
Hymes, Dell 167
hyperlinks 119–120

Iedema, Rick 49, 168, 169

incorporation (supporting incorporation) 83
independence (instantiation) 83, 107
indexing (non-binding reference) 83–84
instantiation (independence) 83, 107
interaction order 19, 21, 22, 24, 32–34
interdiscursivity 12, 79–84, 99, 145–147, 168, 171
interpreters 101, 102
intertextuality 79, 168, 171
Iñupiat (Native American) communities 25

Jensen, Ole B. 168
Jocuns, Andrew A. 168
Johnston, Alexandra 168
Jones, Rodney H. 167, 168
journalistic/media discourses 106–107

Kaktovik testimony 25–36
knowledge axis 134–137
Kress, Gunther 166, 169, 171, 172
Kristeva, Julia 168, 171

Lantolf, James P. 168
Latour, Bruno 49, 168, 169
layered simultaneity 64, 65, 170
legal discourses 85–86
Lehtonen, Jaakko 170
Lemke, Jay L. 168, 170, 171, 172
Lende, Heather 169
letterhead analysis 3–7, 141
lexicogrammar 78, 91
linguistic actions 15
linguistic reduction 46–8

Macnaghten, Phil 74–5, 75, 168, 170
MDA (mediated discourse analysis) 15, 18–24, 36, 166
mediated actions 18

mediated discourse analysis (MDA) *see* MDA (mediated discourse analysis)
Mehan, Hugh 49, 169
metacommunication 53–4
Meyer, Michael 167
Minerals Management Service (MMS) 3, 25
miscommunication 74–5, 170
misinterpretation 61–2
Mitchell, Don 168
MMS (Minerals Management Service) 3, 25
MMS website 118–21
modality: in non-grammatical modes 142–4; in science and politics 137–40; as a term 131–3
modes: communicative 128–30; as a heuristic 78, 91; as a term 131–3
Mooney, Chris 172
multimodal discourse analysis 5, 54, 147, 166, 170
multimodality 140–7, 171
multiple media 60–1
multiple sale documents: *Federal Register* notices 99–104; genre/text types 98–9; Leasing Activities Information memos (LAI) 109–11; MMS website 118–21; news releases 104–9; public testimony 112–18; summary 121–3

National Environmental Protection Act (NEPA) *see* NEPA (National Environmental Protection Act)
Native American (Iñupiat) communities 25
'nature': conceptualization of 74–5
neo-liberal discourse 136, 172
neo-Vygotskian psychology 20, 24, 167, 168
NEPA (National Environmental Protection Act) 8, 25

news release example 3–7, 14, 15, 16,
    57–9, 61, 104–9
nexus analysis 22, 27–36, 36
NGOs 2, 25
Nishida, Kitaroo 18, 168
non-binding reference (indexing)
    83–4
Norris, Sigrid 167, 168, 169
Notice of Sale document 55–57
Novak, Robert 172

oil spill risk analysis example 80–84
Oil Watch Alaska 25
OSRA (Oil Spill Risk Analysis) 111

page layout 55–58
Palmer, Frank Robert 172
'participant' 19
participation 78, 91
passive verbs 110
PCDA (Public Consultative
    Discourse Analysis) xi, 2, 7–10, 12,
    23–4, 36–7, 99, 147, 151–62
'person' 19
Piltz, Rick S. 172
political activism 2
political discourses 87–9, 103–4,
    107–9, 137–40
pragmatics 15
principal receivers 101–2
principals 4, 101
production positions 99
production roles 100–101
public consultation 9, 76–7, 152–3
Public Consultative Discourse Anal-
    ysis (PCDA) *see* PCDA (Public
    Consultative Discourse Analysis)
public hearing 9 *see also* public
    consultation
public testimony 112–18

reality 131, 132–33
reception positions 99, 101, 110
recontextualization 46–53, 169

Reid, Harry 172
resemiotization 49–53, 168
Revkin, Andrew C. 172

Sajavaara, Kari 170
sale of oil and gas leases case study
    24–36
Schiffrin, Deborah 166, 169
Schmidt, Richard 168
Schutz, Alfred 167
science discourses 85–6, 137–40, 171
Scollon, Suzanne Wong 166, 168,
    169, 170, 171, 172
Searle, John R. 167
Silverstein, Michael 167, 168, 169
Smart, Graham 167
social actions 20–21, 170
social interactional analysis 17–18
social languages 168
sociocultural psychology 20, 24
Star, Susan Leigh 169, 171
subordination (binding referential
    incorporation) 83, 100
summarization 46–53, 66
supporting incorporation (incorpora-
    tion) 83
synchronization 63–6, 67, 170
synthetic personalization 60

Tannen, Deborah 166, 169, 170
Thacker, Paul 172
Thibault, Paul J. 168
tiered analysis 170
timescales, multiple 63–6, 170
traditional knowledge discourses
    90–2
trust 75–6
truth 131, 132–3

Urban, Greg 167, 168, 169
Urry, John 74, 75, 168, 170

Van Dijk, Teun 167

van Leeuwen, Theo 166, 169–70, 171, 172
verb forms 110–11
visual semiotics 5, 54, 171
Vygotsky, L. S. 168

Wallerstein, Immanuel 170
websites 60, 61, 118–21

Wertsch, James V. 168
Wittgenstein, Ludwig 48, 65, 167
Wodak. Ruth 167, 168, 169
writer/reader positions 99, 100–3, 105, 106, 110
Wynne, Brian 75–6, 170

Yearley S. 170

Related titles from Routledge

Analysing Discourse
Textual Analysis for Social Research
Norman Fairclough

This is an important text which highlights not only why discourse analysis should be a central method within social science but, unusually, provides the resources necessary for putting this into practice. The book will be an inspiration for social scientists wishing to explore, in a sophisticated way, the importance of language and meaning making in social life. *Annette Hastings, University of Glasgow*

Covers a wide range of important contemporary concepts in social and political theory taken from many different sources and disciplines. I would certainly recommend it to other researchers in the field as a thought provoking contribution to critical discourse analysis. *Ulrike Meinhof, University of Southampton*

Analysing Discourse is an accessible introductory textbook for all students and researchers working with real language data.

Drawing on a range of social theorists from Bourdieu to Habermas, as well as his own research, Fairclough's book presents a form of language analysis with a consistently social perspective. His approach is illustrated by and investigated through a range of real texts, from written texts, to a TV debate about the monarchy and a radio broadcast about the Lockerbie bombing. The student-friendly book also offers accessible summaries, an appendix of example texts, and a glossary of terms and key theorists.

ISBN13: 978-0-415-25892-0 (hbk)
ISBN13: 978-0-415-25893-7 (pbk)

Available at all good bookshops
For ordering and further information please visit:
www.routledge.com